Essays in Maya Archaeology

Essays in Maya Archaeology

Gordon R. Willey

With a foreword by
Jeremy A. Sabloff

University of New Mexico Press
Albuquerque

Library of Congress Cataloging in Publication Data

Willey, Gordon R. (Gordon Randolph). 1913-
    Essays in Maya adrchaeology.

    Bibliography: p.
    Includes index.
    1. Mayas—Antiquities. 2. Indians of Mexico—
Antiquities. 3. Indians of Central America—Antiquities.
4. Mexico—Antiquities. 5. Central America—Antiquities.
I. Title.
F1435.W725   1987   972'.01   86-27255
ISBN 0-8263-0937-2
ISBN 0-8263-0938-0 (pbk.)

Chapters 1, 2, 3, 4, and 6 appeared originally in books published as a result of School of American Research Advanced Seminar Series and are reprinted with permission of the School of American Research, Douglas Schwartz, General Editor.

Chapter 5 originally appeared in *Man,* the journal of the Royal Anthropoloical Institute of Great Britain and Ireland and is reprinted with permission.

Chapter 7 originally appeared in the *Journal of Anthropological Research,* Department of Anthropology of the University of New Mexico and is reprinted with permission.

Contents

Acknowledgments

Jeremy A. Sabloff first suggested, to me and to the officers of the University of New Mexico Press, the idea for this collection of some of my previous writings on Maya archaeology, and I am grateful to him for this as well as for his willingness to write the Foreword to the book. To Beth Hadas, of the University Press, go my thanks for her attention and help in its preparation. As Douglas S. Schwartz, Director of the School of American Research, Santa Fe, New Mexico, was instrumental in the planning and operation of four seminar proceedings which gave birth to four of the essays in the book, I take this opportunity to express my gratitude to him. The same goes for my many colleagues in Maya archaeology who participated in these four seminars, as well as to those who took part in a symposium at the Paris meetings of the International Congress of Americanists in 1976. I owe a special debt, in this regard, to Demitri B. Shimkin who was co-author of one of the Santa Fe seminar summary essays. Two of the essays in the collection were first published in anthropological journals, and I thank the editorial boards of *Man,* the journal of the Royal Anthropological Institute of Great Britain and Ireland, and the *Journal of Anthropological Research,* of the Department of Anthropology of the University of New Mexico, for their permissions to publish these essays. The seven essays are identified as to original source in my introductory essay which follows. Thanks also to Lys Ann Shore, who prepared the index.

1. Gordon Willey, 1970. Photo by Karl Kernberger. Courtesy of the School of American Research.

Foreword

Jeremy A. Sabloff

Although many archaeologists see Gordon Willey as a staid, conservative individual, he is, in reality, a lively, open-minded person. Moreover, in a discipline renowned for its storytellers, he is an accomplished and highly entertaining raconteur. In the isolated setting of the Peten jungle in Guatemala, where I worked with him for four field seasons in the mid-1960s, Gordon was at his best. One of my favorite anecdotes from Gordon's vast repertoire typifies his marvelous sense of humor and offers as telling a comment on the archaeological enterprise as I have ever heard.

In the late 1930s, when Gordon was working for the WPA in Georgia, he spent some time driving around the countryside interviewing people about the location of archaeological sites. One afternoon, at the end of a long day of work, he drove up to a farm house. The farmer was sitting on his porch in a rocker, smoking and looking out over his fields. Gordon pulled up in front of the house, introduced himself, and sat down on the porch to talk to the farmer.

After exchanging pleasantries, Gordon explained that he was looking for the remains of the ancient Indians who had lived in Georgia and
asked if the farmer had noticed any mounds or broken pieces of pottery
on his land. The farmer rocked back and forth and said: "Yes, indeed."
He went on to tell Gordon that he had just run across a small mound the
other day in the back forty and that his plow had turned up all kinds of
debris including pottery. Gordon pulled out his notebook and wrote down
the information. There was a long pause while the farmer kept rocking.
Finally, the farmer asked, "What are you?" Gordon replied that he was
an archaeologist. "What's that?" the farmer queried. Gordon straightened
up a little and proudly explained that archaeologists are scholars who study
the human past. He then went on at some length in youthful enthusiasm
describing the nature of archaeological research and the goals of archaeology. There was another long pause while the farmer digested all this information. He then looked Gordon in the eyes and said, "You do this for a
living?" Gordon answered, "Yes." "You mean you get *paid* for looking
for old remains?" the farmer continued, with disbelief in his voice. "Absolutely," Gordon replied. The farmer continued rocking back and forth without a word for what seemed to Gordon to be an interminable time. At
last, the farmer just shook his head and said, "Well . . . I guess it takes all
kinds of f——ers to make a world."

While any archaeologist will tell you that it does take a particular
kind of person to be a professional, it is clear that Gordon is unusual even
within the profession. Moreover, he seems to have heeded one of the important lessons that can be drawn from his discussion with the farmer. This
lesson is that many people do not recognize what archaeologists do, nor
do they understand what archaeologists accomplish. One of the outstand-
ing features of Gordon's career became his devotion to synthesizing the
nature of archaeological research and the results it produced throughout
the Americas. What is especially remarkable is that Gordon had been able
to combine the writing of numerous important syntheses—such as his huge
two-volume *An Introduction to American Archaeology*—with a most productive field career in Arizona, Georgia, Louisiana, Florida, Peru, Panama,
British Honduras (now Belize), Guatemala, Nicaragua, and Honduras
between 1935 and the present day.

Why has Gordon Willey been so successful as a synthesizer? I believe
that this success is a combination of an extremely bright and agile mind,
hard work, and a devotion to archaeology that has permitted Gordon to
have both a broad control of the archaeological literature of the New World
and in-depth, detailed understanding of Maya archaeology. In addition,
he has exhibited incredible patience in his willingness to listen to and read

every possible source of data on Maya studies. Finally, Gordon has the rare ability to keep his ego under tight reins. This last trait has permitted him to make strong and potentially controversial statements that do not seem to threaten those who might be mortally offended if the same opinion were offered by some other scholar.

Gordon's synthetic abilities are clearly exemplified in the seven papers included in this volume. These abilities are particularly evident in the four syntheses written for the School of American Research Advanced Seminars on ancient Maya civilization. These four papers form the core of this book.

The very successful series of Advanced Seminars, initiated by Douglas W. Schwartz, bring together small groups of scholars—usually ten or so— for week-long in-depth discussions of significant themes in anthropology. The participants are housed in Santa Fe at the School's Seminar House. For five or six days, they live and breath the topic under consideration. The format has worked exceedingly well, and the seminars have prospered over the years. To date, they have produced more than two dozen published volumes, many of which have had significant impact on the field.

The importance of the Advanced Seminars can be seen particularly in the ones devoted to Maya archaeology. *The Classic Maya Collapse* (edited by T. P. Culbert and published by the University of New Mexico Press in 1973) was based on a seminar held in 1970, while *The Origins of Maya Civilization* (edited by R. E. W. Adams and published by the University of New Mexico Press in 1977) derived from a seminar that took place in 1974. It can be argued that these two books marked a major turning point in Maya studies, as traditional views of the development of ancient Maya civilization were discarded in favor of newer ones. In both cases, Gordon Willey served as the moderator of the seminars and prepared the summaries of the resultant volumes. The success of both enterprises clearly was dependent on Gordon's uncanny ability to bring together diverse data and arguments in coherent summary views. In particular, the summary chapter in *The Classic Maya Collapse,* prepared in collaboration with another masterful synthesizer, Demitri Shimkin, had a huge impact on the field and is still frequently referred to in the Maya literature. As Doug Schwartz has pointed out to me, this summary served as a model for subsequent seminars.

In the volume *Lowland Maya Settlement Patterns* (edited by W. Ashmore and published by the University of New Mexico Press in 1981), an important state-of-the-art review of the topic that is heavily used by students of Maya archaeology, Gordon again produced a highly useful summary synthesis. His concluding chapter, "Maya Lowland Settlement Patterns: A Summary Review," is a valiant attempt to synthesize the significant trends in settlement research. On the other hand, in *Late Low-*

land Maya Civilization: Classic to Postclassic (edited by J. A. Sabloff and E. W. Andrews V and published by the University of New Mexico Press in 1986), a volume which challenges much of the accepted wisdom about the Postclassic Maya, Gordon prepared a synthesis of the traditional view prior to the seminar and circulated it to all the participants to use as a baseline for their discussions. Although many of the points raised by Gordon in his general overview were disputed by the conferees, with typical graciousness Gordon allowed his original synthesis to be published without significant revision. His most recent thinking on the subject is presented in his introductory chapter which follows, as well as in the concluding chapter "Changing Conceptions of Lowland Maya Culture History."

In sum, unlike Kent Flannery's humorous figure the Great Synthesizer, Gordon Willey has been able to undertake successfully a huge amount of field research *and* a number of extremely useful syntheses. The utility of the Maya syntheses in particular rests in large part on Gordon's personal knowledge of the "on the ground" data from all over the realm of the ancient Maya. Moreover, Gordon has the intellectual ability to pull all these data together. The *American Heritage Dictionary* (1976) defines "synthesis" as "the combining of separate elements or substances to form a coherent whole." It goes on to define "coherent" as "sticking together . . . orderly or logical." Because of his vast knowledge, fine memory, and orderly, logical mind, Gordon is able to do mental pattern recognition studies on large arrays of Maya archaeological data. With indefatigable energy, he further has been able to translate such studies into clear, written statements. In the pages that follow, the reader is invited to share some of this clear thinking on the development of Maya civilization.

Introduction: Reflections and Reconsiderations

It is with mixed emotions that one looks back on previous archaeological writings—pleasure at the things one got right, dismay at the instances where one went wrong or made foolish statements. So it is in the present case. In these introductory "Reflections and Reconsiderations": I shall review seven essays or articles of mine with the benefit of hindsight. As five of these essays were written in the contexts of seminars or symposia where I drew upon and attempted to synthesize the opinions of various colleagues, I should absolve them of what I say here, which is entirely my own current set of opinions that may or may not coincide with opinions once held or now held by these former collaborators.

The essays were written between 1970 and 1983 and published between 1973 and 1986. I have arranged them in the order in which they were written, which varies slightly from their publication dates (see Table of Contents). In the thirteen years that they span, new discoveries and

interpretations of all kinds indicate the unsettled nature of the Maya archaeological research front. Three of the essays were prepared as summaries
to seminars that were held under the aegis of the School of American
Research in Santa Fe, New Mexico, and a fourth was done for a similar
purpose in connection with an International Congress of Americanists symposium. A fifth was, again, a part of a School of American Research seminar, but this time my paper was prepared as a preview rather than a
summary—a sort of target, as it were, for the other seminar participants
to take aim at in the preparation of their own contributions. The remain-
ing two essays were published in anthropological journals and were unrelated to any seminar or symposium proceedings; however, as both are of
a general and a summarizing or synthesizing nature, they seemed compatible with the present collection.

The seven essays stand essentially as originally written and published.
The only changes are those of a minor editorial nature involving bibliographic referencing in the texts and a compiling of a general bibliography
for the collection.

The Question of the Classic Maya Collapse

The first essay in the present volume, "The Maya Collapse: A Summary View", was written to summarize the proceedings of a seminar on
that topic that was held at the School for American Research in Santa Fe
in October 1970 (see Culbert, ed., 1973). It is the only essay in this present collection that was written with a coauthor, Demitri B. Shimkin, and I
wish to thank him for his willingness to let the essay be reprinted here
and for the fresh insights he brought to it and to the entire seminar. He
was the only one of the seminar group who was neither a Mayanist nor an
archaeologist. A social anthropologist with broad area and theoretical interests, he frequently rescued us from a too-myopic vision of the ancient Maya.

In looking back at the seminar, and in reading over our summary, I
think, perhaps, we were overly impressed with the uniqueness of the ninth-
century phenomenon of the collapse or breakdown of elite Maya culture.
In its magnitude and in the absence of any very impressive recovery of the
centers involved, it is unique; yet when, from a vantage point of research
and thinking of the last fifteen years, we take a look at Lowland Maya
culture growth in long time perspective, we see that the Maya, from Late
Preclassic times onward, were subject to waxings and wanings, periodic
spurts of growth alternating with retrenchments. While we still do not
know the reasons for these oscillations in the Lowland Maya develop-

mental trajectory, such a view helps put the Late Classic collapse in a context that may lead us eventually to a better understanding of it.

Our original summary of the archaeological data on the collapse stands up well enough. After the marked vigor in stelae dedication, major construction, and monumental art which characterized the Late Classic Period and which climaxed between 9.15.0.0.0 and 9.17.0.0.0 (A.D. 731–771), there was a slackening off to about 9.19.0.0.0 or 10.0.0.0.0 (A.D. 810–830) and then, for the most part, a cessation of all such elite ceremonial center or politico-religious center activity. This appraisal was based on the southern Lowlands, but we ducked the issue of the time of the collapse in the north because we could not come to an agreement on how to correlate southern and northern chronologies. E.W. Andrews IV dated his Florescent Period (Rio Bec-Chenes-Puuc) as completely post-Tepeu; others of us argued for what was then the more conventional dating of the Florescent as coeval with Tepeu.

As to the causes of the collapse, I really do not think that the perspective of fifteen years has brought us much closer to answers than we were then. At that time, the seminar members split into two camps: those favoring external pressures of some kind and those favoring internal stresses. It was of course admitted that these two types of factors could have worked in concert. I was in the "external" group and still am. That is, I thought that western or "Mexican" pressures were the most proximate cause of the collapse and still do. I admit I do not understand all of the processes involved in these pressures. An imperial-type military conquest seems most unlikely; the archaeological evidence just does not support it. Occasional military forays, quite probably linked to traders and trading policies, is probably a better speculation. Whatever the processes, I think that the overall picture of reconstructed events of the ninth and tenth centuries A.D. supports the idea of some kind of a western impingement on the southern Maya Lowlands. The far eastern part of the southern Lowlands shows much less evidence of collapse phenomena and foreign incursions than the west. Pendergast's (1981) excavations at Lamanai, in Belize, reveal, in contrast, that that important ceremonial center did not suffer a collapse disruption but, instead, kept right on going with elite constructional activities through the collapse period. I am suggesting that Lamanai's far eastern geographical position, with greater distance from the source of western and Mexican-like influences served as a protection against the cultural changes that were going on elsewhere.

As to Maya Lowland internal weaknesses or stresses, we are still about where we were at the time of the seminar. There Shimkin informed us about disease and nutritional factors. We went over matters of overpopulation, subsistence pressures, soil exhaustion. Since the seminar, I have heard of one new interpretation. This is the suggestion that a maize virus, brought or blown into Maya country from the West Indies sometime shortly before the collapse, had devastating effects on that staple crop (Brewbaker, 1979). Maybe—but I must admit to being prejudiced against all-explaining, catastrophic causes. I favored, and still favor, an explanation that lies in the political, social, and economic realm, to a confrontation of lifestyles between the Maya Lowlanders and the Mexican cultures and societies.

W. L. Rathje offered an hypothesis at the seminar which, I think, could be related to such Maya Lowlander–foreign confrontations. This is what he called his "core-buffer model". Rathje conceived of the "core" of old Maya society as being located in the Peten, certainly the apparent heartland of the stelae cult and related phenomena. Because of the resource redundancy of this tropical rainforest setting—so goes his argument—trade contacts with outside areas were extremely important, not only for exotic luxury items but for basic commodities. Eventually, those zones peripheral to the core, which were more favorably situated for these necessary trade contacts, came to outstrip the core in wealth and political power. Such a process led to the detachment of these peripheral or "buffer" polities from the mother society and their affiliation to what had been the surrounding alien cultures. I am not altogether satisfied with this model. The idea of a resource redundant core could be challenged, and the leading cities or "capitals" of some of the buffer zones—places like Palenque and Piedras Negras in the west or Quirigua and Copan in the southeast—collapsed as early, if not earlier, than the centers of the core. Still, it suggests processes by which old Classic Maya culture could have been adulterated and altered from its original norms.

In our attempts to gain a better perspective on possible or probable causal factors, the seminar, and Shimkin and I in our summary, performed what I think was a useful service in taking an analytical view of Late Classic Maya society. What were its structural features—its subsistence base, its population densities, social and political organization, religion, the institution of militarism, its degree of urbanism and urban functions, its manner of handling trade and marketing? I have no significant revisions on the way we treated these subjects. Viewed dynamically and as a system, we considered the role of the elite, the probable widening gulf that grew between elite and peasantry, the competition between polities, agricultural problems, demographic pressures and problems, and the matter of foreign contacts, especially in the context of trading relationships. While our opinions on all of these things reflected significant changes from the picture of Classic Maya society that archaeologists had operated with up until the 1950s, I do not think that my own opinions have changed much on these matters since the early 1970s. I think that the "widening social gulf" between elite and commoner is a fairly standard developmental corollary in the evolution of political and social systems toward high chiefdoms and states. Our model of the working system of Classic Maya culture and society still seems to me to be a reasonable one as far as it goes, but, as we said at the time, it does not go far enough to give us answers to some basic questions. Why didn't the Maya move on to a centralized state formation in the manner of the Central Mexicans? I cannot explain this now any better than I could in 1970.

The Rise of Classic Maya Civilization

This seminar followed the one on the Maya Collapse, and like the first it was designed by Adams and Culbert. In this one Adams (ed. 1977) edited the proceedings in the volume entitled *The Origins of Classic Maya Civilization*. The seminar was, again, held under the auspices of the School for American Research in Santa Fe, this time in a week in October 1974.

An obvious task in this seminar was to lay out a culture-historical framework in which we could trace the origins and growth of Maya civilization (see the map and chronological chart, Figs. 1.1 and 1.3, in Adams and Culbert, 1977). We set down an Early Preceramic Period (2000–1000 B.C.) but had little to fill it with at that time except speculation. In view of the early occupations in Gulf Coast Olmec country and in Pacific Coastal Guatemala and Chiapas, we asked the question, why not in the Maya Lowlands? Not long after the seminar meeting, Norman Hammond was to argue for a long Swazey phase at the Cuello site, in northern Belize, a Preclassic development that ran from 2000 to 1000 B.C. (Hammond et al. 1979). Swazey pottery was in a general Xe-Mamom tradition, and it has been questioned if it is, indeed, really this early and if for a thousand years or more this pottery tradition showed so little change (Marcus, 1983); however, the deep Cuello stratigraphy and the associated radiocarbon dates speak strongly in favor of the early dating. The seminar, prior to these northern Belizean discoveries, favored two possible sources for early Lowland Maya ceramics—the Gulf Coast Chontalpa country to the west, with its early Olmec linkages, and the Guatemalan Highlands to the south, with such complexes as the El Porton and Sakajut. I think at that time the majority preferred the Gulf Coastal Lowlands as the source; in fact, Hammond (1977b) argued for the beginnings of the Xe complex of the Peten as coming from this locale. The northern Belizean finds have certainly put the matter in doubt and have opened up the possibilities that unknown Lower Central American sources of early pottery may be somehow involved.

In talking about the Maya Lowland Middle Preclassic (1000–300 B.C.) in 1974, we suggested slight evidences for public building at this early date. Since then, with a closer look at our data, I think most Mayanists would concede that special platforms and small pyramids do so date (see Hammond et al. 1979); I know my own review of the Seibal architectural data so convinces me. The Late Preclassic (300–50 B.C.) was depicted as a time of heavy population increase and major ceremonial architectural construction, and everything we have found out about it since 1974 would emphasize these qualities for the period. Since then, the information forthcoming from Mirador, the giant platform and pyramid agglomeration in the far northern Peten, drives home the point even more that the Late Preclassic saw the appearance of politico-religious centers that attest to regional political units as impressive as those of the Classic. In sheer bulk, Mirador is larger than Tikal, and, insofar as archaeologists have yet determined, virtually all of the construction at Mirador is Preclassic (Matheny, ed., 1980; Demarest, ed.,1984). The evidence from there, so far, would indicate this to be Late Preclassic; however, until we have intensive architectural excavations at that site we cannot completely discount the possibility that its substantial constructional beginnings go back to the Middle Preclassic.

One of the things that we noted about the Late Preclassic Period in the 1974 seminar was the variation through time, in population concentration and architectural construction, as we moved from one Maya Lowland region to another and even from one major site to another. For instance, at Tikal in the northeast Peten or at Cerros in northern Belize, the population-constructional peak came early in the Late Preclassic Period, with a subsequent dropoff at both sites; in contrast, at Becan in the Rio Bec region the earlier part of the period saw little major construction, with a boom in such activity later. At Dzibilchaltun, in the Yucatecan northern plains, the Late Preclassic profile was more like that of Tikal or Cerros, but this was not the case with other sites in this part of the Lowlands. With my penchant to seek regularities and generalizations, I was disturbed by this and wrote: "Must our attempts at generalization and our search for developmental regularities be further complicated by site-to-site as well as region-to-region variability?" (Willey, 1977b p. 390) However, I was willing to concede that: "When we construct a finer-grained spatial-temporal framework in which to examine events, we are confronted with variation. This variation is almost sure to have been important in the course of civilizational growth in the Maya Lowlands. (Ibid., p. 391) And this has

been borne in upon us with ever greater force as Maya studies have pro-
ceeded over the decade since the "Origins" seminar. Not only are we confronted with region-to-region and site-to-site variation in the Late Preclassic
but this characterizes the Classic. As is nearly always the case, generalization is easier when we don't know so much.

A striking example of region-to-region and site-to-site variation occurs
with the onset of the Early Classic. The standard markers of that period
in Lowland Maya archaeology have always been Initial Series hieroglyphic
dates, vaulted architecture, and Tzakol polychrome pottery. This complex of elite traits appears in the northeast Peten at ca. A.D. 250. But can
we establish this same "floor" or beginning date for the Early Classic Period throughout the Maya Lowlands? I do not think so. The A.D. 250 date
would appear to hold for the northeast Peten and probably adjacent Belize;
but on the Pasion-Usumacinta drainages I think that the appropriate date
for the first appearance of these traditional Early Classic markers would
be nearer A.D. 450. At least this is the date for the earliest Initial Series
stelae in these regions, and there are good reasons to believe that Tzakol
polychrome pottery was not much earlier there (Lincoln, 1985; Willey,
1985). The same is true for Copan and Quirigua in the southeast. While
we had some information to tell us this in 1974, we were still too prone
to generalize the Early Classic Period and culture type as a fixed and homo-
geneous unit, dating at A.D. 250–600. In this same revisionist spirit, it should
be noted that the "Hiatus" phenomenon of the latter part of the sixth
century A.D. is by no means as uniform for the southern Lowlands as I
then believed (Willey, 1974, 1977b (see, in this connection, the map, Fig.
6, in Mathews, 1985).

On the question of external relationships of the Maya Lowlands during the time of origins and early development, I would still think, following G. W. Lowe's remarks in the seminar, that the probabilities favor the
Olmec and Maya as having been linguistically related in a Mayan-Zoquean
stock. The Olmec-to-Izapan-to-Lowland Mayan iconographic, artistic, and
ideological development in sculptural art that M. D. Coe and Jacinto
Quirarte propounded at the seminar still seems to me to explain at least
part of the story of the rise of Lowland Maya high art although the strict
linearity of the continuity probably was not so simple, and J. A. Graham's
discoveries at Abaj Takalik reveal, although do not iron out, some of the
complexities of what happened (Graham, 1977a,b, 1979). On the matter
of influences from El Salvador to the Maya Lowlands in Protoclassic times,
I think that trade and diffusion is the best way to explain Usulutan and
related ceramic types in the Lowlands rather than large-scale migrations
of peoples (Demarest, 1984 Ms), and this despite arguments about vol-

canic eruptions in the Salvadoran Highlands (Sheets, 1976). I think it is
very difficult—much more difficult than we have conceded—to appraise
the nature of Teotihuacan influence on the Maya Early Classic society and
culture. The monuments and burials at Tikal do indicate some kind of
influence on the elite, politico-religious level (Coggins, 1979), but just how
direct this was from Teotihuacan, as military or even trading power, is
still moot. If I had to sum up the changes in my thinking about the role of
Teotihuacan in Lowland Maya political affairs during the Early Classic
Period, I would say that this influence was less than I thought then. I doubt
if it had any very large part in state formation.

In my seminar summary I tried to synthesize various opinions about
processes of cultural and social growth, especially as these had been voiced
by Sanders, Netting, Webster, and Rathje. Up to a point I agreed with
Sanders, and still do, that population growth in an area that previously
had been unoccupied was a prime mover. This was before R. S. MacNeish
and his colleagues (1980) had published their preceramic discoveries in
Belize, and I was starting from a base-line of Early Preclassic pottery-making
(and presumably agricultural communities). Population at this time would
have been small, and I suppose it would have been smaller still in the
preceramic. Successful agriculture in the tropical lowlands must have been
the principal factor in the population buildup, with new lands constantly
being brought under cultivation. I see no reason to change my mind about
this. In reading back over my concluding summation, I see that I related
the development of elite culture to inter-group rivalry. Competition, including
warfare, must have had something to do with the rise of complex societies,
but if I were rewriting my statement I would prefer to say that the
need for social control, attendant upon population increase, was probably
even more important. I have never been as convinced as others about
the role of trade as a causal force in the rise of the Lowland Maya high
chiefdoms or petty states. I see trade, or at least the trade in elite exotic
goods, as having been handled by the aristocratic lineage leaders or lords
in a redistributive fashion. We first begin to see impressive signs of it in
the Late Preclassic, but I think there are indications now of the beginnings
of non-egalitarian societies in the Maya Lowlands as early as the Middle
Preclassic. I would see exotic trade imports for the elite as coming after
the fact of ranked or stratified societies, rather than the cause of them.
My final words in the 1974 summary were that ideology could not be
ignored in the rise of Maya civilization, and I am still convinced of this.
Since then, the writings of Maya epigraphers (Schele, 1976; Mathews and
Schele, 1975; Jones, 1977) and students of Maya art (Freidel, 1979, 1981c)
have shown us some of the ways ideas articulated with other aspects of

culture to give Maya civilization its form and to provide some of the driving forces behind it. We cannot brush all this off as "epi-phenomenal". An army may march forward only "on its stomach", but I don't believe a civilization can.

Prehistoric Maya Agriculture

This summary essay was written in 1976 in connection with a symposium on this topic organized by P. D. Harrison for the International Congress of Americanists held that summer in Paris (see Harrison and Turner, eds., 1978). I lay no claim to expertise in the subject, but like most Maya archaeologists I am aware of its great importance. Questions about prehistoric cultivation in the Maya Lowlands have been asked, off and on, for some time (Ricketson and Ricketson, 1937), and there had been a renewed interest in them in the early 1970's (Siemens and Puleston, 1972; Turner, 1974). The Paris symposium made it very clear that long-fallow swidden agriculture was not the only cultivation technique used by the ancient Maya in their forested homeland. Populations as estimated from settlement pattern studies were simply not compatible with the swidden model. Various intensive techniques were employed—terracing, artificial raised fields, and "kitchen-garden" cropping. But with these generally agreed upon findings, a number of problems opened up. What was the chronological trend in Lowland Maya agricultural development? Was there a gradual increase in intensification techniques through time, a beginning with swidden cultivation and a subsequent supplementation of this with terraces plots, raised fields, and so forth? There is a superficial logic to such a developmental story, but Norman Hammond (1978), in his symposium paper, offered the counter-suggestion that a technique such as raised field cultivation could have been very ancient. Rather than being more difficult than clearing fields for swidden, it was actually easier, at least on a small scale and in swampy or lacustrine circumstances. In his hypothesis, small villages of the Early and Middle Preclassic were so sustained. Later, with population increases, peoples were forced to move into more heavily forested terrain and to take up swidden clearing. Which is the preferred hypothesis? While there are some Preclassic—mainly Late Preclassic— indications of raised field constructions, the preponderance of the evidence to date suggests that they are largely Classic and, probably, Late Classic.

At the time of the Paris symposium, I offered the opinion that probably all cultivation techniques under discussion were known from early times in the Maya Lowlands but that these varied in application, from period to period and from place to place. I think this was hedging in the face of uncertainty. I do not now think that the highly labor-intensive techniques, such as large scale terracing or raised field construction would date before the Late Preclassic. It is unlikely, if we are correct in our population estimates, that there would have been enough people around in the early periods to have built and maintained them.

Lowland Maya Settlement Patterns

The Settlement Pattern seminar, held at Santa Fe in October 1977, was an idea originally suggested by Wendy Ashmore early in that year. By that time, following the earlier Santa Fe Maya seminars and the Paris symposium on agriculture, it was becoming ever more obvious that settlement sizes and dispositions were crucial in all sorts of questions about the ancient Lowland Maya. Wendy and I planned the seminar together, and she later edited the proceedings (Ashmore, ed., 1981). We considered our theme in much the same way as the "Collapse" and "Origins" themes. We devoted some papers to methodological and theoretical considerations; we went on from these to a series of regional settlement presentations of Lowland data; and we concluded with attempts at a processual understanding of the hows and whys of Maya settlement forms.

From the start of the seminar discussions, it was clear that settlement patterns was a "hot topic" in Maya archaeology. Disagreements popped up all over the place, especially when we began to struggle with definitions of residential units and groupings and the forms and natures of ceremonial or politico-religious centers. No two archaeologists seemed to have thought of these things in quite the same way, yet for all of us there was a certain overlapping of perceptions and concepts. Things were made additionally confusing in that there was no standard nomenclature for settlement units, and, as might be expected, we were plagued by the necessity, in the absence of anything better, to use functional terms over which there was inevitable disagreement. In spite of all of this, I think we did pretty well, and my summary was an attempt to show the degree of consensus that did exist and—it went without saying—to show some of the directions future studies should take. I think if I were writing the summary over again that I would devote more space to the cultural-natural environmental interface and its bearings on settlement, to agricultural strategies, and to population estimates. We did talk about all of these things at some length in the seminar discussions; indeed, they found their way into most arguments. But, as an example, no one addressed questions of settlement densities (on a small, rather than a regional scale) as these might be correlated to terrain types, except Don Rice (Rice and Puleston, 1981) who was not in attendance at the seminar but participated later by completing the late Dennis Puleston's manuscript. One thing that was not treated, although there was probably not enough information on hand to do it, was to examine settlement densities in regions where raised field cultivation was employed and contrast these to regions or locales where there was no evidence of the raised field cultivation technique. With relation to the agricultural terracing technique of intensive cultivation, Adams' (1981) population estimates of persons per sq. km is just about the same as the estimates generally given for Tikal—500 or 600 persons per sq. km. The terracing technique was not employed at Tikal. Was swidden cultivation, supplemented by household "garden-cropping", the only agricultural system at Tikal? Or was there raised field cultivation in the nearby *bajos*? These are questions that we still cannot answer, but they and others that still baffle us help explain why my 1977 summary had to be as inconclusive as it was.

I feel that my summary of "Centers"—the Lowland Maya ceremonial centers, politico-religious centers, organizational centers, cities, or whatever one may wish to call them—is very disappointing, and, again I can only pass a share of the blame on to my colleagues who did not do much with this aspect of settlement in their individual papers or in the discussions. Haviland (1981) was the one exception. He came up with an original idea on the functions of what might be looked at as minor centers within the larger settlement radius of the Tikal main center, suggesting that they might be "dower-houses" for former main center rulers, perhaps collateral kin of some kind still living in aristocratic status but no longer, as it were, "in office". His particular idea is pretty behaviorally specific for the evidence at our disposal, but I think he has opened up the question of multiple aristocratic lineages converging at an important center and one such lineage emerging as paramount. More generally, we need studies of center layouts so that comparisons can be made of these, region-to-region and period-to-period. In making such studies, the degree of urbanism, in its formal or functional aspects, should not be the only question asked. Hammond (1981) in his seminar paper, suggested that certain major centers in Belize featured a bipartite kind of arrangement, with one part of the center devoted to political matters, the other to more sacred or religious themes. This should be followed up as should a suggestion I have made on various occasions to the effect that Late Preclassic and Early Classic center organization may reveal multiple temple-palace complexes, perhaps each relating to a powerful lineage, and that these are then made architecturally, and perhaps politically, subordinate to a single great lineage in the Late Classic.

My 1977 summations of Lowland Maya settlement "micropatterns", attempts at community definitions, is as good as I can do now. Haviland's (1981; see also 1969, 1970, 1972) populations estimates for Tikal—72,000 persons for a 120 sq. km zone consisting of central Tikal and its environs—certainly approaches the physical dimensions of urbanism, even though this lacks the density of Teotihuacan or Tenochtitlan. What were the functions of this urbanism? Who lived in such cities? Almost surely the elite lived there. I think many of the other residents were farmers, but then Millon (1973) thinks that many of the residents of Teotihuacan were also farmers. There is still not much evidence for an urban "middle class", as such a class is usually so defined. Governmental functionaries and servants to the elite could have composed a part of such an emerging class. Some Tikal households have signs of craft manufacturing activities, but there seem to be no barrio sections at Tikal comparable to those of Teotihuacan. So far, the only very good evidence we have for intensive, large-scale craft production comes from the rather small center of Colha, in northern Belize (Hester et al. 1980); but Colha can hardly be considered an urban center. Instead, it looks more like a secondary center in a site hierarchy dominated by a major center, in this case perhaps Nohmul.

The establishment of site hierarchies in the Maya Lowlands seems to be progressing well since what I had to say on the subject of "macropatterns" in the 1977 settlement summary. Much of this advance derives from hieroglyphic textual translation, but the "volumetric" approach needs more examination and analysis in our attempts to determine relative importance and power of centers. We still have little information about residential settlement between centers, and the gathering of this information is bound to be slow-going. I still carry the model of major centers as zones of dispersed-urban clusterings of residences, secondary and tertiary centers as also being the nuclei of smaller clusterings, but what of the interlying hinterlands? There are hints that in some places residential dwellings dotted the landscape in more or less continuous distributions; but there are also indications that there are sizable tracts of Maya Lowland land with no signs of habitations. These latter may have been non-arable tracts, unsuitable for cultivation and habitation; on the other hand, such settlement spacing may have been dictated purely by political or cultural choices.

My ideas about the processual models offered by Adams and Smith (1981), Sanders (1981), and Freidel (1986) are still about what they were. As I have already indicated, I still approve of a general "feudal model" for Classic Maya social, political, and economic organization, and I think that this organization is related to an agriculture that was, to a large degree, so constrained by natural environmental conditions.

I have gone on longer about this seminar, and my summary of it, than I have about any of the others. It is the Maya subject I know best, and I suppose for this reason it is more difficult for me to let go of it or to come to hard and fast conclusions about it. The seminar volume received, as the saying goes, "mixed reviews" when it came out, more so even than the Collapse volume with its quite controversial theme. Most reviewers were disappointed that we had not addressed, or taken into account, many aspects of the Lowland Maya settlement problem or followed approaches, such as that offered by ethnohistory, that we did not pursue. To these criticisms, I can only plead that we made a beginning to a very complex and diverse theme. My colleague Sabloff (1983) feels that the seminar, and Maya settlement pattern studies up to that time, failed to formulate the proper questions and that this has led to the rather diffuse and unsatisfactory state that the subject is now in. I agree, at least in part, and can only hope that such questions will be devised for future research.

Toward an Holistic View of Ancient Maya Civilization

In 1979, with the experience with the four seminars or symposia behind me, I wanted to draw together a statement about the tight integrity, the coherence of ancient Lowland Maya civilization. It was given as the Huxley Lecture at the Royal Anthropological Society, in London, in 1979 and published the next year in the journal *Man* (Vol. 15, 1980). I had been inspired by a remarkable paper written by the late Dennis Puleston (1977) entitled, "The Art and Archaeology of Hydraulic Agriculture in the Maya Lowlands". Puleston had presented a fascinating argument about how raised field cultivation and its aquatic ambience provided dominant themes in the hieratic art and iconography of the time. I attempted to go beyond this and to show the articulation of other aspects of Maya culture—particularly in settlement patterns and socio-political organization—to subsistence, art, and ideology. As a synthesis, the essay was very much related to the Santa Fe and Paris summaries so it seemed fitting to include it in this collection.

The articulations of Lowland Maya settlement patterns with subsistence practices are fairly obvious ones. Residential settlement tends to be dispersed in an adaptation to agricultural fields. Both of these things relate to governance and agricultural management. The hierarchical nature of politico-religious centers is well suited to the control of spatially scattered populations, and I had no hesitancy in accepting the idea of a chain of command, as it were, running from major centers, to secondary ones, to tertiary ones, and on down to farming hamlets, a communication system which must have regulated planting, harvesting, and the appropriate rites and duties in connection with these activities. I still so interpret the subsistence-settlement-governance linkages in the system. I think that the analogy to feudal Europe (Adams and Smith, 1981) is serviceable up to a point. An agricultural economy was managed, and in effect owned, by an aristocratic, hierarchically-ordered leadership. There must have been reciprocal duties up and down the social scale in the operation of the system. The analogy does not go the whole way in giving us a picture of how ancient Lowland Maya society worked (see Marcus, 1983), but then few analogies ever do, at least in human histories.

I think if I were doing the "Holistic" article over again the thing I would change or moderate would be the specificity with which I spoke of Teotihuacan political influence at Tikal. The "foreign-ness" of the ruler "Curl-Snout" is much more equivocal than I wrote about it then. The best of the data implying his Teotihuacan connections are the associations with persons in Central Mexican regalia. The hieroglyphic information on his origins are much less definite (personal communication, Peter Mathews, 1985). I admit to being over-dazzled and over-optimistic about the prospect of dealing with identified personalities of the fourth century A.D. Most everyone in Maya archaeology has responded positively to the recent advances on the part of the epigraphers. The light they have been able to throw upon all kinds of dynastic matters, the births and deaths of rulers, wars and alliances, the determinations of territorial polities—all of these have given a new invigoration to Maya studies; and yet we must temper our enthusiasm with caution, especially those of us who do not directly control the glyphic texts.

I would still emphasize the articulation of ideology with the rest of the Classic Maya system. Whatever "Curl-Snout's" origins, he seems to have been associated with calendar reforms at Tikal, as Coggins (1979) argued, and these calendrical changes appear to be a part of a kind of revitalization movement at the site. As I have noted, Puleston's linking of raised field or hydraulic agriculture to Maya art and iconography was the stimulus for this essay. I suppose his observations are something that can never be proven, but I find them convincing. They argue, in essence, for a functional "fit" between belief systems and other systemic parts of the culture.

The Postclassic of the Maya Lowlands

The Postclassic seminar was planned to be held in Santa Fe in October 1982. Prior to that, I was invited by the seminar organizers, J. A. Sabloff and E. W. Andrews V, to prepare a long preview paper on my ideas about this period in the Maya Lowlands. As a part of my preparations on this, I relied upon the students of my Harvard seminar for the preceding year who were assigned this theme for our semester-long deliberations. They are referred to throughout this preview essay which was written in 1981–82. Following the Santa Fe seminar meeting in 1982, I made some small factual changes and added a little prologue in which I indicated how I had changed some of my ideas about the topic. Here let me add to that prologue.

As I said in my original preview, I have held what could be considered the more or less traditional archaeological views of the Lowland Maya Postclassic Period. I have seen it as a time of cultural collapse and population abandonment in the southern part of the Lowlands, and, with the exception of the great site of Chichen Itza, as a time of collapse in the north as well. In the latter part of the period, the Late Postclassic, I conceded a degree of recuperation in the north, at Mayapan and other sites, but this renaissance always appeared to me to be an achievement well below the architectural, artistic, and demographic peaks of the Classic Period. Our Harvard seminar review of the literature, and my own thoughts concurrent with that seminar, continued to confirm me in this opinion. The Postclassic seminar forced me to change my opinion, at least to a degree.

For me, and I think for some others of us in the seminar, there were two main revisions of the conventional Lowland Maya archaeological picture resulting from the Santa Fe 1982 deliberations. For some of our group, these revisions had already been accepted, or at least seriously considered, at a 1979 symposium at an American Anthropological Association meeting (see Chase and Rice, eds., 1985); but I know that in my own case the Santa Fe seminar was an eye-opener. The first revision—and this takes us back to the "Collapse" seminar of 1970—is that the phenomenon of the Classic Maya collapse does not occur, or at least does not occur at the same time and in the same way, in the northern Lowlands as it did in the south. The ninth century A.D., far from being a time of decline in northern ceremonial center construction, saw the peak of such architecture and art in the Puuc region of northern Yucatan. This climax was then maintained in the north for at least another two centuries.

The second revision concerns the alignment of southern and northern Lowland chronologies. The new alignment, with which most of us are most comfortable, falls somewhere between the old J. E. S. Thompson (1945) matching of southern and northern sequences and the cross-dating advocated by E. W. Andrews IV (1973) at the "Collapse" conference. According to the way we look at it now, the climax of Rio Bec-Chenes architecture occurs coeval with Tepeu 2 and continues with strength into Tepeu 3 (A.D. 800–900). Thereafter, in the Rio Bec-Chenes country there was a decline. Its severity has not yet been fully appraised, but it would seem to approximate what had happened in the Peten a hun dred years earlier. In the far north, however, the Puuc architectural tradi tion continues with force later than this. Just how late the Puuc tradition did continue is still somewhat moot. Charles Lincoln, in his paper for the Postclassic seminar, has argued that Toltec Chichen, as it is generally known—inclusive of the great pyramid, the Temple of the Warriors, the great Ball Court, and other structures at Chichen Itza—was contempora neous with the florescence of the great Puuc sites—Uxmal, Kabah, Sayil, and others. In other words, Chichen Itza and the Puuc sites all represent what E. W. Andrews IV had subsumed together in his Florescent Period, a period which overlapped only with the final century of the Tepeu-defined Late Classic period of the south. Others in the seminar, among whom I would count myself, admit to some chronological overlap between Toltec Chichen Itza and the Puuc sites but are inclined to think that Chichen last ed somewhat longer.

These revisions and these reconsiderations led the Postclassic semi nar group to conclude that the important break in developmental conti nuity in the north is not between the Classic and Postclassic Periods as these have been traditionally defined, but between what was once consid ered the Early Postclassic and the Late Postclassic, or at about A.D. 1250, the date generally considered to be the close of Chichen Itza as the domi nant center of the north. It is probably still too early to consider this new chronological-developmental interpretation absolutely sound; more field investigations are necessary; but I think we are moving somewhat nearer the truth.

As to the question of a Postclassic continuance in the southern Low lands, Arlen and Diane Chase and Prudence Rice, all members of the 1982 seminar, have shown that there was some continued occupation in parts of the southern Lowlands after A.D. 900, continuing, in effect, on up until the time of the Spanish entradas into the lakes region of the southern Peten. Farther east, at Lamanai, in Belize, David Pendergast's work has demon strated occupation and vitality at that site well into what we generally have considered the Early Postclassic centuries. At the same time, it is still my opinion, as I stated in my preview essay, that this continuance in the southern Lowlands was of a greatly reduced nature, especially in contrast to elite activities of the Classic Period. In the north, while I must admit to substantial populations and elite constructional and ceremonial activi ties throughout the Late Postclassic, continuing through the building of Mayapan and even afterward, I see Lowland Maya society of this period as drastically changed from its earlier norms. It is a reduced and redirected version of what went on before in the great Puuc sites and at Chichen Itza. We shall continue to be concerned with how and why this transformation took place. As I have said, I feel it had something to do with the Mayans inability to successfully adapt to a world that was more and more becoming an extended sphere of Central Mexican power.

Changing Conceptions of Lowland Maya Culture History

This essay was written in 1983 although published later (Willey, 1984). It is, in itself, a review and general consideration of the trends in thinking in Maya archaeology, from earliest times down to the present. As such, I have little to change although Maya archaeologists could enter into extended discussion from many of the points touched upon so briefly in the article. One such take-off point is the matter of the Olmec and Olmec-Maya relationships. Did a precocious Olmec peoples, presumably centered on the Gulf Coast of Mexico, bring civilization to other groups of the Mesoamerican area somewhere back in Middle Preclassic times? Arthur Demarest (1986), in his summary to an Olmec seminar on the Olmec, views such an interpretation with caution. He argues that several regions of southern Mesoamerica—the Pacific Coast of Chiapas and Guatemala, the Grijalva Trench in Chiapas, Oaxca, and perhaps even the Maya Lowlands—were already on their way to complex, stratified societies before they were so blessed with Olmec enlightenment. I think we have to heed his statements. Whatever the facts of archaeology that emerge in continued research on this early period in Mesoamerica, we are certainly dealing with important questions of process as we address this point.

Related to this, and moving on into the Late Preclassic, what did happen between the Maya Highlands and Pacific Coast and the Maya Lowlands, especially in the spread and acceptance of elite elements of culture?

The Lowland Maya, Teotihuacan, and Kaminaljuyu have fascinating Early Classic relationships. How will we continue to interpret these? What was the nature of Teotihuacan power and what effect did it have, if any, on the processes of state formation in the Maya Lowlands?

How are we to interpret Lowland Maya-Central Mexican relationships during the Late Classic and Postclassic Periods? For some time it has been obvious that the art and iconography of the Late Classic northern Lowlands exhibited Mexican-like traits (Proskouriakoff, 1951; Sabloff and Willey, 1967; Sharp, 1981). We have generally considered these traits to have resulted from contacts antedating the presumed Toltec influence at Chichen Itza. Is this correct? What was the nature of these contacts or interactions? There is evidence available now from the site of Cacaxtla, in

Tlaxcala, to suggest that this interaction was much more complicated than a simple Central Mexican invasion into the Maya Lowlands (Quirarte, 1983). Closely related to these questions about Mexican influence is, of course, the problem of the chronological correlation between northern Lowland and southern Lowland sequences, just referred to in my comments on the Postclassic seminar.

As we consider these and other questions, and reflect on the changing conceptions of Lowland Maya culture history and archaeology, I think the one thing that is brought to our attention most forcefully is that as the culture-historical framework is extended and improved we are in a better position to ask other kinds of questions about the ancient Maya and their neighbors. In turn, as we ask these questions, we come back to correcting and improving the culture-historical framework. In this way, in spite of many errors and false starts, I think the Maya archaeological enterprise can look forward to a good future.

Harvard University
April 1986

1 The Maya Collapse: A Summary View

Gordon R. Willey

Department of Anthropology
Harvard University

Demitri B. Shimkin

Center for Advanced Study
in the Behavioral Sciences

Introduction

The purpose of this chapter is to perform a synthesis of the opinion and argument presented and developed in the preceding chapters (see also Willey and Shimkin 1971a, 1971b). It will be organized along three axes: historical, analytical, and hypothetical. The findings of archaeology which bear upon the Maya collapse and failure of recovery will first be presented in a chronological and descriptive-historical manner. Secondly, we will analyze the nature of ancient Classic Maya society and culture from the standpoints of their structural features and of their dynamic aspects. Thirdly, we will construct our hypothetical model of the processes involved in the Maya collapse. We will close by posing a series of new questions, generated by our inquiry, for future research.

We feel—and the other authors in this volume concur in this—that the problem of the Maya collapse, besides being of unusual culture-historical interest in its particulars, has a broader significance for archaeology and anthropology at large. What we have attempted in our discussions, essays, and this summary is to develop a social anthropology of the Maya, particularly of prehistoric culure change, from archaeological data. To whatever extent we have been successful, our findings should have a bearing on other questions of a similar nature.

A Historical Synopsis of Classic Maya Civilization and the Collapse

EARLY CLASSIC PERIOD ANTECEDENTS

As has been related elsewhere in this volume, Maya civilization appeared in the Southern Lowlands in its developed form by the third century A.D. Its development was in situ, although influenced to a significant extent by stimuli from outside the Southern Lowlands. In the Early Classic Period (A.D. 250–550) the elements characterizing the elite aspects of this civilization spread throughout the Southern and Northern Lowlands. Although some population movements may have been involved in this spread, it seems most likely that the process chiefly involved the relatively rapid acculturation of a number of Maya-speaking communities that were already interrelated by a common Late Preclassic culture base.

During the Early Classic the Maya Lowlands maintained trade contacts with the major political and economic power of that time–Teotihuacan in Central Mexico. Tikal, especially, was a focus of such contacts and of Teotihuacan influences. In the sixth century A.D., with the waning of Teotihuacan power, these influences disappeared from Maya culture. For a brief period of from 40 to 60 years, the Classic Maya seem to have undergone a period of crisis, quite probably in the course of a readjustment of trade routes and patterns that had been occasioned by the weakening—and eventual death—of Teotihuacan; but beginning with the *katun* ending of 9.8.0.0.0 (A.D. 593),[1] Maya culture in the Southern Lowlands enjoyed a vigorous renewal in the Late Classic Period. Thus, it is quite likely that the decline of Teotihuacan opened the way for an era of Maya florescence. Conversely, the reemergence of Central Mexican political and commercial hegemony, at the close of the Late Classic Period, hastened and intensified the Maya Lowland collapse.

THE LATE CLASSIC PERIOD CLIMAX

While Maya Late Classic culture shows a clear continuity with Early Classic, there are differences in degree and in structure. For one thing, there are indications that Late Classic society was more sharply differentiated into elite and commoner strata than had been the case in Early Classic times. Multiroomed buildings or "palaces," presumably residences for the aristocracy, are more numerous in the Late Classic. Rathje (1970; 1973) has noted Early Classic to Late Classic changes in the variables of age, sex, tomb or grave types, elaborateness of burial accouterments, nature of burial ornament symbolism, and the location of graves with reference to temple, palace, or ordinary domestic structures; and these changes point to a solidification of class lines and an increasing trend toward ascribed as opposed to achieved status. Another supporting line of evidence for this trend can be seen in the hieroglyphic inscriptions and associated sculptural representations. Early Classic inscriptions tended to be short, frequently little more than dedicatory dates; those of the Late Classic, insofar as they can be translated (Proskouriakoff 1963, 1964; Kelley 1962), tell of royal lineages, ascensions to kingship, dynastic struggles, and intercity wars. In sum, our inferences from the evidence lead to a picture of a hereditary artistocracy steadily increasing its influence in the early part of the Late Classic Period.

As this process of an elite consolidation went on, the Maya Late Classic social order must have become more complex, with a related development of a class of bureaucrats and craft specialists. The clues to craft specialization, both in the nature of the products themselves and in the urban-type settlement findings, indicate that the presence of full-time artisans is a reasonable possibility. The institution of long-distance trade—both in luxury Items and in more general produce—probably involved the services of a large staff of bureaucratic officials. Certainly, if Rathje's (1973) and Webb's (1973) theses are accepted, we must believe this increase to be the case. While we are still of the opinion that a redistributive system, controlled at the top by the aristrocracy, was the basic form of Maya economics, such a system would have engaged the services of many persons; and such a system was probably undergoing expansion during the first 200 years or so of the Late Classic Period.

The proliferaton of ceremonial centers during the Late Classic Period indicate trade and political expansion. New sites sprang up in numbers, especially along the western, southern, and eastern peripheries of the old Maya Lowland Peten "core." The sites of the Usumacinta drainage did not come into prominence as important centers until the Late Classic; in the south and east the centers of southern British Honduras (Lubaatun, Pusilha), of the Motagua-Chamelecon (Copan, Quirigua), and of the Ulua periphery were being settled for the first time or rising to importance.

This political and commerical expansion of the Lowland Maya, as seen in the rise of many new sites, undoubtedly reflects population growth.

From those regions where we have adequate settlement surveys, such as in the Belize Valley (Willey et al. 1965), at Tikal (Haviland 1965, 1969), and at Seibal (Tourtellot 1970), there are indications of an increase in the number of domestic quarters from Early Classic to Late Classic times which is most reasonably interpreted as an absolute increase in population numbers. Proportionately, however, the rate of this increase, in view of the already substantial Early Classic population, was not as great as that which occurred in the Maya Lowlands from Middle Preclassic to Late Preclassic times.

The Late Classic Period in the Southern Lowlands is subdivided chronologically. The earliest part of the period, from 9.8.0.0.0 (A.D. 593) to 9.13.0.0.0 (A.D. 692; see Rands, 1973a, Fig. 6), is most frequently referred to by the ceramic phase name and number, Tepeu 1. Pottery of Tepeu 1 shows definite linkages back to antecedent Early Classic (Tzakol) styles, but there are also a number of changes. The earlier basal-flange bowl disappears, and figure painting—with scenes of men, gods, and animals—becomes quite common in polychrome decoration. Tepeu 2, dating from 9.13.0.0.0 (A.D. 692) until 10.0.0.0.0 (A.D. 830), marks a climax in polychrome figure painting, especially in the production of handsome cylinder jars, often ornamented with hieroglyphic inscriptions, as well as with life or mythic scenes.

For most of the Southern Lowlands the climax of Maya Classic civilization occurred in Tepeu 2 times, and especially within the earlier part of that subperiod, or from 9.13.0.0.0 (A.D. 692) to 9.17.0.0.0 (A.D. 771). For example, more dedicatory monuments or stelae date from the 9.17.0.0.0 *katun* ending than from any other; and, considering all of the Southern Lowland ceremonial centers, it is probable that the sheer mass of architectural construction dating to this earlier part of Tepeu 2 was greater than for any other equivalent period of time in Maya history, before or since. There is, however, some regional and zonal variation in this tempo of cultural growth, and some centers appear to have begun to "boom" earlier than others. For instance, the greatest Late Classic building surge at Tikal may have been in Tepeu 1, rather than in Tepeu 2, times,[2] and the same seems to be true for Palenque (Rands, 1973b) and Altar de Sacrificios (Adams, 1973b). But, whatever the finer chronological subdivisions of events, there is no question but that Tepeu 1 and 2—or the centuries from approximately A.D. 600 to 800—saw the spectacular climax of Lowland Maya civilization in the south.

During this two centuries of climax, Maya civilization in the south was integrated at the elite level in a more impressive fashion than ever before. The various regions and centers were linked by a monumental art style in stone sculpture and by a variant of this style in the polychrome figure-painted pottery. The same mythic or god figures are represented in this art; and this, together with the same hieroglyphic and calendrical systems, often expressed from center to center in identical texts and in the same complex lunar count formulations, leaves little doubt of a shared religion, ritual, and history.[3]

However, some signs of regionalism in this culture of the elite are apparent. "Emblem" glyphs, which appear to be the heraldric insignia of the different centers (and/or their ruling families) suggest such feelings of regional identity; and portrayals of warfare, on wall paintings and in monumental carvings, in which Maya are obviously fighting other Maya, imply a degree of rivalry. Such regionalism or localism is further reinforced—but with implications for a commoner level of society—by differences in ordinary domestic ceramics between ceremonial centers. Very likely, there were rules and regulations in the elite tradition which attempted to restrain or control such rivalry, and the widespread popularity of the ball game in the Maya Lowlands in Late Classic times may have served the function of mitigating intercity strife. But, as we shall see later, it is highly probable that competition between centers and regions was a definite dynamic factor in Maya Late Classic life.

In the later part of the Tepeu 2 subperiod (after 9.17.0.0.0 or A.D. 771) and in the Tepeu 3 subperiod (10.0.0.0.0–10.3.0.0.0 or A.D. 830–889) Maya civilization in the Southern Lowlands descended rapidly from its Tepeu 1–Tepeu 2 climax and, eventually, collapsed completely. In the light of the details presented in the accompanying symposium papers, let us review the events of this decline and collapse.

THE COLLAPSE

In considering the events of the collapse as these are registered in the archaeological record, we shall refer to the chronological charts presented by Rands (1973a, Figs. 5–8).

The Western Data   Beginning on the left hand side of these charts— at what represents the western edge of the Southern Maya Lowlands—are the columns for Trinidad, Palenque, and Piedras Negras. The Trinidad column, which subsumes information from that site and from Calatrava and Tierra Blanca, is known chiefly from ceramic information. A Taxinchan Phase is contemporaneous with the later part of Tepeu 1 and dated (although without benefit of directly associated Long Count dates) from 9.10.0.0.0 to 9.13.0.0.0 (A.D. 633–692). (These are the mean or standard dates offered on Rands's chart, Fig. 5. For the possible range of "slippage" or error for these and other dates discussed in this section see Rands's

2. Maya Collapse seminar, 1970. Photo by Karl Kernberger. Courtesy of the School of American Research. (left to right front row: William T. Sanders, Malcolm C. Webb, Gordon R. Willey, Jeremy A. Sabloff, E. Wyllys Andrews IV, Robert L. Rands, John A. Graham, left to right, back row: William R. Bullard, Jr., T. Patrick Culbert, Dimitri B. Shimkin, Richard E. W. Adams)

Fig. 6.) Taxinchan is Peten-oriented in some of its polychrome ceramics; however, even at this early date there are some temperless or fine paste wares in the complex. At this point it should be noted that a fine paste tradition in pottery making begins earlier in the Usumacinta sector than it does farther to the east and that these earlier fine paste types are not the Terminal Late Classic Balancan, Altar, and related Fine Orange and Fine Gray types which help define the Tepeu 3 horizon.

The Naab Phase—9.13.0.0.0–9.19.0.0.0 (A.D. 692–810)—follows the Taxinchan and marks a break away from Peten-oriented ceramic traditions. Naab pottery is predominantly fine paste (of the earlier fine paste styles); however, late in the phase some true Fine Gray appears. Fine Orange does not make an appearance at either Trinidad or Tierra Blanca, but it is well represented on the Jonuta horizon at Calatrava. In general, the cultural decline in which we are interested is not seen clearly in these sites in Terminal Late Classic times although, as Rands (1973a,b) points out, the disappearance of the Taxinchan polychromes correlates with the fading out of Peten-like polychromes elsewhere in the Southern Lowlands. It is possible that the late Naab influx of Fine Gray may mark a cultural displacement, occurring just antecedent to the Jonuta horizon.

At Palenque the latest Long Count date is a 9.18.9.0.0 (A.D. 799) reading from an early fine paste vessel of the Balunte Phase. In Rands's opinion, the climax of the site's architecture occurred in the late Otolum—early Murcielagos phases, or between about 9.11.0.0.0 and 9.15.0.0.0 (A.D. 652–731), corresponding to late Tepeu 1 and early Tepeu 2. After that, building slacked off and then all elite activity ceased at the break between the early and late Balunte Phase. This cessation is dated on the chart of 9.19.0.0.0 (A.D. 810), although Rands is of the opinion that it may have occurred slightly earlier—at about A.D. 800. This effective abandonment, along with that at Piedras Negras, is one of the earliest which occurred at a major ceremonial center in the Southern Lowlands.

The latest date at Piedras Negras is 9.18.5.0.0 (A.D. 795); at Bonampak 9.18.10.0.0 (A.D. 800); at La Mar 9.18.15.0.0 (A.D. 805); at El Cayo 9.19.0.0.0 (A.D. 810); and at Yaxchilan, somewhere between 9.19.0.0.0 and 10.0.10.0.0 (A.D. 810–840).

At Piedras Negras the cessation of activities at the site came at just about the end of the Chalcahaaz Phase. Early fine paste wares are found in the succeeding Tamay Phase; however, in this case, the horizon-marking Altar Fine Oranges do not appear until post-Tamay times, or until about 10.3.0.0.0 (A.D. 889).

Thus, in the west we see the extreme northwestern sites, those of the Lower Usumacinta, being somewhat atypical in the brand of Classic Maya hierarchical culture which they display. This is especially true of the smaller centers (Calatrava, Trinidad, Tierra Blanca) in their lack of monuments and great art; and even Palenque virtually lacks stelae and is without such very Mayan traits as caches of eccentric flints and obsidians. We see the Peten-like polychrome pottery tradition being terminated early in the northwest. The elite collapse occurs at Palenque at about A.D. 800, that of Piedras Negras, farther up the Usumacinta, at just about the same time, and the other Upper Usumacinta sites follow rapidly. The appearance of some fine paste wares begins very early on the Lower Usumacinta sites, with the switch from polychromes to fine pastes constituting the changeover from Classic to Postclassic. These, however, are early fine paste wares, presumably the prototypes of the later Altar and Balancan Fine Gray and Fine

Orange wares which constitute the ninth century A.D. Fine Orange–Fine Gray horizon.

The Altar de Sacrificios and Seibal Data   Altar de Sacrificios, at the confluence of the Pasion and Chixoy rivers, had a thriving stelae cult and was a center for fine Maya polychrome pottery in the Pasion Phase (9.9.0.0.0–9.17.0.0.0 or A.D. 613–771). Pasion is correlated with Tepeu 1 and the earlier half of Tepeu 2. After 9.17.0.0.0 there were no more dated monuments at the site, and the pottery of the Boca Phase (estimated at 9.17.0.0.0–10.4.0.0.0 or A.D. 771–909) dropped off in the quantity and quality of polychrome ceramics. The site was by no means abandoned, and some ceremonial construction continued after 9.17.0.0.0; but it is fair to say that there was a decline in the old-style elite activities.

Fine paste pottery first occurred in the site sequence in the Boca Phase, apparently coming in as trade and being used along with polychromes. However, this earlier fine paste ware was not the Fine Orange–Fine Gray horizon material, which appeared about 10.0.0.0.0 (A.D. 830), or halfway through the Boca Phase. Following 10.4.0.0.0 (A.D. 909), with the advent of the Jimba Phase, major construction at Altar ceased, and the site was occupied by groups whose total ceramic complex was in the Fine Orange–Fine Gray tradition (as opposed to the earlier Boca Phase occurrences of Fine Orange–Fine Gray as trade). Site abandonment is estimated at about 10.6.0.0.0 (A.D. 948).

Seibal, at the great bend of the Pasion River in the south-central Peten, flourished as a typical Peten-type Maya ceremonial center from about 9.12.0.0.0 (A.D. 672) until 9.18.0.0.0 (A.D. 790)—the Tepejilote Phase. Ceramics are affiliated with the northeastern Peten, and it may be that Seibal's Late Classic population actually came from the Tikal-Uaxactun region.

At some time between 9.18.0.0.0 (A.D. 790) and 10.0.0.0.0 (A.D. 830) Seibal was probably invaded by non-Classic Maya peoples. These newcomers may have been from Yucatan. Their leaders are protrayed on the stelae at the site, and the monuments showing this influence are some of the most impressive sculptures of Seibal, dating from the 10.1.0.0.0 (A.D. 849) *katun* ending. The persons depicted are garbed in a basic Maya Classic manner, though their countenances are quite non-Maya. Significantly, and quite at variance with other Southern Maya centers of the time, Seibal enjoyed a very great boom of pyramid and platform building activity and monument dedication in these early decades of the ninth century, the beginning of the Bayal Phase; and the Fine Orange pottery of this phase is to be correlated with the Fine Orange horizon occurrence in the Boca Phase of the Altar de Sacrificios Sequence. Stelae dedication continued at Seibal until

10.3.0.0.0 (A.D. 889) or slightly later (Graham, 1973). The carvings on the 10.2.0.0.0 (A.D. 869) and 10.3.0.0.0 (A.D. 889) monuments include figures dressed in the Classic Maya style as well as others whose accouterments and general appearance are more like those seen in the carvings of western Yucatan and Campeche. Quite probably, these figures represent Maya, but they are not the Classic Maya of the Southern Lowland artistic tradition. Throughout the Bayal Phase, which may have lasted until about 10.5.0.0.0 (A.D. 928), Fine Orange–Fine Gray wares increase in occurrence, and there is a disappearance of polychromes. Seibal, and its nearby sustaining area, were abandoned after this phase.

In summary, we can say that typical Peten Maya Classic activities declined in these two Pasion River sites after about A.D. 771–790 with the decline setting in a little earlier at Altar de Sacrificios. Some construction continued at Altar for a time after that but stopped by A.D. 909, after which the site was occupied by foreigners, who probably came from the Gulf Coast. At Seibal, stelae and construction activities enjoyed a florescence after A.D. 771–790, but this florescence seems to have been under foreign tutelage. Seibal was no longer important after A.D. 889. Both Seibal and Altar were abandoned altogether about A.D. 928-948. In this Terminal Late Classic time both sites were influenced by fine paste wares, Altar earlier than Seibal; however, the inception of the Fine Orange–Fine Gray horizon pottery can be dated at about A.D. 830 at both sites.

The Tikal and Uaxactun Data　The great building period at Tikal, according to Culbert (1973b), was between 9.13.0.0.0 (A.D. 692) and 9.16.0.0.0 (A.D. 751). This 60 years marked the first half of the Imix Phase, corresponding to the first half of Tepeu 2 at Uaxactun. Building at Tikal continued for a time, with some big construction probably occurring as late as 9.19.0.0.0 (A.D. 810), but no building occurred after 10.0.0.0.0 (A.D. 830). The Eznab (corresponding to Tepeu 3) architecture at Tikal is extremely impoverished, and Culbert estimates that the population at Tikal in Eznab times (A.D. 830–909) was reduced by as much as 90 percent from its Imix Phase maximum. A probable Eznab monument is dated at 10.2.0.0.0 (A.D. 869).

At Uaxactun, in the Tepeu 3 Phase, there is a dated monument at 10.3.0.0.0 (A.D. 889). After this date there are no more Long Count stelae at either site. The Maya polychrome pottery tradition of the Imix and Tepeu 2 phases carried over, in reduced fashion, to Eznab and Tepeu 3; but both phases are also marked by Fine Orange–Fine Gray horizon types.

In brief, Tikal and Uaxactun show signs of decline in stelae construction by 9.19.0.0.0 (A.D. 810). Over the next 80 years this decline became ever more rapid, and by the close of the ninth century (A.D. 889–909) both sites were virtually abandoned, although a desultory and probably inter-mittent occupation of Tikal by Postclassic Period groups continued for some decades. Culbert emphasizes the point that the Tikal decline seems to have been under way before the first signs of fine paste wares and sev-eral decades before the first appearances of the Fine Orange horizon mark-ers of the Altar and the Balancan series.

The Belize Valley Data   In the Belize Valley the Early Spanish Look-out and Benque Viejo IIIB phases correspond in time to Tepeu 2 and show the last full vigor of polychrome styles. These polychrome styles, while recognizably linked to those of the Peten tradition, are divergent from those of Tikal and Uaxactun. In the Late Spanish Lookout and Benque Viejo IV phases, polychrome pottery disappeared. These phases are cross-dated with Tepeu 3 and Eznab and probably can be bracketed between 10.0.0.0.0 and 10.3.0.0.0 (A.D. 830–889), although it is possible that late Spanish Lookout lasted somewhat longer. Probably Benque Viejo, the major cere-monial center in the Belize Valley, was largely abandoned shortly after 10.0.0.0.0, for many of the buildings seem to have fallen into disuse and disrepair in the Benque Viejo IV Phase. In other words, signs indicate that hierarchical culture came to a close in the Belize Valley at about A.D. 830; however, the domestic occupation at Barton Ramie (the principal site from which Spanish Lookout is known) continued on with vigor for 60 years or more. There is no fine paste pottery in these Belize Valley sites, in either the late Spanish Lookout or the Benque Viejo IV phases—which is the time horizon on which it might be expected—or in any other.

The New Town Phase, which follows Late Spanish Lookout at Bar-ton Ramie, is represented by a much-reduced ceramic complex, and no ceremonial center components appear in the valley that can be attributed to this phase. The New Town Ceramic Complex, which has no fine paste wares, is a part of what Bullard (1973) has designated as the Central Peten Postclassic Tradition.

Summary   On a factual and descriptive level, we can sum up by saying that marked cultural decline, as reflected by curtailment of ceremo-nial center activities and population loss, began on the northwestern and western frontier of the Southern Lowlands at some time between 9.18.0.0.0 and 9.19.0.0.0 (A.D. 790–810). Palenque and Piedras Negras collapsed at about this time, and the other Upper Usumacinta sites were effectively deserted very soon after. Altar de Sacrificios suffered a decline after 9.17.0.0.0 (A.D. 771), although populations continued to live there and to do some building until as late as 10.4.0.0.0 (A.D. 909). At Tikal, farther to the east and north, decay, marked by construction decline and popula-tion loss, was registered between 9.19.0.0.0 and 10.0.0.0.0 (A.D. 810–830), with virutally complete abandonment by A.D. 909. In the Belize Valley, at the very eastern edge of the Maya Lowlands, ceremonial center functions apparently stopped by 10.0.0.0.0 (A.D. 830) or shortly after; but here outlying domestic dwelling sites continued to be occupied until the middle or later part of the tenth century A.D..

On the same factual and descriptive level, we record the earliest appearances of fine paste wares in the northwest, their somewhat later occurrences as one moves east, and their absence in the extreme east in the Belize Valley. It should be pointed out that the earliest of these fine paste wares dates some two centuries before the appearance of Fine Orange and Fine Gray horizon-marker Altar and Balancan types. These later types effect a nearly horizontal time-band on the chart (Rands, 1973a:Fig. 8). Their first occurrence is at about 9.19.0.0.0 (A.D. 810) in the west, and they are slightly later in occurrence to the east, where they appear a little after the first signs of the collapse.

THE FAILURE OF RECOVERY

There was no recovery of Classic Maya civilization in the Southern Lowlands following its eclipse. It is true that the area was not entirely abandoned, and some Postclassic centers were established, especially in those territories peripheral to the old Peten "core." Some of these centers were on the northwestern frontier, as at Potonchan and Izamkanac (Thompson 1967) This was Chontal Maya country, and Chontal were strongly influenced by the Central Mexicans and their ruling families and intermarried with them (Thompson 1970). A few other Postclassic Maya centers were established elsewhere: on the eastern coast of the Yucatan Peninsula near Chetumal; in the southeast near the mouth of the Chamelcon River; and even in the old Southern Lowlands proper at Tayasal and Topoxte. Topoxte, which is better known archaeologically (Bullard 1970), seems to be allied in its architectural styles to Yucatan rather than to be a continuation of the old local Classic traditions. Both its ceramics and those of Tayasal were of the new Central Peten Postclassic Tradition. Tayasal is assumed to have been a settlement of the Itza after their flight from northern Yucatan. According to Spanish accounts (Thompson 1967), Tayasal and the Lake Peten Itza were important politically and militarily, but on a small, local scale. They also controlled trade to some extent, but not to the degree attributed to former Classic centers.

There are some indications that reduced populations lived in or near the old centers and communities of the Classic Period after the collapse. This seems to have been the case at Tikal, Altar de Sacrificios, and Seibal— three Southern Lowland centers where extensive housemound surveys have been carried out. It is also true that there was a Postclassic dwelling site occupation at Barton Ramie, in the Belize Valley (Willey et al. 1965; Willey, 1973). Named the New Town Phase, this period of occupation appears to postdate the abandonment of the nearest major ceremonial center at Benque Viejo. We have been uncertain as to just how long this New Town Phase lasted, but Bullard's (1973) definition of the Central Peten Postclassic tradition has helped in this regard. New Town pottery belongs to this tradition, and the great bulk of the pottery belongs to the earliest ceramic group within the tradition, the Augustine. The somewhat later, probably Middle Postclassic, pottery group of the tradition, the Paxcaman, is present at Barton Ramie but is restricted to a very few housemounds and probably is to be attributed to occasional later reoccupation of house sites by relatively small numbers of people.

PROBLEMS AND SPECULATIONS

We have recounted the archaeological facts that appear to bear directly on the Maya collapse and the failure of recovery. These facts bring to mind immediate questions. One of these is what the relationship was between the Terminal Late Classic appearance of fine paste horizon wares, Fine Orange and Fine Gray, and the collapse of the cities of the Southern Lowlands. Were these wares brought by an invading people from the west, and were these invaders the cause of the downfall? The answer would appear to be no. For instance, Culbert (1973b) points out that Tikal was already in decline before the horizon wares appeared at that site.

Are we then to conclude that the Fine Orange–Fine Gray pottery types are in no way a clue to the events of the collapse? Again, we would answer no. There can be little doubt that such wares developed in the Tabasco lowlands, in a region immediately adjacent to that of the Lower Usumacinta. It is in the Lower Usumacinta region that we have our first signs of the replacement of the Maya Classic ceramic traditions by the fine paste wares. In some sites this replacement was rather gradual, and there was no abandonment; but Palenque, the greatest of the old Maya ceremonial centers of the region, collapsed as this time, among the first of the Maya Classic centers to be deserted. These circumstances suggest that alien peoples, or at least peoples with a culture not typically that of the Classic Maya, were in some way involved with the Maya decline on the northwestern frontier of the Southern Lowlands.

The fact that deeper within the Southern Lowlands evidences of the decline precede appearances of the foreign fine paste pottery tradition could be interpreted variously. The conquest on the northwestern frontier might have frightened peoples within the Southern Lowland core into withdrawing to other regions, leaving their cities vacant. But the sequence of the collapse events in most sites does not appear to have been quite that rapid, and such a sudden flight seems improbable. More likely, a series of events occurred on the northernwestern frontier which transformed the local Maya cultures through conquest and acculturation. Old patterns of behavior and of sociopolitical and commercial control were changed. A traditional seat of power such as Palenque was abandoned. In effect, a former segment of the Maya Classic system was detached from the old body, and this segment was so situated geographically as to be able to destroy the trade routes and relationships on which the peoples of the central and northeastern Peten were dependent.

Such an interpretation follows Rathje's (1973) argument that in the course of the evolution of a redundant resource zone, like the Peten, its core will eventually be shut off from areas of more diversified resources by the development of "buffer" zones which drain off or hold these resources so that they never reach the core. There is logic to the argument, but we also feel that in this case evidence suggests that the process was put in motion and hastened when the northwestern frontier or Lower Usumacinta "buffer" zone fell under the domination of the alien peoples of the Fine Orange and Fine Gray pottery.

Another major problem which arises from a consideration of the facts of the collapse is what happened to the people who lived in the Southern Lowlands and were so numerous at the Tepeu 2 climax of Maya civilization. It is, indeed, possible that many were lost, over the century of the decline and collapse, through the economic and social disruptions that ensued in the period of crisis. Intensified competition among cities, intercity fighting, crop loss and destruction, malnutrition, and disease—this chain of events, as Shimkin (1973) has argued, could have reduced population greatly. Would it have been enough to result in the decimation implied by Culbert's 90 percent reduction estimates for Tikal?

Sanders (1973) does not think so and favors migration out of the disaster area. Where, then, did they go? His suggestion of a movement into the northern Guatemala Highlands (the Alta and Baja Verapaz regions) is not supported by archaeology, according to Adams, who has worked in these regions in recent years. Could the movement have been to the north?

This last question raises a very old hypothesis about the Maya, one associated with the earlier writings of Morley and Spinden—that of the Maya "Old Empire" and "New Empire." According to this hypothesis, the "Old Empire" in the south (what we are calling the Classic Maya civilization of the Southern Lowlands) was abandoned at the end of the ninth century A.D., at which time the Maya moved north into the empty Yuca-

tan Peninsula and built there the great cities of the Puuc, Chenes, and Rio
Bec cultures. This idea tended to be discredited when it was shown that
there was a long history of cultural development in the Northern Lowlands from Preclassic times on; however, the fact that there was already
some population in the north need not preclude later populations from
moving in to join them. Andrews's (1973) interpretation of Maya culture
history is readily reconciled with this "New Empire" view or a modifica-
tion of it. In brief, did the populations of the Southern Lowlands move
north to take up residence around emerging new centers in the Rio Bec,
Chenes, and Puuc regions in the ninth century A.D.? G. L. Cowgill suggested something like this a few years ago (Cowgill 1964), with the added
speculation that they might have done so under foreign or non-Classic
Maya direction.

     This interpretation of a northern movement of Classic populations
out of the southern Lowlands at the end of the Late Classic Period leads
us into the problem of the correlation of Southern Lowland and Northern Lowland sequences which we have not yet considered. At this point, it
might be well for us to consider this correlation problem, for the whole
matter is closely bound up with Andrews's (chapter 12) views of Maya
culture history as seen from the north. The crux of the Northern and Southern Lowlands chronological alignment controversy is in the placement of
what Andrews calls the Northern Lowland "Pure Florescent Period"
(embracing the Puuc, Chenes, and Rio Bec developments) in relation to
Southern Lowland Tepeu. Most of the archaeologists writing for this volume prefer to see the Northern Pure Florescent as being essentially coeval
with Tepeu; Andrews, in opposition to this, maintains that it is largely
post-Tepeu. Lack of sufficient Long Count dates in the northern sites has
led archaeologists to seek a solution to the question through pottery associations and comparisons, but this solution has been made difficult by the
divergences between southern and northern Late Classic ceramic traditions.
As of now, the debate is still unresolved, and Rands (1973a):Figs.5–8)
has not attempted to chart the Northern Lowland columns alongside those
of the south; but the question is closely related to the formulation of any
hypotheses about south-to-north migrations.

     With the conventional chronological alignment of southern and north-
ern sequences, the collapse of the Puuc-Chenes-Rio Bec sites would have
been more or less synchronous with the Southern Lowland collapse. Toltec
Chichen would then have been established after the northern cities had
died. With the Andrews alignment, the Puuc-Chenes-Rio Bec florescence
would have taken place after the abandonment of the southern cities, and
Toltec Chichen would have been established as a conqueror's city in the

context of a thriving Pure Florescent culture. It is, of course, possible that the truth and the proper alignment lie somewhere in between. That is, the northern Pure Florescent centers of Puuc-Chenes-Rio Bec affiliation could have had their start in the Tepeu 3 Period (10.0.0.0.0 to 10.3.0.0.0 or A.D. 830–889) as groups of southerners abandoned the old Classic leadership around sites like Tikal and moved north to cluster around the viable centers of Yucatan which, under a non-Classic Maya domination, were a part of new trading networks. This dating would mean that the whole Pure Florescent Period in the north was relatively brief. lasting between 100 and 200 years. At the close of this period the Puuc-Chenes-Rio Bec sites may then have been—or may not have been—in decline before the Toltec conquered Yucatan.[4]

All of the above must remain highly speculative—an attempt to account for the massive population losses in the south. There is, however, one line of supporting evidence. This comes from Seibal which, it will be recalled, displayed a quite different pattern of events during the time of the collapse than that of other southern centers. Seibal's heyday was in the Bayal Phase, especially from 10.0.0.0.0 to 10.2.0.0.0 (A.D. 830–869), or in the Tepeu 3 Period. The Seibal stelae of this time show definite ties to Yucatan (see Sabloff 1973b and Graham, 1973), and there are also Seibal-Yucatecan architectural resemblances (Andrews, 1973). It is suggested that non-Classic Maya invaders, perhaps peoples of Maya speech but acculturated to Mexicanized ways in the Gulf Coast or Yucatecan regions, assumed positions of leadership at Seibal in the ninth century A.D. and that under their tutelage that site had a brief remission of the illness that was affecting other southern centers at this time. In fact, Seibal even enjoyed a small florescence. This was short lived, however, and it may be that such a non-Classic Maya leadership withdrew to Yucatan or perished along with the site.

These problems are some of the most immediate and major posed by the data of the collapse, and we could detail variations on these, as well as on many others. Quite obviously, we do not have the data with which to answer these questions. Rather than pursuing this line of speculative inquiry further, it is more to our purpose at this time to construct a hypothetical model of the Maya collapse, a model which will accommodate the widest possible range of the data now available and which will also suggest new directions for research. Before we can do this, however, it is necessary to take another view of Classic Maya civilization. We have already presented it in historical synopsis. Let us now take an analytical view of its structure and its dynamic aspects.

An Analytical Consideration of Late
Classic Maya Society and Culture

It is evident from the chapters in this volume that there has been much new fieldwork in Maya archaeology in the last 20 years, that many new findings have resulted from this work, and that new interpretations have grown out of these. One point which has emerged from the preceding chapters is the extent to which these new data and opinions have confirmed or changed our previously held conceptions of Maya culture. Maya civilization is colorful and spectacular; it has received a large share of attention relative to other pre-Columbian cultures; and it is fair to say that over the years a standard body of opinion has tacitly grown up among Maya scholars about certain features of the structure and organization of Classic Maya society. This shared opinion is apparent in the general and semipopular books on the Maya, and has tended to be accepted as a given in most of the considerations of the Maya downfall discussed by Adams (1973a) and Sabloff (1973a). Although most of the authors had doubts about parts of these assumptions, we had continued to accept the basic framework. In retrospect, one of the most valuable aspects of this volume is that it has led us to examine the old image of Classic Maya cvilization and to revise this image. For in discussing the collapse it has become apparent that we must be quite specific about the nature of the society that collapsed. Old assumptions had to be reconsidered; and in the process, the gaps and disjunctions among them became evident.

The old model of the Maya Classic civilization had two major weaknesses. First of all it lacked a convincing systemic structure. Its various segments were not interconnected in any necessary relationships, and it was difficult to understand the actions of one part of the system in terms of the other parts. For example, it was not easy to explain the actions of the commoner segment towards the elite in terms of the role the elite was considered to have played. Second, the application of explanatory principles, particularly those starting from natural environment and subsistence, frequently led to disjunctions with the actual data. A good example of these explanatory disjunctions is the difference between maximal population densities predicted on the basis of the subsistence system assumed to have been used and the higher population densities computed from settlement pattern studies at several sites.

But to examine these disjunctions more systematically, let us consider the features of the conventional and revised models of Classic Maya society and culture under a series of semiseparate but interdependent parts. We will first analyze the structural features or conditions of the society and, after this, the dynamic aspects of the interactions among these features and conditions.

STRUCTURAL FEATURES

Subsistence   The conventional model of Maya Lowland subsistence held that the subsistence system consisted of slash-and-burn agriculture with maize as the staple crop. This viewpoint was based upon analogy with presently used agricultural practices in the Maya Lowlands and in neighboring ecologically comparable areas. It was also based upon the apparent absence and presumed impracticability of such labor-intensive features as irrigation and terracing, both of which are crucial features of agriculture in the rain-poor Mesoamerican highlands. According to this conventional view, the primary constraints upon such a subsistence system were declining yield after the first year of cropping, the length of fallow time necessary, and the amount of land unusable for agriculture because of seasonal flooding or lack of sufficient soil.

But the high population density estimates which have been derived from settlement pattern studies in recent years have demanded a reevaluation of this traditional subsistence picture. Actually, this is not an altogether new line of argument. When Culbert (1973b) states that the settlement density for Tikal could not have been sustained by the ethnographically known model of slash-and-burn maize farming, one is reminded of Ricketson's similar pronouncement of more than 30 years ago (Ricketson and Ricketson 1937). Ricketson, too, conducted settlement pattern studies, in his case around the Uaxactun center, and this was an important factor in leading him to consider the possibility that the Classic Maya had practiced more intensive methods of cultivaton. At the time, Ricketson's settlement and population figures were held in doubt, but as Adams, in his review of downfall hypotheses (1973a) observes, most Maya archaeologists today believe that Ricketson's estimates were much too low.

What are, or were, the possibilities for more intensive cultivation or more abundant subsistence resources in the Southern Maya Lowlands? As Shimkin (1973) indicates, studies of the agricultural potential of these lowlands are still far from adequate, but the very facts of marked regional variability in soil potential and rainfall "give strong grounds" for attributing some variability of farming and food-getting techniques to the Maya. Sanders also notes that some of Peten soils are very much richer than others. Such regions or localities, through high crop yields, could have allowed for rapid population buildups, and this, in turn, could have provided an incentive for grass-swiddening, or the relatively short-term fallowing, cutting, and burning of fields that were allowed to return to grass and weeds

but not to trees. This grass-swiddening requires enormous labor time, especially with the stone tools available to the ancient Maya; but Sanders is of
the opinion that the Maya did shift to it, at least in some regions, in Late
Classic times. This system is also destructive of the land if fertilizers are
not added, through degradation of nutrients, erosion, or both. This hypothesis is, of course, closely related to Ricketson's hypothesis about the Maya
collapse.

Another possibility for subsistence improvement in Maya Classic times
was in crop diversificaiton. Bronson (1966) has made the case that manioc and sweet potatoes were important dietary supplements to maize; and
Puleston (1968) has established the importance of the breadnut tree even
more convincingly. Although Sanders, in his present paper, is inclined to
feel that Puleston has overestimated the breadnut resource, he admits its
very probable importance at Tikal and goes on to say that the site density
in the northeastern Peten region, which is *ramón* or breadnut tree country, may be related to this protein food supplement.

Finally, Culbert, Shimkin, and Sanders all mention the possibility that
Maya food resources in the core of the southern Lowlands may have been
supplemented by imports of foodstuffs from neighboring areas. In this
connection, fish, a high protein source, are especially mentioned (see also
Lange 1971).

The conventional view of Maya subsistence is, thus, seriously chal-
langed. Regional and local population densities, as these have been carefully derived from settlement studies, are clearly too large to have been
supported by *milpas* or swidden maize farming alone. More intensive cultivation, possibly grass-swiddening as opposed to forest-swiddening, or
possibly the utilization of swamp or *bajo* lands for farming, is suggested.[5]
Considerable regional variation in subsistence potential is also suggested.
Root crops and breadnut harvests are very likely supplementary food possibilities; and, finally, the importation of foodstuffs as a part of a trading
network can no longer be completely disregarded.

Population Density   As noted, low population density is linked
to the kind of subsistence practices that the old Maya were believed to
have followed, and the conventional Classic Maya model was one of low
population density.

Sanders, in commenting on settlement evidence, says:

> What the data do suggest, even allowing for the noncontemporaneity
> of house groups, is that the population density of the Maya Low-
> lands in Late Classic times was considerably higher than most earlier
> writers have thought and, most importantly, exceeded most estimates
> of the potential of the area to support populations with long-cycle

swidden maize cultivation. I would suggest that the overall density of the 250,000 sq. km. area that made up the Maya Lowlands was probably not below 20 people per square kilometer and that the densities found in the core areas were probably well over 100 persons per square kilometer, probably closer to 200 in some small sectors of the core (1973: 331–32).

In commenting upon Sanders's position it should be noted that the 250,000 square kilometers of the lowlands at large includes those sections of poor farming lands, or lands impossible for farming, as well as the good farm lands. By "long-cycle swidden" Sanders is referring to forest-swidden, in contrast to short-cycle grass-swidden. "Core areas" and "core" refer, especially, to the great sites of the northeastern Peten and also to some of the centers of the Usumacinta and Palenque zones. However, these figures do not refer to the very heavy concentrations in the inner zone of a site such as Tikal, which are estimated at much higher than 200 persons per square kilometer. In these observations it should be noted, also, that Sanders tends now (within the last 10 years) to be on the conservative side in these estimates. Although any population figures are, indeed, relative, and figures for Mesoamerican upland areas are substantially higher, the estimates given here indicate a surprisingly dense population for a lowland jungle terrain.

Sociopolitical Organization Reasoning from the assumptions of low subsistence yield and low population density, the conventional model of the Maya Classic provided for little administrative organization in sociopolitical or economic matters. Since the long-cycle swidden agricultural system involved neither large-scale labor nor techniques unavailable to the family-level farming unit, it was assumed to be largely self-regulating on the commoner level. The one possible articulation of the commoners or peasantry with the elite stratum of the society was believed to have been in the guidance the former received from the latter concerning seasonal planting and harvesting, although even here there was some doubt about how esoteric such knowledge may have been. In general, the elite were considered to have led a life of their own that was of little concern or interest to the lower classes—a separatist view quite possibly promoted by the long reseach emphasis in Maya archaeology on such esoterica as astronomy and hieroglyphic writing. Of course, the lower classes maintained the elite and constructed the great ceremonial centers under their direction. This, it was believed, was motivated largely by fear of religious sanctions or by religious zeal. On the more strictly political scene, it was held that political units were small—city-states, in effect—each under the direction of a major ceremonial center. The relationships between such states were pictured as concerning only matters of interest to the elite classes, such as the exchange of calendrical information and trade in luxury goods.

Were the attitudes and functions of the Maya elite as introverted and as limited as this conventional model implies? It seems unlikely. Shimkin (1973) has drawn an analogy between the Classic Maya and the small central Asian states of the first millennium A.D. These Asian states had social components of a hereditary aristocratic leadership and a pious peasantry, and the loyalty of the peasantry to the aristocracy was maintained in large degree by religious feeling. Nevertheless, the management functions of the leadership were of key importance in the workings of the society. They allocated labor and resources; sponsored craft manufactures, graphic artistry, and elaborate ceremonialism; dispensed justice; and arranged for measures of social security.

Any serious considerations of the range, variety, and complexity of Classic Maya material remains in a great ceremonial center suggests that neither Maya agricultural labor nor labor for other purposes could have been "self-regulating." Labor demands and labor allocations would, inevitably, have been in conflict without careful and planned scheduling; and, in our opinion, labor demands would have been great. Allowances surely had to be made not only for land clearance and agricultural tasks but also for road and monument construction and maintenance and for crafts, food preparation, ceremonial activities, and the education of an intellectual and management class. Another very important management function must have been the maintenance of trade.

As to the nature of the Maya Lowland "state," and the relationships between such states, it now seems very likely that there were regional "capitals" exercising economic, religious, and political hegemony over other, lesser ceremonial centers. Culbert (1973a) suggests the probability of such a role for Tikal. Copan, Palenque, and Yaxchilan are other possible "supersites" or "capitals." Such centers of power and prestige would have been key points in trading networks. The presence of the emblem glyph of Tikal at a number of lesser ceremonial centers hints at its "metropolitan" importance. That such hegemony had a dimension of military and political force and dynastic involvement receives support from Proskouriakoff's (1963) analyses of the hieroglyphic texts, dates, and sculptures at Yaxchilan (see Graham, 1973).

The conclusion must be that we have tended to underrate the mundane, but highly important, functions of the Maya aristocracy. There were numerous and crucial articulations between the aristocracy and the farming commoners and, probably, between it and an emergent "middle class" of craftsmen and bureaucrats. At the same time, the degree to which such an aristocracy had the ability to enforce its dictates—Webb's criterion for separating the "chiefdom" from the "state"—is still a moot point. In attempting to refashion the model of the Maya elite as a separate "other-wordly" group we should take care not to go too far in the opposite direction.

Religion   In the standard model, religious statuses were seen as the keys to prestige and power, and, as we have seen, religious sanction was conceived of as the true basis of the body politic. In comparison to other Mesoamerican societies, and especially those of the Postclassic Period, Maya Classic investment of labor and goods in religious activities was considered to be very high.

We feel that this appraisal still has considerable merit. Webb, (1973) in his accompanying paper, points out that the most advanced societies on the "chiefdom" level tended to be the most theocratic. In other words, the structure of the society had grown to a complexity that demanded sanctions; force could not be resorted to in the manner of the "state"; the result was an intensification of religious sanctions.

Without subscribing altogether to the chiefdom-state dichotomy and assigning the Classic Maya to one or the other, we think this reasoning may be applicable to the Maya religious and social order. Although a method for measuring the investment of labor and goods given to religious activities, as distinct from secular ones, has not been devised, we are of the impression that such investment in Classic Maya times was very high. Similarly, there can be little doubt that religious status was the key to prestige and power; at least, individuals who seemingly held positions of high status appear, always, closely associated with symbols and paraphernalia connected with religious contexts. The degree to which religious and secular persons, or religious and secular functions in the same person, can be separated in the Maya archaeological record is still undefined.

Militarism   The old view, consistent with the sacred rather than the secular power of the chiefdom (or the state), was that militarism was poorly developed among the Classic Maya.

This view is, indeed, "old," for archaeologists have been pointing out for some time that the "peaceful" and "pious" Maya engaged in their share of violence. Late Classic stelae representations of brutal treatment of prisoners or captives are quite common, and it is likely that these depict the military and political subjugation of one group by another. Battle scenes also occur in Maya art, as in the murals of Bonampak.

Still, there is little in Maya art, or elsewhere in the archaeological record, to indicate that there was anything resembling the professional military orders of Central Mexico, or that Maya governments, in either their internal or external policies, depended upon the services of "standing armies."[6]

Urbanism   It was formerly thought that Maya ceremonial centers were, indeed, just that—religious or politico-religious precincts with little or no domestic population. Such a view was in keeping with the image of Maya elite as a segment of the Classic Maya society remote from the sustaining peasantry. It also conformed to the picture of a sacred, rather than a secular, leadership.

The intensive settlement studies in and around Tikal now leave little doubt that the "vacant town," or the pure ceremonial-center-without-resident-population, image does not apply there. In this volume both Culbert and Sanders refer to these studies (made by Haviland, Fry, and others) in considerable detail; and although there is some difference of opinion between the way Haviland (1969, 1970) and Sanders (1973) estimate population densities from the "housemound" findings, there can be no denying that Tikal had urban dimensions. A core zone of approximately 63 sq. km., immediately surrounding the major constructions of the center, is densely dotted with small platform structures, many of which on excavation have proved to be housemounds or domestic sites. Haviland estimates a population of 39,000 persons for this 63-sq.-km. core, a density on the order of 600–700 persons per square kilometer. An outer periphery, surrounding the core zone and adding another 100 sq. km. to it, shows a thinner distribution of housemounds, but raises the figure from 39,000 to about 45,000 people for a greater Tikal. This greater Tikal was bordered on the east and west by natural *bajos* or swamps, but the strong possiblity that the inhabitants of the site had a concept of some kind of "city limits" is seen in defining walls or earthworks at distances of 4.5 km. and 10 km. from the north and south of the center of the city, respectively.

Sanders's differences of opinion with Haviland arise principally from the lower figure of persons per family which he applies to the housemound settlements and housemound countings. He thinks that an overall greater Tikal maximum of from 20,000 to 25,000 persons would be more realistic. Although we appreciate the importance of the differences in these formulae for estimating population sizes from settlement data and sampling, we cannot, in the present context of discussion, become overly concerned in this debate. Even Sanders's halved figure is within the range of preindustrial urbanism and bespeaks urban functions of some sort, not an empty ceremonial precinct.

The matter of urban functions is, perhaps, even more important than sheer size, although the two undoubtedly are related. Certainly Haviland must be correct in arguing that not all of the inhabitants in the core zone of Tikal were food-producers. At least it is difficult to conceive of them as having been maize farmers, though many of them may have cultivated *ramón* or breadnut trees. Haviland also has some evidence for socioeconomic differentiation within the city zone in that some dwelling clusters appear to have housed families specializing in different crafts; and Tikal may also have had a marketplace. Nevertheless, these evidences of socioeconomic diversity within the city, which, in Sanders's opinion, are the key criteria of urban life (Sanders and Price 1968), are relatively weak in contrast to the evidence present in a huge urban agglomeration such as Teotihuacan in the Mexican central highlands. This difference, according to Sanders, correlates with the lesser population density of the Tikal city zone in contrast to that of Teotihuacan. While evidence at Tikal would indicate a density of 600–700 (or at most 1,000) persons per square kilometer, that at Teotihuacan indicates an estimated 5,000 persons.

In our opinion, the Classic Maya had made some important steps on the way to urban life. In their greatest center, Tikal, they enjoyed a form of urban life, although this form differed from what we know, and can reasonably infer, about a place like Teotihuacan. The extent to which the Tikal pattern can be extended to other Maya centers is unknown, although it seems probable that some other Classic Maya "supersites" or metropoli had population congestions in their immediate environs; however, other centers, of a somewhat lesser size and extent in their ceremonial constructions, seem to have lacked these congestions (Bullard 1960).

Trade and Markets   According to the old model, trade and markets were little developed among the Classic Maya. This lack of development was believed to be linked to the lack of ecological zoning within the lowland setting and, as a result, the lack of product diversity seen in the Mesoamerican highlands, where the trade-market institutions were highly developed. Some long-distance trade was admitted, involving regions outside the lowlands, but was seen as being devoted to low volume, luxury goods that were distributed largely to the elite.

How has this model been modified? A closer look at the archaeological data, expecially the new data now coming in from recent excavations at Tikal, on the Rio Pasion, and elsewhere, shows more hard evidence for trade than was present, or at least appreciated, before. Obsidian was definitely imported into the Maya Lowlands as a raw material, being brought or traded from sources in the Guatemalan Highlands, and Central Mexico. The extent to which it was a luxury and a ritual item or, instead, a necessity is debated. Sanders (1973) considers obsidian to be a luxury item, arguing that chert, which was available in the limestone beds of the low-lands, would have provided for all of the cutting tools necessary for life in the rain forests; Rathje (1973) sees it as a necessity or near-necessity. We feel that while life in the Peten was possible without the fine-cutting-edge tools that obsidian provided, it would not have been possible to maintain the level of technico-artistic competence that characterized Maya civilization without these tools.

Salt was, indeed, a necessity. If it were obtained from sources in the Guatemalan Highlands a considerable trade organization would have been needed for its regular procurement; even if it came from the Yucatan coast or from deposits on the Salinas River, not far above Altar de Sacrificios, its transport into the central Peten would have involved substantial distances—too far, at least, for a day's walk or a day's canoe trip. Fish and shellfish, we know, were imported to the Peten from the coasts. Igneous rocks for *metates* could have been obtained from the Maya Mountains, a short journey, or from the Guatemalan Highlands, a relatively long journey. Other highland items were traded into the Maya Lowlands. Most of these, including jade, were luxury items. Items traded out of the lowlands included Maya polychrome pottery and, probably, textiles, cacao, and tropical feathers.

The significant change that we see in all this, in contrast to the old model about Maya trade, is that several commodities obtained in long-distance trade may have been more basic to Maya economy than what we usually think of under the heading of "luxuries." We think this view might be conceded even if there are some reservations about the Rathje hypothesis that long-distance trade was the underlying cause for the development of complex society and an elite class in the lowlands.

So far we have been talking about long-distance trade, and the produce of long-distance trade could have been distributed without market-places. As yet, we do not know if the Classic Maya had markets or not, although there is a tentative identification of one at Tikal (W. Coe 1967). It seems reasonable to assume the existence of such a mechanism for the exchange of local food produce, if for nothing else; however, there may have been food distribution arrangements without markets. Finally, it is also possible that food staples were brought into some parts of the Maya Lowlands from other regions, in the manner of long-distance trade. Culbert (1973b) has suggested the possibility for Tikal. It cannot be demonstrated as yet, but it is a possibility to be kept in mind.

Maya Isolationism   Isolationism is a condition rather than a structural feature. While the conventional model of Maya Lowland culture recognized the Early Classic Period influence of Teotihuacan, the Late Classic

Maya were thought of as having been little influenced by, or having little influence upon, other Mesoamerican societies until the time of the collapse. In fact, some scholars looked upon the Terminal Late Classic Mexican or Mexicanoid influences as essentially incidental to the problem of the fall of Maya civilization.

This isolationist view can no longer be maintained. Although we do not yet fully understand the Teotihuacan-Classic Maya relationships, they must have been of considerable importance. After the recession of Teotihuacan influence, the Maya Lowland centers appear to have suffered a brief crisis, and when the lowland Late Classic culture resumes its stride it shows definite signs of change. Sanders (Sanders and Price 1968; Sanders, 1973) has argued that this Teotihuacan influence instituted the development of the state among the Lowland Maya; and Webb (chapter 16) would consider this the process whereby a "secondary state" (in which he would class the Maya) arose from contact with a "primary state"—with the principal vehicle of contact being trade.

As to later foreign Mexicanoid influences or impingements upon the Maya Lowlands, several chapters deal with the subject in detail. Webb and Rathje, convinced as they are of the importance of trade in the growth and decline of Maya civilization, demand that the Maya be considered only in the larger context of Mesoamerica. Sabloff, Adams, Rands, and Graham all point to specifics of non-Mayan influences. And even those of the seminar group more "internally" oriented in their views of Maya culture history and the Maya collapse acknowledged the importance of wider Mesoamerican relationships in the discussions.

DYNAMIC ASPECTS

With these revisions of the structure and conditions of Maya society and culture in mind, we want now to analyze the dynamic aspects of the structure. In so doing we will be attempting to visualize the stresses and strains that must have existed within Maya civilization in its Late Classic climax period. In this analysis we feel that the most vital of these aspects were: (1) the roles of the elite class, (2) the widening social gulf between the elite and the commoners, (3) the competition between centers, (4) the agricultural problems, (5) the demographic pressures and disease burdens, and (6) the changing effects on the Maya polity of external trade.

The Role of the Elite   In the preceding section we have referred to the role of the elite in the sociopolitical structure and in religion, militarism, trade, and markets. Here we wish to focus on selected aspects contributing to the Maya climax and collapse. The multiplicity of the roles of the Maya elite, in contrast to the specialization of the elites in Mexico, is brought out by these several references to the Maya aristocracy in the above contexts. Such a multiplicity of roles was made possible by the prestige of artistocratic descent and the conduct of protracted training. Longevity contributed importantly to the effectiveness of the elite and validated their differential access to improved food, housing, clothing, and other resources. Given all these circumstances, whether or not polygamy was a practice, a member of the elite would have had more surviving offspring than a commoner. The expansion of the hereditary elite population was clearly a major force in the geographical expansion of Late Classic Maya civilization. Moreover, as long as resource margins were ample the growing elite would have harnessed these resources, and the commoners would have benefited as well. However, in the later phases of Maya Classic culture, and especially in the populous central regions, the role of the elite must have become increasingly exploitative as resouce margins declined.

The Widening Social Gulf   Consistent with the above would have been a widening social distance between the Maya Classic elite and the commoners. Such is an inevitable accompaniment of the evolution of a ranked, and probably kin-based, society to a class structured one (see Rathje 1970b; 1973). Such a widening gulf need not have led to a "peasant revolt," as some earlier workers have hypothesized (Thompson 1966), to have had deleterious effects on the Maya system. A growing upper class (Haviland 1966b), together with its various retainers and other members of an incipient "middle class," would have increased economic strains on the total society (Willey et al. 1965: 580–81), particularly in conjunction with ecological-demographic stress factors. In some areas, it is quite possible that by the end of the Late Classic the numbers of commoners were being maintained only by recruitment and capture from other centers. Yet the upper class continued to grow, to expand its demands for luxury and funerary splendor, and to strive to compete with rival centers and aristocracies. This expansion required the allocation of considerable resources, including resources for the conduct of long-distance trade and the production of fine manufactures for export in such trade.

Competition Between Centers   There was undoubtedly considerable competition between ceremonial centers or cities in the Southern Lowlands. Overt signs of this competition are to be seen in pictures of captives, such as those on the wall paintings at Bonampak or in the numerous Late Classic stelae representations of crouching bound figures being stood upon by haughty and imperious conquerors. All such representations show both sides as clearly Maya in physical type; the prisoners are not foreigners in the sense of being non-Maya. The competition is to be seen more covertly in the magnificence of the ceremonial centers themselves. The centers represent great numbers of man-hours in both unskilled labor and skilled craftsmanship and, on the highest social level, of priestly-aristocratic scholarship.

As expounded by Rands, especially in the seminar sessions, the priest-ly leaders of these great centers, in their efforts to outdo each other, to draw more wealth and prestige to themselves, and to bring more wor-shippers and taxpayers into their particular orbits, must have diverted all possible labor and capital to their aggrandizement. New emerging centers and ruling lineages—and these, as we have noted, sprang up in numbers during the Late Classic Period—needed particularly to consolidate their statuses through ceremonial splendor. And this competition, too, involved more mundane and crucial matters such as foodstuffs, a point at which this stress relates to the previous ones. Add to all this the competition for trade, which Rathje and Webb propose as a dynamic element in Maya culture history and development, and we can see the situation brought to a fighting pitch.

Culbert (chapter 5), gives an imaginative insight into the plight of the great city of Tikal in such a sea of rivalry. The largest and strongest of all the Maya centers, it was also the most vulnerable in that its great size and prestige demanded the services of more adherents; and as these were lost to jealous rivals the effect could have been a rapid down-spiraling to extinction, not unlike what indeed did happen.

Agricultural Problems   We conceive of Maya agricultural prob-lems as being of a four-fold nature. First, expansion from the prime lands, which were probably occupied by the end of the Early Classic, if not before, was associated with increasing demands on agronomic knowledge and tech-nique in the handling of the poorer soils, of areas subject to erosion, and of wet lands. In addition, the expansion of land clearance, for either per-manent use or slash-and-burn agriculture, might have reduced the avail-ability of forest resources and, especially, the supply of land game.[7] This process would have been accelerated in areas of high population density where potential fodder was gathered for fuel.

Second, the expansion of crop lands to marginal areas and the prob-able shortening of fallow periods, in zones of high population, promoted both weed and insect infestation and the probability of plant disease. It must be noted that, while the Maya apparently brought a variety of crops, such as breadnut trees, into cultivation, there is no evidence that they prac-ticed plant selection to improve yields or resistance to disease. Maize, in particular, would have been subject to serious infestation in low-lying areas; cotton also is vulnerable to both disease and insect pests.

Third, the question of climatic variability in the Maya Lowlands and its effects on agricultrual production is still unresolved; but quite certainly the different regions of the lowlands would have been susceptible in varying degrees to drought or to major damage from hurricanes.

Fourth and finally, the variations in population distribution and in agricultural production made increasingly necessary augmentation in the capacity and network of food storage and distribution. This, again, would have required investments of labor and materials and placed additional burdens on management.

These agricultural problems notwithstanding, there is no real evidence that Classic Maya farming ever reached the absolute limits of its productive capacity. What we are indicating, instead, is that as the expansion of Maya agriculture in the Late Classic became more costly and less reliable, the consequences of managerial mistakes or natural disasters would have become increasingly serious. In brief, there was no margin of safety.

Demographic Pressures and Disease Burdens   From the data at hand it would appear that there was essential continuity in Maya populations, with those of the Classic Period being the descendants of the earlier Preclassic colonists of the lowlands. The overall pattern of population growth is still uncertain, but indications point to a decline in growth rate through the Classic Period, largely because of increased mortality.[8] Nevertheless, the large population base, which had been assembled by the end of the Late Preclassic Period, permitted substantial absolute population increments so that Late Classic populations, as we have said elsewhere, were the largest of all.

Evidence for heavy disease burdens is most extensive in regard to malnutrition (Saul, 1973), which had massive effects on infant and maternal mortality. Deficiencies of animal proteins were most severe and had considerable effects on the work capacity of adults. In addition, urbanization and, especially, sedentary life in thatched structures provided environments suitable for insects, particularly the triatomid bugs, the carriers of Chagas' disease, which is both an acute illness and a source of chronic disability through endocarditis. Less certain is the possibility, particularly in the wake of land clearance or hurricanes, of epidemics of jungle yellow fever (Shimkin, 1973).

Disease exposures and malnutrition were highly differentiated, as far as we can judge, first, between old areas of intense colonization and the more marginal regions and, second, between commoners and the elite. The resulting differences in mortality surely led to differential population trends, both geographically and by social class. In consequence, population trends acted in four basic ways as dynamic cultural factors: (1) population growth increased the demand on resources; (2) the growth of able-bodied manpower, a varying fraction of the population, was the foundation of economic expansion; (3) the differential growth and longevity of different social classes and regions brought about changes in the balance of power within the Maya Lowlands; (4) efforts to compensate for manpower shortages, and the shortages of wives, were increasingly important causes of warfare.

External Trade   There has been considerable interest in trade in recent Mesoamerican archaeological writings, including an article dealing specifically with Lowland Maya trade (Tourtellot and Sabloff 1972); and in our reappraisal of Maya civilization, we have just argued for its importance. Webb (1973) and Rathje (1973) see it as the paramount institution in the rise and in the fall of Maya civilization. Rathje has argued that the demand for such items as obsidian and salt was the lever that started the Maya on their way toward the organization of a complex society, and Webb sees the choking off of trade into the core of the Southern Lowlands as the prime proximate cause of the collapse. If one accepts these hypotheses, one must concede to trade, and its stoppage, the key role in the Lowland Maya collapse. If trading entrepreneurs were able to elevate themselves to positions of power by the control and distributon of goods, and if this trade was instrumental in maintaining the positions of such an elite, it was a most integral part of the Maya system. It demanded time, wealth, and administrators or managerial personnel. It was both a great benefit and, at the same time, a point of great vulnerability for the system. For if trade routes were changed or disrupted the structure of the civilization would be bound to change.

Some authors in this volume, Sanders in particular, were disinclined to see trade, and especially trade in symbolic status items, as being this crucial to the maintenance of the system and of the elite who directed it. In his opinion, such an elite could have held their positions of leadership without the symbols of status. Others seem inclined to side with Webb and Rathje and see trade, with its prerogatives for the disbursement of goods to all levels of the society, as the real mechanism for keeping a Maya elite in power and for keeping the system going.

Trade, as a key mechanism in Maya society and as a potential stress factor for that society, leads us directly into the matter of potential external pressures upon the Maya Lowland Classic civilization. Foreign trade put Maya society into contact with the more dynamic and aggressive societies to the west and north. We have already mentioned these contacts with Teotihuacan in Early Classic times. Following the fall of Teotihuacan, Maya trade with Mexican or Mexican-influenced cultures continued, especially in the northwest along the Gulf of Mexico. It is uncertain just what

Mexican civilizations were dominant on the political and trading scene at this time. Webb has suggested several as exercising important roles: Xochicalco, Tajin, Cholula. In general, better craft organization, and often, access to superior resources made these Mexican societies formidable competitors. Along the Gulf Coast and on the Lower Usumacinta, these societies were in a position to develop peripheral Maya peoples as allies, and it would appear that they did so. The representatives of these Mexican and Mexicanized groups were shrewd professional merchants, probably often backed up by military force, in the Mexican trading manner, and eager to profit from Maya wealth and disunity. Their presence, on the northwestern frontier of the Southern Maya Lowlands, did not bode well for the Classic Maya.

A Model of the Collapse

With this historical and analytical preparation, we come now to our model of the collapse of Late Classic Maya civilization.

A *model* (and, admittedly, in some of the foregoing discussion we have used the term more loosely) is a precise statment of the characteristics and dynamics of a system. Its precision makes possible more exact and testable propositions. Through its mathematical properties, the model suggests, by analogy with other systems of the same type, certain predictions which can be further tested.

The model which we are here proposing is a qualitative and general one which will be compatible with the known facts and which will suggest leads for more complicated models and, particularly, for models which will be ultimately quantified. For example, our model is more general than, but nevertheless compatible with, the quite specific economic model that Rathje has proposed (1973).

In briefest form, and in general terms, our model attributes to a special development of elite culture a primary role in the generation of the climax manifestations of Maya Lowland civilization. The success of the system produced growths of population and of competing centers which led to increasing rigidity in the system as it was subjected to internal stresses and external pressures. The system failed through inadequate recognition of these stresses and pressures and through inappropriate responses to them. The economic and demographic bases of the society were weakened; the consequences were the collapse of the system, the decimation of the population, and a retrogression to a simpler level of sociopolitical integration.

This model is not unique to Maya culture history. It is, in fact, an example of the general model of sociopolitical collapse proposed by Karl W. Deutsch (1969:28–30).

The model, as it can be detailed, comprises the following:

1. After the withdrawal of Teotihuacan influence (and power?) from the Maya Lowlands, the managerial functions of the Maya elite were intensified in two ways. First, they contributed to the growth of the Maya economy by promoting central place development, agriculture, manufacturing, and long-distance trade involving commodities for both general and elite consumption. Second, they intensified a system of economic motivation through the competitive splendor of ceremonialism and ceremonial centers.

2. At the beginning of the Late Classic Period the Maya elite approximated a corporate body which shared like training, mutual recognition of prestige, common beliefs, and systems of interregional cooperation which acted to control warfare and promote the geographical expansion of Lowland Maya civilization. All of these characteristics of the elite increasingly separated them from commoners.

3. Throughout the course of the Late Classic Period, the general growth of population, pressure on natural resources, and urbanization generated increasing competition between the elite leadership of the various regions. This competition engendered prestige-building activities to attract resources to the various regional centers. Concurrently, the pressure on resources decreased the productivity of labor, and increasing allocations to prestige-building activities were at the expense of the commoner population.

4. As a result, malnutrition and disease burdens increased among the commoner population and further decreased its work capacity. This decrease, in turn, intensified elite pressures through the competitive exploitation of the commoners by the elite.

5. Despite these internal stresses, the Maya of the Late Classic Period apparently made no technological or social adaptive innovations which might have mitigated these difficulties. In fact, the Maya managerial elite persisted in traditional directions up to the point of collapse. A contributing factor in this failure was clearly the inadequacy of bureaucratic technology—the systems of information gathering, record keeping, decision making, and control—to cope with an increasingly complex and unstable social situation. It is also quite likely that the very nature of managerial recruitment in Maya Classic society—presumably restricted to a small aristocratic elite—further contributed to these problems.

6. Up to now, we have been considering the Maya Classic system from an internal point of view; however, the Maya were also a subsystem

of a greater Mesoamerican system. During the Late Classic Period, Central Mexican peoples and cultures were impinging with increasing intensity on the western frontier of the Maya Lowlands. The full consequences of these impingements are not as yet understood. But it is clear that a minimal effect was the disruption of Maya trade patterns to the west. As we have already noted, this trade was a critical element in the maintenance of Maya Classic elite prestige and, possibly, important for the effective operation of commoner households.

7. As a result of these internal stresses and external pressures, the Classic Maya polity, a level of sociocultural integration encompassing the lowlands and maintaining a partly urbanized population of as many as five million people at its peak, was no longer viable.

8. Our analysis rules out a single "internal" or "external" phenomenon as the agent of the Classic Maya collapse. Rather, the coincidence of an array of disturbing factors—trade disruptions, social unrest, agricultural difficulties, disease—appears to have coalesced to administer a shock to the Maya polity, around 9.17.0.0.0 (A.D. 771) to 9.18.0.0.0 (A.D. 790), which exceeded the recuperative capacity of the Maya Lowland sociocultural system, especially its capacity of elite management. Despite some few partial continuities of the Maya elite tradition in the lowlands, no general recovery of the Late Classic Maya civilization took place.

Clearly, our model is incomplete. For example, and as we have related earlier, we do not know the degree to which populations of the Southern Maya Lowlands either died out or migrated. Quite possibly, a part of the old Classic populations of the south moved north where they contributed to the florescence of the Rio Bec, Chenes, and Puuc cities of the Northern Lowlands; but we have no proof of this migration, and indispensable to this question is the resolution of the alignment of southern and northern sequences. Also unclear are the factors which must have inhibited a Classic-type recovery in the south. It is our belief that difficulties in the accumulation of critical resources—manpower, skills, and materials—were engendered by the rise of competing Mexican states, but we cannot yet be sure.

Our model-building seeks economical and plausible synthesis of the known facts about the Classic Lowland Maya. On a more general level, and at the same time, we have suggested that the Maya collapse exemplifies phenomena recurrent in culture history. We have cited Karl Deutsch's general model, and we have elsewhere in this volume drawn attention to broad similarities between this history and that of the rise and fall of Angkor. We must caution, at this time, against the temptation to draw unwarranted conclusions evoking the traditions of Spengler and Toynbee. There are many unknowns in the Maya collapse. Why, for example, was the turbulence of the Late Classic Period not terminated by the emergence of a unified state? Why did the Maya pay so little attention to the improvements in labor productivity available within the known technology of their times in Mesoamerica? Questions such as these call for much tentativeness: we believe we are contributing to history, but we are uncertain of the degree to which we have illustrated evolutionary determinism.

Research Directions for the Future

In general, we believe that the model formulated above provides the best possible fit with the established and evaluated data that present knowledge permits. Our previous discussions have pointed out a number of research questions. At the same time, additional research appears worthwhile on the following questions related to and arising out of the study (see also Adams 1969).

1. How can presently collected data and future excavations be utilized and future research designed to provide firmer evidence directed toward understanding the Maya cultural collapse?

2. How can comparative historical and ethnographic data contribute to the search for better understanding of this collapse?

3. How can experimental archaeology and model construction best be utilized? What hazards need to be avoided with these techniques?

4. What light can analysis of the collapse of Maya Classic civilization throw upon the general (or "genetic") history of the Maya people as a whole? On the regional history of Central America and Southern Mexico? On the comparative understanding of cultural history in the wet and wet-dry tropics?

Let us examine these questions in more detail. Our model of the collapse itself suggests a good many ideas which need to be confirmed by better evidence: the implied contrasts between Early and Late Classic in expansion and solidification of the elite class, the exploitation of commoners by the elite, the extent of malnutrition, the kinds of disease, and so on. To determine with greater reliability and in greater detail the basic facts of what happened, where, and when, we need to employ the kinds of refined descriptive techniques that have been developed for pottery studies. For example, the breakdown of observations to directly reportable and measurable attributes seems particularly important in the development of comparability for settlement analyses and population estimates.

Specifically, we urge that space be reported as *covered*—with the amount given over to housemounds and monumental structures separately calculated (structures of determined use, sweat-baths, chapels, and so on, should be subdivided again)—and as *developed open space*—such as plazas, "ceremonial" causeways, and so on. The data so developed would not only eliminate intervening uncertainties about, say, unsupported and varying estimates of family size, but would also provide new analytical indices. For example, a settlement in which the ratio of housemound ground space, monumental covered space, and developed open space ran, say, 100, 20, and 300 would indicate profoundly different politico-economic properties from one with ratios of 100, 50, and 100, respectively. Obviously, the development of such indices would be a complex task. A topographic factor, among others, would have to be brought into this formula, and corresponding estimates of the volumes of building, by types—housemound, pyramid, and so on, would also be of great interest.

The broad outlines of architectural variability laid out by Pollock (1965) need to be supported by more fully plotted distributions and by refined analysis. In particular, the distribution and detailed variations of ball courts need fuller study. Water management—reservoirs, ditches, aqueducts, bridges—also merit special attention.

Within settlements and structures, the distribution of economic activities needs much better definition. Food preparation (*manos*), spinning (spindle whorls), tool manufacturing, pottery making, and other crafts need to be mapped to establish the presence of household, ward, or other patterns. Related to this type of study is the need to collect soil samples and cores, to observe vegetational clusterings, and to establish local hydrological conditions. In short, local environmental data closely related to settlements and activities are a needed prerequisite for meaningful ecological interpretations.

All of these observations have, of course, been made in particular investigations. The need is to establish comparable regional and temporal data. This can be done with good economy by utilizing the data from carefully studied localities as spatial models for the design of sampling schemes for new surveys.

Data of standardized nature, from pottery onwards, should be used to develop *indices of resemblance and difference* between localities and over time. Such indices could be used to examine, for example, the degree to which the links expressed by identical city glyphs denote corresponding similarities in other realms of culture. In general, routes and boundaries indicated by various sources need to be correlated as a basis for better understanding of socioeconomic and sociopolitical structures and spatial

organizations. The time-space correlation of the distribution of exotic articles can also give important information on the relative significance, the
rise and fall, of long-distance communication centers. In particular, the
careful comparison of nearby sites, such as San Jose (Thompson 1939)
and Benque Viejo (Thompson 1940), which seemingly show very different levels of involvement in long-range trade, should be fruitful.

Finally, the profound results of the dynastic interpretations of hieroglyphic texts may justify the search for indications of drought, famine,
war or other, especially dated, events in these monuments.

The data obtained in these ways could be aggregated into structural
models that would yield basic information on space-time continuities and
breaks, the keys to politico-economic and historical interpretation. To tie
these structural models more effectively into estimates of population dynamics, labor-force utilization, and inferences of stress will require further materials. These materials include especially the continued analyses of skeletal
data; and the judicious use of comparative historical and ethnographic
data, and of experimental archaeology. The end results would be the formulations of dynamic models of Maya culture and its history.

The utility of models or formally stated sets of compatible hypotheses has been discussed in this volume; Rathje (1973) exemplifies this use
of a very promising market model. Here it is important to stress the utility of models in locating data gaps and inconsistencies in some cases and in
defining the more probable alternatives in others. Models force the research-
er to define how a phenomenon is supposed to have taken place. Often,
unfortunately, failures of imagination block the most plausible answers.
An illustration is the question of manpower needs in monument building
as stated by Erasmus (1968) and Heizer (1960). These authors accept a
totally implausible span of continuous activity in order to hold labor-
force needs to a minimum; the reverse views, that the sustaining area had
many more people or that the building activity mobilized manpower
from beyond the area, seem in fact to be demonstrated by the calculations
of these authors.

Underlying model-building is the need to look at archaeological data
in functional and operational terms. If we look at the plan of Central Tikal,
for example, in W. R. Coe's book (1967), the great width and length of
the causeways—35 m. to 50m., up to 2 km., respectively—must be related to the masses of users that might be visualized by its builders. Certainly, a procession of fewer than 5,000 persons on foot or in litters would
look puny on the Maudslay or Mendez causeways. The plaza at the foot
of the Temple of Inscriptions, some 17,000 sq. m. in area, would hold
15,000 to 25,000 spectators without difficulty. This level of design seems

compatible with the 3,000 plotted structures and the 9 reservoirs located so far, and with an estimate of a minimal sustaining-area population of about 50,000.

In general, the most fruitful models to aid the better understanding of the Maya zenith and collapse might be the following:

1. A labor-force supply and demand accounting which would disclose a total population, a distribution of that population by age and sex, and an inventory of activities. Such a model would be useful in providing reasonable structural estimates, for example, that "ceremonial site" (in other words, central-place) populations did not exceed 10 percent of the total (Sanders, 1973). Our suggested model might also help in perceiving the possible effects of perturbing changes, such as hurricanes or the loss of able-bodied men through raids.

2. A much more difficult model would be that of capital investment, capital coefficients (that is, ratios between the costs of the investment measured, say, in manpower terms, and its incremental contribution to output), and capital durability. Underlying this model is the realization that investments in land (clearance, cultivation, tree-planting, and so on), water resources, manufacturing and storage facilities, "infrastructure" (sites for social interaction and social regulation), and manpower (particularly specialist education) had specific yields of an economic nature, and that these yields varied. Moreover, since the investments had varying durabilities (for example, the rate of weed infestation versus the life expectancies of priestly agronomists) and varying possibilities and consequences of deferral, choices would be available on a short-time basis (for example, more temple building versus more ramón-tree planting) that could have cumulative effects of a decisive nature. Finally, the interdependence of capital needs to be stressed—reducing some key component below a level of need would reduce the capacity of the entire system, provided compensatory inputs could not be gained from other areas. At the present time, no more than a very approximate capital model appears attainable. Yet even this approximation seems worth a research effort for the kinds of questions it might raise.

3. A different, much needed, type of model is that of the structure and dynamics of sociopolitical control. This model requires an examination and perhaps a differentiation of functional places: were the "ceremonial sites" at Tikal and Jaina similar? Or could the contrasts of Athens and Delos be useful analogies? How important were the local and regional integrations and controlled competitions developed through the ball games? Not only are the Olympic games and gymnasia of Greece to be recalled, but also the passionate involvements in ball games of the towns

in southern United States (Natchez, and so on) need to be remembered (Swanton 1946).

4. Finally, rising out of the other models are those of the actual pathways, the reconstructed histories, of social downfall. In the Maya case, the evidence for mass invasions or other physical catastrophes is largely negative; the question as to whether or not a concatenation of smaller upsets is sufficient needs more formal testing than our volume has been able to undertake. Central to such a model of fragility is the idea of close-to-equilibrium conditions—high death rates and high birth rates, high agricultural bioproductivity and intense weed and disease problems, and (sociopolitically) the balancing options of "command" versus "market" economies and of "gardening" systems of low labor and high land productivity versus "*milpa*" systems of high labor and low level productivity.

The data requirements of these models are large and cannot be satisfied by direct archaeological materials alone. Consequently, a variety of comparative and experimental information must be used.

It is suggested that such data be used at two levels. The first is one of critical suggestions, wherein widespread sources can be used without too much reference to context. The second is that of controlled comparisons, wherein systems that appear analogous are matched after careful examination of their differences.

In all cases, the great importance of protohistorical and early historical information on the Maya area must be stressed. While these data reflect the changes imposed by Toltec and, in part, Spanish impact, and by some important changes in technology, especially the use of metals, their basic validity seems fundamental. While the data on the Yucatec clearly have first importance in this regard, it appears also that materials on the Cakchiquel and Quiche (Miles 1965b) may have substantial relevance to the lowlands as well. In particular, the data on the kinship system (Miles 1965b:280–82) appear to be most compatible and applicable. The contemporary ethnography of the Lacandon and the Tzotzil are of immense relevance, as is well known; however, it is important here to take more account of such factors as the inhibitions on centralization imposed by Ladino dominance. The problem is essentially one of reconstructing a "Great Tradition" from remnants found in "Little Traditions"; comparative studies (see Shimkin 1964) would indicate that the identification of apparent inconsistencies, for example, where a bridegroom is referred to ceremonially as "the leader of 1,000 men," may be especially important.

For other areas, the most fruitful comparisons would, we believe, include Polynesia (especially the Marquesas) for technology and economic organization; the Yoruba of Nigeria for sociopolitical organizations (especially the intercity kingly ties and the rural-urban interactions [Bascom 1969]); and Angkor, as previously mentioned (Shimkin, 1973), for the general model of peaking and collapse.

Experimental archaeology has advanced the understanding of tool types and provided important clues to past astronomical knowledge; it has been much less persuasive in its reconstructions of labor-force use and organization. At present, one of the most promising areas of such investigations would be the determination of the degree to which measures, volumes, and weights may have been standardized. The spans of such standardizations would give a fundamental guide to the corresponding spans of economic management, tribute collection, and commercial law. This standardization can often be of great persistence: the Greco-Roman storage jar continued as the basic Russian volumetric measure to 1917.

Assuming that additional fieldwork, including environmental studies and the model-building suggested, is undertaken and better knowledge of the Maya collapse is gained thereby, what would be the significance of these advances?

First we would gain a better understanding of the Maya people in *genetic* terms, that is as a partial integration through time and space of languages, other cultural features, and biological populations. Such a genetic approach is inherent in all major taxonomies of culture—the "Romans," the "Arabs," the "Chinese,"—yet it is rarely defined. For the Maya, work on this problem is still at a pioneering level, despite the contributions made to it in the Vogt-Ruz study (Vogt and Ruz 1964), and in Juan Comas's critical assessment, *Características Físicas de la Familia Lingüística Maya* (1966).

The relations between linguistic history and other components of the climax cultural features of the Maya remain unclear. A careful phonological analysis and interpretation of the calendrical vocabularies (Satterthwaite 1965) is an immediate need. Our impression is that these words are relatively late secondary loans within the Maya stock. Their relation to the model of Maya differentiation would be likely to contribute heavily to the understanding of Classic culture; likewise, the better understanding of the break down of the "Intertribal Tzolkin" could well lead to important suggestions about the mechanics of the decline. Similar studies of the vocabularies of chieftainship, priesthood, and ballcourts drawn from the protohistoric and specialized ethnological literature also would have great promise.

In general, while the genetic model of the Maya is by no means a developed concept, it has substantial theoretical promise not only for general understanding but for the specific issues of the downfall problem.

The relation of the present study to the regional history of Middle America has already been raised, especially in a previous paper (Willey and Shimkin 1971a). We believe, however, that much more can be done. The coincidences of population growth and decline in the highlands as well as the lowlands of Guatemala present a research area. In addition, the degree of complementarity and exclusive competition between the great centers—Teotihuacan, Kaminaljuyu, Tikal, Dzibilchaltun; later, Tula, Chichen Itza, and Mayapan—needs, and would probably reward, more formal specification. Some kind of balance exists here between market and influence possibilities and the limits of resource generation for urban life which needs further specification. Finally, while we are concerned about the dangers entailed in a too enthusiastic evolutionary view in regard to social systems, we feel that a more extended look at specific technical and social inventions and their potential effects may be rewarding. We have in mind such questions as molds and other serial-production techniques in pottery, the acceptance of cacao as a general currency, or the introduction of large coastal canoes for trade.

A few words on the broadest levels of comparisons. An understanding of the comparative histories and cultures of humid tropical areas—in the Americas, West Africa, south Asia, and, above all, Southeast Asia—is of great importance in correcting the culture-historical bias of all anthropology toward temperate-lands foci. In addition, the significance of tropical flora and fauna as genetic pools for man's future use, combined with their vulnerability to destruction as population growth continues, add a dimension of pragmatism to the study of disasters such as the Maya and Angkor downfalls, Man-land relations in the tropics do have a very general relevance. That our findings to date indicate that these downfalls involved complicated interactions with sociopolitical events rather than simple environmental causation simply requires a broader definition, not a negation, of this work as a study of human ecology.

Notes

1. Throughout we use the 11.16.0.0.0 or Goodman-Martínez-Thompson correlation of Mayan and Christian calendars.

2. Haviland (1971, personal communication) tends to see the building peak of Tikal in Tepeu 1; Culbert (1973b), in Tepeu 2. This difference of opinion is not, however, crucial to our thesis of a Late Classic climax.

3. An excellent example of this sharing of hierarchical culture is seen in a burial at Altar de Sacrificios where an apparent great lady of that site was buried

with high mortuary rites, and her funeral was attended by dignitaries from other major Maya Lowland centers (Adams 1971:159–61).

4. The 12.9.0.0.0 or Spinden correlation of Mayan and Christian calendars would allow more chronological "room" for the Puuc-Chenes-Rio Bec development, and for this reason Andrews tended to favor it; however, the 11.16.0.0.0 correlation is preferred by all other authors in this volume, and it allows a seemingly adequate, if compressed, span of time.

5. Puleston and Puleston (1971) describe and illustrate riverine lowlands, along the Lower Usumacinta and Candelaria rivers at the northwestern margin of the Southern Maya Lowlands, where cultivation ridges are visible. These imply farming methods of a more intensive sort than the slash-and-burn system. According to the Pulestons' argument, such riverine lowlands, peripheral to the central Peten, were the locations of the first Maya Lowland settlements in the Preclassic, and the subsequent settlement of the heart of the Peten, distant from any such riverine lowlands, was made possible by an intensive use of the *ramón* nut.

6. David Webster, whose views were brought to our attention by R. E. W. Adams, would see militarism as definitely "institutionalized" by the time of the Late Classic Period in the lowlands. He bases this opinion on the evidences of ceremonial center fortifications of Early Classic date at the Rio Bec center of Becan, in Campeche, and upon inferences which can be made involving demographic pressures, competition between centers, and the growing importance of centers as the organizational means of controlling and protecting dispersed farming population. We cannot present his ideas in full here, but it is to be hoped that he will develop them in a future publication.

7. It may be that slash-and-burn clearance could actually increase some species of game (especially deer and brocket) by providing a greater variety of fodder, especially young growth. What is needed, with reference to this question and with reference to arguments that have been raised by the Pulestons (1971) about the importance of wild game in the Maya Late Classic, are studies on kinds and volumes of animal remains by regions and time periods.

8. Unlike peoples of many early agricultural civilizations of the Old World, the Maya give no clear evidence of having been concerned with the promotion of human fertility ("fertility cults" and so on) in Classic times. The only Maya figurines that would appear to qualify as "fertility" fetishes would be those of the much earlier Middle Preclassic Period.

2 The Rise of Maya Civilization:
A Summary View

This chapter is intended as a summary and, to a degree, a synthesis of the exposition, argument, and discussion that have been presented in the foregoing chapters and that were developed in the course of the seminar proceedings.[1] Its organization follows that of the book and falls into the same three essential parts, covering (1) the basic archaeological data from the Maya Lowlands; (2) the external influences that are presumed to have impinged on Lowland Maya cultural developments; and (3) the cultural processes involved and the models that have been designed to explicate them.

As will be evident to the reader, there is a descending scale of agreement among the seminar participants as we progress in this organization. For the most part, there is a concordance on the archaeological data bases although even here divergences in interpretation may set in at primary or low levels of inference. Beyond this, disagreement arises as we attempt to understand the nature of external influences that bore upon Maya cultural growth and upon cultural process in this growth. I have indicated some of this disagreement, but, in the interests of summarization and brevity, admit to not having done full justice to it all. Thus, whatever I have done, my summary is biased, although I have tried to keep my biases to a minimum and can only urge the reader to return to the individual chapters to appraise various lines of argument.

As what I have to say here is obvioulsy based on the preceding papers, I shall not cite these papers specifically in all instances; however, where speculation and theoretical opinion come to the fore, I will refer to specific names. Additional backup literature will not be referred to, as a rule, since it is cited in the other papers, but I will provide references for those few occasions which were not so covered.

The Lowland Maya Data Bases

The basic data, especially as presented in the chapters by Culbert, Hammond, Adams, Ball, Willey, and Rands, pertain to the Mesoamerican cultural subarea known as the Maya Lowlands. This territory, of southern Mexico and portions of Central America, is well defined in many source books, and it has been very specifically plotted and subdivided into regions or zones in an earlier work by Culbert 1973 ed.:Fig. 1).[2] As each of the above authors has provided a regional or zonal presentation. I shall not recapitulate here in that fashion, but instead will summarize by horizons or time periods. These periods correspond to those of Mayan (and Mesoamerican) archaeological chronology. The reader's attention is called to J. W. Ball's chronological chart (1977a, Fig. 1.3), with its zonal columns, major period divisions, and B.C.–A.D. dates. This chart is an important adjunct to the study of this summary or to the reading of any of the chapters in this volume.

THE EARLY PRECLASSIC PERIOD (2000–1000 B.C.)

There is, as yet, no clearly defined cultural horizon for the Maya Lowlands prior to or during the Early Preclassic Period. Scattered possible preceramic finds have been reported, but these "assemblages," if they can be dignified by that name, are neither well defined nor dated. Hammond (1977b) has referred to a radiocarbon date on a maize pollen core from Lake Yaxha, in the Peten, which is given as 2000 B.C.; but we need to know more about the cultural context of this date—as well as to have others of a comparable chronological range—before we can arrive at any well-grounded conclusions. Besides this, there are hints that pottery-making peoples may have been present along the western and eastern margins of the Maya Lowlands a little before 1000 B.C. The earliest Chontalpa-region pottery, on the western side of the Maya Lowlands proper, dates to the Early Preclassic Period (Molina and Palacios phases—see Ball, 1977, Fig. 1.3); from Cuello, in northern Belize, Hammond (1977b) reports an early radiocarbon pottery date of 1020 B.C. This last, of course, is a single date, and it is close to the Early Preclassic–Middle Preclassic dividing line. The fact that pottery-making and farming peoples were well established in the Early Preclassic Period in other southern Mesoamerican subareas, at no great distance from the Maya Lowlands, does make it strange that these lowlands were not also so occupied at the same time; but such are the facts to date.

THE MIDDLE PRECLASSIC PERIOD (1000–300 B.C.)

The earliest firm and reasonably abundant evidence for Maya Lowland occupation comes from the Pasión Valley region or zone of the southern Peten Department of Guatemala. This is the Xe pottery complex of the sites of Altar de Sacrificios and Seibal. Xe pottery occurs as unslipped or monochrome wares, occasionally incised and punctated, and featuring flaring-sided, flanged-rim plates and *tecomate* jars. It is similar to Early Middle Preclassic pottery of the Gulf Coast Chontalpa country, which, in turn, derives from the tradition of Chontalpa Early Preclassic pottery to which we have just referred (see Ball, 1977, Fig. 1.3). The wider relationships of this ceramic tradition are with other early southern Mesoamerican pottery groups of the Chiapas Pacific Coast and to Gulf Coast pre-Olmec and Olmec levels. The Middle Preclassic Chontalpa pottery (the Puente and Franco phases) may have provided the source for the Xe pottery of the Maya lowlands, via early settlers from the Gulf Coast–Usumacinta country. The Chihuaan phase of the Trinidad locality may be a link in such a line of relationships which lead on up the Usumacinta River to the Pasión drainage. Hammond argues for such a Xe entry, suggesting that these earliest immigrants into the Maya Lowlands were following out and exploiting a landscape that would offer aquatic riverine as well as terrestrial resources. Subsequently, in the course of Middle Preclassic cultural change, they, or their descendants, were forced into less desirable nonriverine, as well as other riverine, site locations. An alternative source for Xe ceramics, and for a first peopling of the Maya Lowlands, is out of the highlands to the south, in Salvador or Guatemala. Xe-like pottery is reported from the Guatemalan sites of El Porton nd Sakajut. I have tended to prefer this as the starting point for the Xe immigrants, although the majority of the seminar participants argued for a Gulf Coastal source. The relative datings, which would be crucial to the resolution of such a question, are still too uncertain for a final decision, at least to my way of thinking. One difficulty in all of this is that we are dealing with an interrelated southern Mesoamerican ceramic evolution, one that has earlier manifestations in the Early Preclassic potteries of the Chiapas Pacific Coast (Barra, Ocos), as well as on the Gulf Coast (Ojochi, Bajío, and Molina), so that there is a strong possibility that descendant complexes may have been carried into the Peten from either direction.

Pottery definitely identified to the Xe ceramic sphere has not yet been reported elsewhere in the Maya Lowlands. Culbert (1977) describes the Eb complex, the earliest at Tikal and a possible contemporary of Xe, as being distinct from Xe although showing some resemblances to it. The same could be said for the early facet of the Jenney Creek complex of the Belize Valley. Hammond's (1977a) Cuello pottery, which he dates to his pre-Mamom-horizon Swasey complex, is also described in preliminary comments (postconference commentary from Hammond) as being distinct from Xe. In reviewing the situation as a whole, the seminar group tentatively agreed that, while a Gulf Coastal or northwestern source seemed the most likely, it remained a distinct possibility that the earliest ceramics of the Maya Lowlands may have had diverse origins—as did the people who brought these ceramics with them.

Xe and Eb sites are small and few. They are, in effect, small refuse areas and house locations found beneath later cultural deposits at Altar, Seibal, and Tikal. The inferences drawn from this are that the first Peten settlers were few in number and widely scattered. It is highly probable that these people were farmers. They built perishable houses either on the ground level or on very low artificial platforms. No clearly identifiable public architecture was found at any of the sites, although it is just possible that an inner mound platform (within a much larger and later structure) at Tikal does date from late Eb. However, owing to the very limited excavation exposure (a tunnel), and the possibility of earlier sherds being included in later fill materials, the Eb-phase identification remains uncertain. The settlement and architectural implications for Xe and Eb are, thus, those of peoples living in simple, egalitarian societies. At the same time, we should not forget that Xe and Eb peoples must have been aware of more complex societies in the contemporary communities of the Gulf Coast Lowlands or Chiapas. Here, the village-cum-ceremonial-center settlement system and at least the beginnings of nonegalitarian social orders were in existence in the Middle Preclassic Period and had been even earlier. That there were contacts with the outside as early as Xe-Eb times is attested by the fact that obsidian was traded into the Maya Lowlands on this horizon.

By about 700–600 B.C., Xe ceramics began to be replaced by those of the Mamom pottery sphere. Mamom appears to have developed out of Xe, and it persisted throughout the latter part of the Middle Preclassic Period. In the Central Zone and the Pasión Zone, as well as elsewhere, ·Mamom pottery marks a trend toward greater uniformity and standardization in manufacture. Ball (1977), however, viewing the situation from Yucatan, is inclined to reject this "uniformity" as superficial, and stresses, instead, regional differences. From his descriptions, these differences do, indeed, set the north apart from the south at this time. He relates this regionalism to segmentary tribal settlement of the Maya Lowlands as the descendants of the original Xe riverine communities spread away from the river locations into the internal hinterland and filled up the Maya Lowlands. While I am in agreement with Ball's concepts of fission and spread of tribal societies, I do think that there is a discernible overall trend from ceramic heterogeneity to homogeneity in the three to four hundred years of the Mamom horizon. That there should be such a trend is not surprising. As populations increased and the country became filled, communication between communities must also have increased.

Mamom-sphere pottery has little that suggests sumptuary wares for burial or trade. This is in keeping with the profile for other archaeological remains of the sphere. The sites themselves, while more numerous than those of the Xe horizon, are still small village areas. Public architecture is lacking or rare and of modest size. At Altar de Sacrificios there is an artificial platform, four meters high, that dates from late Mamom (San Felix), and this is in a modest ceremonial-center-type setting of a plaza arrangement with other, smaller mounds. At Nohoch Ek, in west central Belize, there is a small Mamom-horizon platform with cut-stone masonry and lime-stucco plastering, constructional traits that continue and flourish with the Maya (Coe and Coe 1956). In northern Yucatan the Nabanche phase at Dzibilchaltun has some platform structures that also look like corporate labor constructions. Elsewhere, however, even this small-scale elite architecture is lacking. This applies to such Mamom-sphere phases as the Escoba at Seibal, Tzec at Tikal, Mamom proper at Uaxactun, Jenney Creek in the Belize Valley, López Mamom in northern Belize, Acachen in the Rio Bec, and the pre-Picota and Xet phases in the Northwestern Zone.

THE LATE PRECLASSIC PERIOD (300–50 B.C.)

The chronological definition which Ball (1977, Fig. 1.3) has given to this period is a compromise and reconciliation of a number of regional sequence columns. The authors of the several data-base papers offered slightly varying dates, and this was complicated by the fact that some, but

3. Gordon Willey, 1974. Photo by David Noble. Courtesy of the School of American Research.

not all, operated with the concept of a Protoclassic Period. Ball has included such a period on his chart (50 B.C.–A.D. 250), and it is a useful device in our tracing out the events leading up to the Maya Classic Period; however, some authors in their descriptions of local phases often melded Late Preclassic and Protoclassic together. Here I shall be at pains to try to make a distinction, and we shall take up the Late Preclassic first.

Chicanel and Chicanel-like ceramics are the diagnostic of the Late

Preclassic in the Maya Lowlands. Chicanel very clearly develops from the Mamom sphere. For the most part, the pottery complexes of the Chicanel sphere are highly standardized. The ware has a characteristic "waxy" surface, usually in red, black, or cream monochromes. There are also bichrome wares, and these tend to be more common in the later facets. To generalize further about the Chicanel-linked cultures, this was a time of marked population increases. Sites become more numerous, are individually larger, and the first major ceremonial center architecture appears. Specific architectural features herald later Classic Period developments. There is a trade now in luxury items, such as marine shells and stingray spines from the coast and jade imported from the highlands. Differentiations in grave goods signal status differences. The implications of all this are those of a society, or series of related societies, expanding and developing a nonegalitarian sociopolitical structure.

At the same time there are notable regional differences to these generalizations. Indeed, these were some of the most important findings to emerge from the seminar, bringing together as it did regional specialists from all parts of the Maya Lowlands. Among these differences were the pace and timing of population expansion, ceremonial center construction, and indications of elite-commoner dichotomies. At Tikal, in the Central Zone, it is the early part of the Late Preclassic Period, the Chuen phase, that sees the big population upswing. This was accompanied by public architectural construction, including such anticipations of later Classic Period features as apron molding on pyramid-platforms and corbeled-vaulted tombs. Such tombs were presumably the burial places of members of an emerging elite class and were accompanied with such things as jades and stingray spines. In contrast, the latter part of the Late Preclassic Period, the Cauac phase, was a time of either population stabilization or, perhaps, decline. This Tikal diachronic configuration of the Late Preclassic differs from that of the Pasión Zone as seen in the stratigraphic record at Altar de Sacrificios, where there are indications that ceremonial elaboration, and probably population as well, built up through the Late Preclassic, climaxing at its very end. In Belize, also, in the northern Corozal–Orange Walk sector, the Cocos Chicanel phase, which shows a fourfold increase in site-unit occupation over earlier Mamom-sphere times, seems to show a more or less steady growth, or at least there is no noticeable decline in the latter part of the period. In the Northwestern Zone we know the Chicanel pottery is associated with the first sizable mound structures of the region, in the vicinity of Palenque, in the Chacibcan phase of Trinidad, and in the Pinzon complex nearer the coast; however, there is still too little information to say anything about the timing of developments within the Late Preclassic Period.

The Northern Plains Zone has a Late Preclassic developmental profile more like that of Tikal or, perhaps, even more pronounced. The Komchen phase, which Ball (1977) dates at 250–100 B.C., was a cultural peak, with large populations and architectural constructions of great size. The ceramics of Komchen, while showing some relationships to Chicanel, differ from those of the south. In the succeeding Xculul phase, which Ball dates at 100 B.C.–A.D. 250 and thereby carries over into the Protoclassic Period, there are indications of population decrease and a cessation of public building. It should be noted, however, that this developmental pattern derives from the great site of Dzibilchaltun. Elsewhere in the north, at Soblonke and Yaxuna, for example, the Xculul drop-off is not apparent.

In the Rio Bec Zone, in the south central part of the Yucatan Peninsula, there is still another developmental story. While the Pakluum phase of the Chicanel sphere registers a population increase over earlier times at its inception, there is no major architectural development at all in the 300–50 B.C. period. This all comes later (50 B.C.–A.D. 250), in the Protoclassic Period.

This regional irregularity in Late Preclassic Period developmental profiles is most interesting and certainly not yet well understood. Tikal peaked in the first half of the period (Culbert, 1977). One wonders if this was true of all of the northeast Peten region, or Central Zone. Dzibilchaltun, in northern Yucatan, did the same. Were the causes similar? In this connection, it is worth noting that the two phenomena do not seem to have been closely related historically. Dzibilchaltun was, in its Komchen phase, the most divergent of any of the early Late Preclassic ceramic complexes, with its Chicanel-sphere status most dubious. At Tikal the Cauac phase of the later part of the Late Preclassic was at best a time of stabilization of population. At Dzibilchaltun the contemporaneous Xculul phase was definitely one of population drop-off and cultural decline. At the same time, this was not the case in other sites in the Northern Plains Zone. This latter finding is both interesting and disturbing. Must our attempts at generalization and our search for developmental regularities be further complicated by site-to-site as well as region-to-region variability? In the Pasión Valley the Late Preclassic has been adjudged to be a time of mounting population growth and constructional buildup, with the climax at the end. The same seems to hold for the Rio Bec Zone, as this is measured at Becan, although the pace is slower, and the climax, at least for ceremonial architecture, is delayed until the succeeding Protoclassic Period. The best we can come up with out of all this is that while the Late Preclassic Period was the time of the first rise toward population density and the kind of settlement organization and public construction one associates with civilization, this must be viewed in broadest chronological perspective. When we construct a finer-grained spatial-temporal framework in which to examine events, we are confronted with variation. This variation is almost sure to have been important in the course of civilizational growth in the Maya Lowlands.

THE PROTOCLASSIC PERIOD (50 B.C.–A.D. 250)

In Maya archaeology there has been some conceptual confusion about the "Protoclassic." It has three aspects of meanings. A Protoclassic Period of time has generally been defined as the early centuries A.D. This is the chronological definition on Ball's chart—50 B.C.–A.D. 250. Obviously, all Maya Lowland regional cultural continua passed through such a period. A second meaning of the Protoclassic pertains to cultural content. This content refers mainly to ceramics, to vessel-form features such as mammiform tetrapodal supports and to surface decorative techniques in the Usulutan-resist manner or to positive painted imitations of this. There are also a distinctive orange monochrome ware and red-and-black-on-orange polychromes (e.g., Ixcanrio) which presage the Early Classic Maya polychromes. One of the better known ceramic complexes of this kind is the Floral Park of the Belize Valley. Holmul I and the Salinas phase at Altar de Sacrificios also fit here. It is generally thought that these pottery traits were introduced into the Maya Lowlands from the Salvadoran-Guatemalan Highlands. A third Protoclassic meaning is a little harder to define, but it has, essentially, a cultural-stage connotation. It refers to the terminal climax of the Late Preclassic Period and to the transition from that period into the Maya Early Classic. This is expressed in architectural forms, as well as in ceramic decoration, and in tomb paraphernalia and other indications of the rise of an elite class. As we review the several lowland zones, let us keep these three definitions or meanings in mind.

At Tikal the Floral Park kind of ceramic complex is present during the late Cauac and Cimi phases, which date to the 50 B.C.–A.D. 250 time bracket; however, this kind of pottery does not appear in sufficient volume for Culbert (1977) to postulate a site-unit intrusion of people bearing such a complex. Nor was there any population growth or major increase in architectural activity at Tikal during this period. Still, some of the Protoclassic "stage" developments do make an appearance in such things as tomb and temple wall paintings of the Cimi phase. These depict individuals in the high-status dress and paraphernalia, similar to those of the succeeding Classic Period, and in some of these paintings there are defi-

4.   Origins seminar, 1974. Photo by David Noble. Courtesy of the School of
      American Research. (left to right, seated: Michael D. Coe, Robert L. Rands,
      Gordon R. Willey, Gareth W. Lowe, William T. Sanders. left to right, standing:
      Jacinto Quirarte, T. Patrick Culbert, Joseph W. Ball, R.E.W. Adams, Robert
      McC. Netting, William L. Rathje)

nite clues to Izapan stylistic influence. Uaxactun, the other major Central
Zone politico-religious center for which we have detailed information, has
much less Floral Park or Holmul I–type pottery than Tikal; but the stucco-
ornamented E-VII-sub temple at that site undoubtedly dates to the Protoclassic Period, and its sculptures are another indication of the Protoclassic
"stage" transition into the Classic.

        Along the Peten-Belize border, as at Holmul, and in both the Belize
Valley and the Corozal-Orange Walk district to the north, the Floral Park
ceramic complex is present at several sites. In the Belize Valley this was a
time of population increase in the house clusters of Barton Ramie. To the
north, in the Corozal–Orange Walk sector, Hammond (1977b) reports
the presence of the Freshwater Floral Park–phase ceramics at several sites,
including the important center of Nohmul, where they are associated with
major architecture. In his opinion, a center such as Nohmul was in process of becoming an important governmental locus at this time for the
direction of agricultural production and the control of trade for the region.

Here it is of interest to note that agricultural intensification, as indicated by the ridged fields of the Río Hondo locality, dates as early as this. Hammond makes the point that not all sites in northern Belize show the Floral Park ceramic complex. While its absence might possibly mark a hiatus between Late Preclassic and Early Classic in their occupation, he feels that this is unlikely—and so do I. Apparently here, as to the west at Tikal and Uaxactun, the time period designated as the Protoclassic (50 B.C.–A.D. 250) was not everywhere characterized by Floral Park–complex pottery. In Hammond's opinion the cacao production of the Belize Zone was an important trigger in the processes leading to the rise to civilization, not only in northern Belize, but indirectly, for the rest of the Lowland Maya.

The other place where the specialized Floral Park–like ceramic content of the Protoclassic Period is found is in the Pasión Valley, at Altar De Sacrificios (Willey, 1977a). The ceramic relationship may express a connection out of original highland prototypes rather than a direct one across the southern Peten. While no case can be made out for a population increase, Salinas was a phase of architectural activity which set the local scene for the Classic; but, while this was going on at Altar de Sacrificios, Seibal, some distance upstream to the east, was undergoing a definite population decline and cessation of building activities in the late facet of the Cantutse phase.

In the Northwestern Zone, Rands (1977) says, Protoclassic pottery (presumably that of Floral Park–Salinas styles) is rare but present. This does not, of course, necessarily indicate any population or cultural decline along the Usumacinta at this time. The Northwestern Zone sites, like those of the Central Zone, may simply have been too remote from, or in some other way out of the orbit of, Floral Park–Salinas ceramic styles.

In the Rio Bec, the later Pakluum-phase facets mark a cultural peak, both in the ceremonial-center constructions at Becan and in the peopling of the surrounding countryside. Becan at this time consisted of a ceremonial center of plazas, platforms, and pyramids covering some forty acres. This was surrounded by a moat and wall of obviously defensive purpose—the earliest defense work, at least of great size, in the Maya Lowlands. Thus, in the sense of a developmental climax, the Protoclassic is well represented in the Rio Bec Zone. At the same time, as both Adams (1977) and Ball (1977) stress, the Protoclassic Floral Park–like pottery is not found.

For the Northern Plains we have already recounted what happened at Dzibilchaltun during the Xculul phase, which subsumes the Protoclassic Period. It was a time of population and constructional decline at that great site—trends which are in no way consistent with the Protoclassic buildup in the south. This decline, however, is modified somewhat by the apparent continued heavy activity at other Northern Plains sites during the same period. In ceramics the north did not participate in the Floral Park or any closely related sphere.

The overall Protoclassic Period picture for the Maya Lowlands, as I see it, then goes something like this. In the south, particularly in the Peten, the Protoclassic phases come at the end of a Late Preclassic era of populational growth and cultural buildup. In this growth and buildup Tikal and the Central Zone had taken an early lead and then slacked off somewhat; along the Pasión these upward trends seem to have continued more or less steadily up to the Protoclassic. The Protoclassic was a time of stabilization and crystallization, with the latter term applying to the fact that certain cultural forms take on a definite "Classic" appearance at that time. Along the far eastern edge of the Peten and in western Belize the Protoclassic cultures were given a new and somewhat different "flavor" by the appearance of exotic ceramic traits, generally thought to be of Salvadoran or Guatemalan Highland origin, and referred to, collectively, in the Lowlands as the "Floral Park complex." The Belize Protoclassic cultures enjoyed a florescence at this time, and it is possible that they served to transmit new ideas of various kinds, along with new ceramic elements, into the Central Zone of the Peten, where Maya Classic culture was to make its first appearance a century or two later. Floral Park–like ceramics are also seen in the Protoclassic along the far western edge of the Peten at Altar de Sacrificios. In the Rio Bec Zone the Protoclassic Period was a time of cultural climax, both demographically and architecturally; however, there is no sign of the Floral Park ceramic complex in this zone. In the Northern Plains the data indicate a populational and cultural buildup beginning early in the Late Preclassic. At Dzibilchalturn this buildup is terminated in the Protoclassic, which is a period of decline for that site; elsewhere, however, there is the strong possibility that such a buildup was maintained. This zone is without Floral Park ceramics.

THE EARLY CLASSIC PERIOD (A.D. 250–600)

The formal definition of the inception of the Early Classic Period is the appearance of Initial Series-dated monuments in the Central Zone, especially at Tikal and Uaxactun, in the half-century between A.D. 250 and A.D. 300. These monuments may be said to have put the seal of official and authoritarian recognition on the social and political hierarchies that had been developing during the Late Preclassic and Protoclassic, especially in the three centuries of the latter period. While concerned with astronomical events to a degree, their hieroglyphic texts and Long Count calendric dates were the validations of a ruling aristocracy. In the Central

Zone the Tzakol ceramic sphere replaced the Chicanel sphere. Culbert (1977) notes that many of the new ceramic traits had been present before, in the Protoclassic Period at Tikal, but that now these formerly minor traits assume a position of numerical dominance. Many other new Tzakol features would appear to have been introduced via Floral Park influences, and there are also Teotihuacan ceramic features as early as Early Manik (the beginning of the Tikal Early Classic). But Culbert sees this Tikal Early Classic development as a local synthesis and rejects the hypothesis of a new population influx of the site-unit intrusion type. The Early Classic brings demographic changes at Tikal. Early Manik gives little evidence of population growth over the antecedent Cimi phase, but by Middle Manik times Culbert postulates a doubling of former population. Architectural construction enjoys a boom, but actual ceremonial center layout and architectural features continue in the plans and modes that had been laid down as early as the Late Preclassic.

The Central Zone "stela cult" of Initial Series dedicatory monuments had spread to Altar de Sacrificios on the lower Pasión by A.D. 450, as had Tzakol pottery, including the polychrome vessels (of Floral Park ancestry) and the tripod jars (of Teotihuacan inspiration). The Early Classic was not a time of population growth at Altar de Sacrificios, but, judging from the hieroglyphic monuments, the site continued as an important center. During this time, Seibal, the other major Pasión Valley center, located upstream from Altar, was virtually abandoned (Willey 1977a).

The Early Classic and the Nuevo-Tzakol ceramic sphere are well represented in Belize. While the stela cult does not seem to have spread this far to the east, at least on this time level, the ceramic ties binding the Central and Belize zones are strong (Hammond, 1977b).

In the Northwestern Zone, Rands (1977) describes the Picota complex as being essentially unlike the Tzakol, although contemporaneous with it. No Picota-phase architecture has yet been identified at Palenque, although refuse and fill sherds suggest that ceremonial construction probably began this early somewhere in the site locality. In the succeeding Motiepa phase (the latter part of the Early Classic Period) there was an introduction of the Peten Gloss wares of the Tzakol sphere, plus some polychrome pottery. These new traits, however, are modified and integrated into local patterns and styles. There is large-scale construction identified with Motiepa. Elsewhere in the Northwestern Zone, as along the Middle Usumacinta, the Early Classic seems to have been a time of population decline. Rands considers the possibility that this might be a nucleation of population into fewer but larger sites, but he is inclined to reject this hypothesis for lack of indication of sociopolitical complexity in the sites that are occupied. Again, however, regional or even subregional differences must be commented upon. Northward, on the Gulf Coast, the Early Classic is better represented; and southward, in the upper Usumacinta Zone, the site of Piedras Negras was an important Early Classic center. The stela cult is represented by Early Classic Piedras Negras monuments, and the pottery belongs to the Tzakol sphere. In all of this, Piedras Negras, as well as Yaxchilan, farther upstream, are much more closely allied to Altar de Sacrificios than they are to the Northwestern Zone sites.

In the early part of the Early Classic Period in the Rio Bec Zone the population expansion and architectural florescence that had characterized the preceding Protoclassic Period came to a stop. At some point in the A.D. 250–450 period, known as the Chacsik phase, the inhabitants of Becan appear to have been, in effect, besieged in their fortified city. There is no evidence of the stela cult, hieroglyphics, or other distinctive Peten Central Zone traits. Later, in the Sabucan phase (A.D. 450–600), the political situation may have changed. There is evidence to indicate that the great defensive moat at Becan was no longer maintained as it had been formerly. This may have been related to more peaceful conditions, although Webster (1977) cautions that this neglect may reflect only higher priority labor use elsewhere, and continued reliance on a fortification which even in a somewhat shoddy condition remained perfectly defensible.

In the Northern Plains Zone, Dzibilchaltun, which had declined notably in the preceding Xculul phase, was abandoned in the earlier part of the Early Classic (A.D. 250–450); however, we know that other northern sites, such as Yaxuna and Acanceh, were active at this time, so events were not uniform for the entire zone. Nevertheless, looking at all of the north, including the Puuc, Chenes, Rio Bec, and Northern Plains zones, Ball (1977) makes the generalization that the early Early Classic saw a reduction in the number of ceremonial centers and in individual size of sites. A little later (A.D. 450–600), Dzibilchaltun was reoccupied during the Piim phase, and, in general, the late Early Classic saw something of a revival in the north. Throughout, the cultural changes are those noted for the Rio Bec Sabucan phase. Southern, or Peten, influences appear in ceramics and occasional stelae and hieroglyphic inscriptions.

THE CLASSIC HIATUS PHENOMENON (A.D. 534–593)

The Classic hiatus in stela dedication lasted from shortly after 9.5.0.0.0 (A.D. 534) until 9.8.0.0.0 (A.D. 593). This is the end of the Early Classic Period following Ball's chronological chart (Ball, 1977, Fig. 1.3); however, the short hiatus interval might be said to form the dividing line between Early and Late Classic. In the data chapters I was the only one to direct much attention to the hiatus. It is a phenomenon of the Southern Low-lands, especially the Central, Pasión, (upper) Usumacinta, and Southeast-ern zones. From Piedras Negras, in the west, to Copan, in the east, there is a marked drop-off in stela carving and dedication for an interval of about sixty years; there is evidence to indicate that ceremonial construction also slackened during this time. Elsewhere, however, the hiatus either is not clearly registered in the archaeological record or fails to exist. It is not noticeable in the Palenque sequence, where the late Early Classic Motiepa phase seems to have been a time of growth and construction. Nor is it present in any clearly defined way in the north. In fact, in some northern sequences the sixth century A.D. is, relatively, a time of cultural vigor, as in the Sabucan and Piim phases. Without attempting to offer explana-tions or processual statements at this point in the summary, but merely trying to set down the basic data, it appears that the Classic Hiatus is a southern phenomenon and, especially, a Peten phenomenon.

THE LATE CLASSIC PERIOD (A.D. 600–900)

This period takes us essentially beyond the story of the rise of Maya civilization, but its configurations are of some interest. Throughout the Maya Lowlands it was a time of demographic growth and cultural elabo-ration. For most regions this Late Classic peaking, in contrast to develop-ments that had gone before, was most impressive. In fact only in the Central Zone, at Tikal and perhaps Uaxactun, and probably in the Belize Zone do Early Classic achievement and growth even come close to rivaling those of the Late Classic. The Late Classic was the time of the Tepeu ceramic sphere,[3] and the centuries of growth and climax were the Tepeu 1 and 2 subphases of that sphere (ca. A.D. 600–800). In general, ceremonial cen-ters multiplied in numbers and were individually enlarged architecturally. Outlying house-mound occupations, insofar as we have archaeological infor-mation on this, increased in number in almost all parts of the lowlands. In the south this was the era of the stela cult in full glory, with sculptural portraits of rulers and hieroglyphic texts recording the deeds and pedi-grees of royal personages. In the south and especially the north the Late Classic saw the largest and most impressive architecture. Palenque, Pie-dras Negras, and Yaxchilan in the west, Copan in he east, and the Rio Bec, Chenes, Puuc, and Northern Plains centers of the north grew in size to rival Tikal.

In the latter third of the Late Classic Period, the time of the Tepeu 3 subphase (ca. A.D. 800–900), a decline set in that led to the desertion, or near desertion, of the southern cities by the end of the ninth century. This "Maya collapse" has been discussed and documented at length in an ear-

lier seminar presentation (Culbert 1973a). In the north this decline seems
to have been somewhat later. Here it occurred somewhat earlier in the
southern zones, such as the Rio Bec and Chenes, later in the Puuc and
Northern Plains. In the latter regions substantial ceremonial construction
lasted until A.D. 1000, or into the Early Postclassic Period. After that portions
of the north fell under Toltec dominance for a time (Chichen Itza) and then
continued in a Mexican-Maya cultural tradition (Mayapan, Tulum).

External Influences on Lowland Maya Cultural Growth

In the foregoing section we have referred, by way of descriptive identification, to the presences of what are unmistakable external cultural influences in the Maya Lowlands and in the Maya Lowland cultural continuum.
Except for the evidences of the earliest cultural remains, and the question
of the "first peopling" of the lowlands, we have offered no discussion of
these influences. In this section of the summary I will bring together what
I consider to be the salient points of the seminar's opinions about these
matters. The principal sources and source areas for the foreign influences
that impinged upon the Lowland Maya are: (1) the Olmec Gulf Coast;
(2) southern Chiapas; (3) the Guatemala-Salvador Highlands; and (4) central Mexico. While it would be possible to take up the questions of external influences under each of these headings, a better integrated and
interactive picture of events through time can be obtained by organizing
our discussion period by period, in the same manner that the basic *in situ*
lowland data were presented.

SOUTHERN MESOAMERICA IN THE EARLY
PRECLASSIC PERIOD (2000–1000 B.C.)

Some background on the Early Preclassic Period in southern Mesoamerica is a prerequisite to our understanding of the influences that
created Maya Lowland culture. The earliest known ceramic complex of
southern Mesoamerica is the Barra of the southern Chiapas coastal region,
dating to 1600 B.C. (see Fig. 1.3) or even earlier. It and the immediately
later Ocos-phase pottery of the same region represent an early pottery
tradition that may have spread from southern Chiapas, across the Isthmus of Tehuantepec, and into the Gulf Coastal Olmec country of southern Veracruz-Tabasco. The Gulf Coastal Ojochi, Bajío, and Chicharras
phases are developments out of this tradition, as are the later San Lorenzo
A and B phases of "classic" Olmec (M. D. Coe, 1977) and the Cuadros
phase of southern Chiapas. Lowe (1977) regards this ceramic tradition
as the creation of peoples of Zoquean (Mixe-Zoque-Popoluca) speech.

Zoquean, along with Mayan, belongs to the more inclusive Macro-Mayan language group. This cultural-linguistic linkage is a speculation, but a speculation based upon the geographical position of Zoquean-speaking peoples in the historic period, especially with reference to the position of the Maya; upon archaeological continuities; and upon the probabilities that tribes speaking these Zoquean languages were the old residents of this territory, antedating such nations as the Chiapanec and Nahuas. Others of us in the seminar, including myself, have suggested that the Early Preclassic Olmec were Mayan-speaking. This is, of course, a possibility, although I admit to being impressed by Lowe's line of argument. It should also be kept in mind that Zoquean and Proto-Mayan may have been much more closely related in the 1600–1000 B.C. period than were Maya, Zoque, Mixe, and Popoluca in historic times.[4]

Other southern Mesoamerican ceramic complexes that may relate to this Barra-Ocos-Ojochi (possibly Zoquean) tradition include the Molina of the Chontalpa country (to which we have already referred in discussing Maya Lowland origins), the Pre-Chiuaan of the Trinidad locality, the Cotorra of the Grijalva Trench (Chiapa de Corzo), and the Tok of Salvador. All of these complexes are thought to be Early Preclassic in date. It is also possible that the Salama Valley complexes of the northern Guatemala Highlands which have been described briefly by Sedat and Sharer (1972), and to which Lowe (1977) refers in his chapter, date this early; however, some seminar members expressed doubt on this point. Pottery-making villagers do not appear to have been this early in the central Guatemalan Highlands, nor is there a matching occupation in the Maya Lowlands (excepting the Chontalpa and Trinidad finds as essentially marginal to those lowlands).

The general culture status of all of these Early Preclassic peoples of southern Mesoamerica is not fully known; however, there are indications that some of them already had hierarchically ordered, nonegalitarian societies. This certainly was true of the Olmec-region peoples during the San Lorenzo phases, with their large earth constructions and monumental stone art, and in M. D. Coe's (1977) opinion, it was probably also true of the earlier Chicharras and Bajío phases. In southern Chiapas earth mounds are associated with the Ocos phase, although Lowe (1977) can identify no definite ceremonial centers.

THE MIDDLE PRECLASSIC PERIOD (1000–300 B.C.)

It is to these surrounding regions, which were participating in an early southern Mesoamerican pottery tradition and which were, at least in some places, the settings for centrally controlled, hierarchical societies, that we must look for the first settlers to the Maya Lowlands. As has already been stated, the Xe and Eb complexes of the Peten appear to have been derived from this same early southern Mesoamerican pottery tradition. Xe-Eb pottery is, of course, of Middle Preclassic date, rather than Early Preclassic, and its closest resemblances are to the contemporaneous Middle Preclassic phases of the surrounding extralowland territories—to Duende, Conchas I, and Dili, of Chiapas; to Nacaste of the Olmec region; to Puente in the Chontalpa; and to Colos of Salvador. Based on pottery criteria, it was the unanimous opinion of the seminar that the Xe-Eb pottery-making immigrants first entered the Maya Lowlands at the very beginning of the Middle Preclassic Period.

Lowe (1977) suggests that these earliest settlers were groups who were marginal to or disaffected from the somewhat more prosperous and advanced societies to the west and south. Indeed, he argues, they were "commoners," and "desperate commoners," who were moving out into hitherto unexplored lands, motivated essentially by hunger resulting from increased population pressure in the "old lands." As we have seen, the Xe and Eb communities were small and their cultural repertory modest. There are no public structures, no sumptuary goods. The social profile is an egalitarian one. Yet if Lowe is correct, and I am inclined to think that he is, these Peten "pioneers" were aware of more complex social structures than their own. Archaeological evidences of extra-Lowland contacts bear this out. Furthermore, these commoner settlers aspired to greater things; and, following Lowe's thesis, these aspirations fired an ethnic rivalry between the emigrants and their more established relatives that led to the rise of a separate Maya Lowlander religious and political identity in the succeeding Late Preclassic Period.

Exactly who were these first settlers of the lowlands, and where did they come from? Lowe concurs with his colleagues that Olmec ceramic traits (Nacaste phase) were carried into northern Yucatan from the Gulf Coast at this time and that the Usumacinta, Pasión, and Peten may also have been peopled from this direction at the beginning of the Middle Preclassic. However, with reference to this last point, he expresses a preference for another migration down from the Salvadoran-Guatemalan Highlands. These migrations, in his opinion, mark a split between Zoquean- and Mayan-speaking populations; seen in this light, the highland-to-lowland route was the most likely one for Mayan groups to have taken.

THE LATE PRECLASSIC AND PROTOCLASSIC PERIODS (300 B.C.–A.D. 250)

Both Coe (1977) and Quirarte (1977) make convincing cases for Olmec iconographic elements and themes in the later art of the Classic Maya. One of the problems of southern Mesoamerican archaeology is just how this transfer took place. As Coe points out, there seems to have been little direct contact between Olmec and Maya. For one thing, this could not have been possible on a Classic Period level. By that time the ancient Olmec were long gone. The first Olmec horizon, so designated by Coe, was between 1200 and 900 B.C., the period of the San Lorenzo A and B phases. As far as we can tell, this was prior to the first settling of the Maya Lowlands. The second horizon, from 900 to 400 B.C., is pretty much the period known as the Middle Preclassic. La Venta was the dominant Olmec center during this time. It was during this time that the Maya Lowlands were settled, at least in part by peoples who were marginal Olmecs or related to the Olmecs; however, virtually nothing of Olmec art or symbolism seems to have been carried by these Middle Preclassic settlers. The jade bloodletter that Coe mentions, which was found in a Xe cache at Seibal, is one of the few truly Olmec ritual items found in a Maya Lowland Preclassic context. It is, of course, possible that Olmec religious and ritual concepts were a part of the ideological heritage of the first Maya Lowland settlers, even though they brought or made little attendant material paraphernalia to accompany this mental culture. Lowe (1977) suggests this possibility with his hypothesis that early concepts involving the jaguar were carried into the Maya Lowlands from Olmec country at this time. Later, these jaguar concepts were replaced by others in the Olmec–southern Chiapas Zoquean territory but were retained by the Lowland Maya as unifying cultural symbols in their ethnic confrontations with the Zoqueans. By this time the period is that of the Late Preclassic, and the Maya Lowlanders had adopted or evolved (both, probably) an elite class system and were constructing major ceremonial centers. By this time, also, Maya Lowland Late Preclassic cultures were in contact with the Izapan culture of southern Chiapas and its related manifestations in the Guatemalan Highlands at Kaminaljuyu. This Izapan culture was an important and demonstrable link between Olmec and Lowland Maya.

Both Coe (1977) and Quirarte (1977) stress the Izapan linkage between Olmec and Maya, and there can be little doubt but that contacts between Pacific Chiapas and the Guatemalan Highlands, on the one side, and the Maya Lowlands, on the other, were vital in introducing a certain ideological content and form to Classic Maya civilization. This could have taken place even though the bearers of Izapan culture were Zoqueans and the Late Preclassic Lowlanders were Mayans. Modes of religious and political organization can transcend ethnic rivalries, as can the iconographic elements and motifs that may be used to express them. Indeed, these rivalries may even promote borrowing, although, as Lowe argues, the patterns and emphases may be different. In the Izapa–Lowland Maya contacts it is also highly probable that Kaminaljuyu, in the Guatemalan Highlands, was a vital node in the transmittal of ideas. The odds are that Late Preclassic Kaminaljuyu was Mayan rather than Zoquean, and it is significant that an Izapan-style monument at that site (Stela 10) also bears hieroglyphs very similar to those of the slightly later Classic Lowland Maya stelae. Coe has listed iconographic elements and themes shared by Olmec and Maya; and many of these, as Quirate indicates, such as the U-shaped moon symbol, the composite creatures of saurian, serpentine, and feline forms, and the feather-winged deity impersonators, are also present in Izapa art. In Coe's opinion the Olmec had a "proto-writing" and also some elements of Mesoamerican calendrics. Long Count dating and hieroglyphic systems probably developed in Izapan and related Late Preclassic cultures on the western and southern borders of the Maya Lowlands. In these inventions the role of Oaxaca and the Zapotecs is not to be discounted, although the geography of the situation would suggest the Izapan and epi-Olmec cultures of the Gulf Coast played a more direct role in the influencing of the Maya.

As we have seen in the basic lowland data papers, Maya iconographic and architectural elements that are the obvious immediate antecedents to those of the Classic begin to appear in the Late Preclassic ceremonial centers and come into better definition in the Protoclassic. It cannot be denied that the synthesis of these takes place in the lowlands and is peculiarly Maya, just as it cannot be denied that there has been borrowing and influencing from the Late Preclassic and Protoclassic Period cultures lying outside the Maya Lowlands. This Late Preclassic–Protoclassic influence can be definitely identified, in many instances, as we have already noted, as Izapan in style; quite possibly it passed to the lowlands via Kaminaljuyu. It is also probable, following Lowe's (1977) hypothesis, that earlier the Olmec-Maya Middle Preclassic established certain ideological bonds that made for a more ready acceptance of the Late Preclassic Izapan-Olmecoid traits in the Maya Lowlands.

Two other currents of influence affected the course of Maya Lowland development in the Protoclassic. One of these is best registered in ceramic traits—Usulutan wares, imitation positive-painted Usulutan, polychromes, and specialized vessel forms such as the mammiform tetrapodal bowl and the Z-angle bowl—in brief, what is sometimes called "Protocalssic Period pottery" or, now, the Floral Park complex. In the regional data papers we have noted particularly heavy occurrences of these traits in Belize and along the Belize-Peten frontier, on the eastern side of the Maya Lowlands; they occur, also, at Altar de Sacrificios, on the western or southwestern edge of the Lowlands, Their source almost certainly is highland, in Guatemala or Salvador. Usulutan ware, one of the Floral Park–complex traits, dates back to the Kal complex in Salvador; this dating is Middle Preclassic, or substantially earlier than its appearances in the Maya Lowlands. In the Altar de Sacrificios sequence the Floral Park influences make a first and somewhat minor appearance in the Late Preclassic Period but become pronounced in the Protoclassic. Does the appearance of these new ceramic traits in Belize, on the eastern edge of the Peten, and at Altar de Sacrificios signal an invasion or partial population replacement? It is a question that has vexed Maya archaeologists for some time and that, as the papers in this volume indicate, is still with us (see Hammond, 1977b). That the Floral Park pottery, of Salvadoran-Guatemalan Highland inspiration, should occur on the very threshold of the changes that usher in the Classic Period suggests the invasion hypothesis—the arrival of groups with an elite social class organization who subjugated the simpler resident Lowland Maya and, in effect, "lifted" them up to the status of civilization. This is a possibility, but I am inclined to doubt it. Many important sites and regions show little of the Floral Park complex. Tikal and the Central Zone are prime examples. Here we can trace a very steady buildup in cultural elaboration from the Late Preclassic, through the Protoclassic, and into the Early Classic Period with little or no tangible sign of the Floral Park complex. Of course, it could be argued that only certain rather marginal sites were directly affected by the "invaders" and that these marginal establishments, along the Belize-Peten border or at Altar de Sacrificios, in turn influenced more centrally located sites and regions. It is possible that physical anthropological research on skeletal series may some day be able to help us resolve this "invasion or diffusion" question. As yet, however, such research has not been done. Appraising the evidence that is available at present, I am inclined to see the Floral Park ceramic complex as an indication of extraterritorial trade and contact, processes that were increasing as Lowland Maya culture grew more centralized politically and more differentiated socially. In saying this, however, I should call the reader's attention to Ball's (1977) statement that he thinks a Protoclassic Period invasion of a new population group into northern Yucatan is a distinct possibility, so that the question, important as it may be for an understanding of the rise and growth of Lowland Maya civilization, must remain an open one for the time being.

The second current of influence referred to derives from Central Mexico, in particular from Teotihuacan. I use the term "current of influence" because, again, as with the Floral Park–complex case, the processes of this influence are not clearly understood; however, for Teotihuacan I believe that direct contacts, brought by emissaries from that Mexican Highland metropolis to the Maya Lowlands, are highly probable. As Teotihuacan influence upon the Lowland Maya was heaviest in the Early Classic Period, I will refer to these probable processes of contact below. For the Protoclassic Period we know there were some contacts, direct or indirect, between Teotihuacan and the Lowland Maya. A cache of specialized obsidian artifacts from Altun Ha, in Belize, can be cited as hard evidence. Just how important these early Teotihuacan contacts may have been in transforming Lowland Maya Protoclassic culture to the Classic stage is more difficult to determine.

THE EARLY CLASSIC PERIOD (A.D. 250–600)

As indicated, Teotihuacan continued to exert a major influence upon the Maya Lowlands in the Early Classic Period. It is highly likely that this influence was in some way mediated by or involved with the great site of Kaminaljuyu in the central Guatemalan Highlands. Sanders describes two sequent "waves" of Teotihuacan influence at Kaminaljuyu. The first left its imprint in architecture, and Sanders is inclined to relate this to the presence and power of important Teotihuacan nobles or emissaries at Kaminaljuyu. The second wave is documented in ceramics and manufactures and, perhaps, represents the descendants of the Teotihuacan visitors in a more settled or acculturated situation in the Highland Maya cultural context. It is possible that these two waves are also registered in the Tikal record. Some of the earliest Teotihuacan influences there are seen in stela inscriptions and portraiture, dating to the late eighth and early ninth baktun, or very early in the Early Classic Period. These Teotihuacan evidences might very well pertain to the arrival, presence, and intermarriage of Mexican Highland aristocrats. Subsequently, in the range of A.D. 400–500, Teotihuacan influence is fairly common in ceramics. It is this later kind of influence that is found in most other Maya Lowland sites and regions, so that the strongest Teotihuacan ceramic impress in the Tzakol sphere pertains to Tzakol subphase 2 and the early part of 3.

The question referred to in our discussion of the Protoclassic Period—to what degree is Maya Lowland civilization indebted to Teotihuacan for its origins and growth?—is also important for the Early Classic. Was Teotihuacan influence or tutelage, in either the Protoclassic or Early Classic periods, responsible for the centralization of Lowland Maya polity? Again, this is a question that must be left open. While it is true that the strongest "wave" of Teotihuacan influence, insofar as this can be measured in the archaeological record, is in the A.D. 400–550 time band, there are stelae and other indications of a Teotihuacan presence a century or two earlier—early enough to have been significant in the crystallization of Classic Maya culture. After A.D. 540–50, the beginning of the hiatus, Teotihuacan influence disappeared from the Maya Lowlands. Did a break with Teotihuacan precipitate the hiatus or semicollapse, as I have suggested in my chapter? Or did Teotihuacan influence stop because of a locally generated crisis within the Maya Lowlands? Once more we are puzzled by, and seek information about, the Teotihuacan–Lowland Maya relationship.

THE LATE CLASSIC PERIOD (A.D. 600–900)

During most of the Late Classic Period no single external area influenced the Maya Lowlands more than any other. To some extent the lowlands may be said to have flourished in "splendid isolation" for two hundred years. This does not mean that there were no contacts or exchanges with other Mesoamerican subareas. In both raw materials and manufactures there was a vigorous commerce with the Guatemalan Highlands, and there must also have been contacts with and knowledge of Oaxaca, Gulf Coast, and central Mexico. The results of some of these contacts are seen in the Late Classic art of the Maya, particularly along the western edge of the Maya Lowlands and spreading into the Yucatan Peninsula (Proskouriakoff 1951; Sabloff and Willey 1967). Alien, or at least non–Classic Maya, elements appear integrated into Classic iconography. Anything like an invasion seems an unlikely explanation; perhaps we are seeing a reflection of the assimilation of some foreign elite persons into the local Maya aristocracies.

In the last century of the Late Classic, along with the decline of Classic civilization in the Southern Lowlands, there are various clues to foreign presences in some sites. Fine Paste pottery wares, made in Tabasco or the Gulf Coast Lowlands, are a part of the Tepeu 3 (A.D. 800–900) pottery complexes along the Usumacinta and in the Peten. A new figurine style, associated with the Fine Paste wares, depicts a non-Classic Maya individual. At Seibal, on the Pasión River, stela portraits of the ninth century are those of nontypical Maya personages. J. E. S. Thompson (1970) has suggested the Chontal, or Putun, Maya, from the Gulf Coastal region, as being responsible for these alien introductions into the heart of the Maya Lowlands, and most Mayanists agree, at least in general, although some prefer variant interpretations (see R. E. W. Adams 1973b: Sabloff 1973). This Terminal Late Classic impingement on the Southern Maya Lowlands is the theme of the previous seminar on the Maya (Culbert 1973), and several of the papers issuing from that conference evaluate the degree to which this late external influence was responsible for the fall of Classic Maya civilization. As an epilogue to the story, the central Mexican Toltec

invaded northern Yucatan a century or so later, at about A.D. 1000, and
this invasion had a profound effect on Maya civilization in the Northern
Lowlands.

Processes and Models

The chapters by Sanders (1977), Netting (1977), Webster (1977), and
Rathje (1977) are all concerned primarily with processes of culture growth
and change, and these processes and the formulation or selection of models to explicate and systemically relate them will provide the core of the
discussions that follow in this section of the summary; however, as is evident from a reading of the papers in this volume, all seminar participants
were involved with processual interpretations, and I will try to integrate
their views in my comments.

I have arranged these comments under five headings: (1) ecology-
subsistence-demography; (2) warfare; (3) trade; (4) ideology; and (5) what
I have called the "overarching model," or my attempt to interrelate opinion and interpretations into a unified synthesis. Such a breakdown is
designed for clarity and emphasis in presentation and, as the several authors
have made clear, does not indicate a faith in monocausal explanations on
the part of any of my colleagues. On the contrary, all authors have been
at some pains to place their particular models and the processes which
these subsume into broader contexts of systemic interaction.

ECOLOGY-SUBSISTENCE-DEMOGRAPHY

Sanders sees the natural environmental heterogeneity of the Maya
Lowlands as the underlying reason why Maya civilization developed as it
did. This lowland heterogeneity is by no means as marked as that of some
other Mesoamerican subareas, such as the central Mexican Highlands; nevertheless, it is a condition, too often overlooked, that had an important
effect in social and cultural growth. Man's ecological adaptation to the regional diversity of the Maya Lowland natural environment related directly
to subsistence and demographic systems and patterns; and this systemic
complex of ecology-subsistence-demography, in turn, provided a matrix for
the growth of Maya civilization that was, in many of its features, restric-
tive and determinative. Sanders's (1977) evaluation of environmental heterogeneity is based on soil analysis. While he admits that this is not a
total environmental evaluation, he feels that it is, within the Lowland Maya
setting, the crucial factor in appraising agricultural adaptation. The soil
analyses classify soils by types and subtypes and rate these on a fertility
scale, especially with reference to the swidden farming of maize. These

various soil types are plotted on a map of the Peten, following the research of Simmons, Tarano, and Pinto. Unfortunately, comparable data were not available for other portions of the Maya Lowlands.[5] With the data at hand, however, Sanders notes an exceptionally good soil fertility rating for the northeast Peten, or the Central Zone of the Maya Lowlands—the region in which Tikal, Uaxactun, and a large number of other major Maya ceremonial centers are located and in which Classic Maya civilization first emerged. The total acreage of highly favorable soils for this zone exceeds that of any other Peten zone.

According to the Sanders model, which is an adaptation of the Boserup model, this natural environmental advantage of the Central Zone made possible a population buildup which, in turn, resulted in a shortage of agricultural land, which led to competition, and thus to inequities in control of the land, and so on to social ranking and ultimately stratification. Such a sequence also transpired elsewhere in the Maya Lowlands, but it occurred earliest, or got off to an earlier start, in the Central Zone. A review of the archaeological evidence, at least in the Southern Lowlands, supports this contention. Of course, it is a circumstance that was known a priori, and Sanders's hypothesis and model are attempts to explain it. The one other lowland region where there was a contemporaneous developmental precocity (as measured by population concentration and architecture) is the Northern Plains of Yucatan. Here, however, the developmental upcurve seems to have been broken prior to full Classic-type achievements. In the Central Zone, the Tikal data show a continuity, although there is, perhaps, a slackening or lag in population growth in the latter part of the Late Preclassic and Protoclassic periods. At the same time there was, however, a Late Preclassic and Protoclassic development of what is interpreted as centralization and ranking which led into the Early Classic.

Culbert (1977) was the only contributor to challenge Sanders's basic environmental appraisal. He did this by citing the high fertility potential of the Southeastern Zone (the location of Copan, Quirigua) which, he states, did not have a well-developed Late Preclassic occupation. The nature of Southeastern Zone soils are not specified, and, as I have said, this portion of the Maya Lowlands was not included in Sanders's soil map. My own opinion of the fertility of the zone, based on a brief survey of the Copan Valley, would correspond to Culbert's; however, we need more information on the Preclassic there, for its developmental status might be somewhat better than Culbert's rating. Nevertheless, Classic Maya civilization does not appear to have been established in the Southeastern Zone until one or two hundred years later than it was at Tikal and Uaxactun, so Culbert has a point. Why didn't the apparently favorable soil conditions

make the Southeastern Zone the "cradle of Maya civilization"? We cannot give a certain answer to this question, but I suggest that it has something to do with geographical marginality, quite possibly related to ethnic
differences. The Southeastern Zone is on the edge of the Maya Lowlands,
and it may not have been a part of the territory settled by the Middle
Preclassic pioneers who moved into these lowlands from the Gulf Coast,
the Guatemalan Highlands, or both. It is possible that it was not occupied
in Early Preclassic times; and in Middle Preclassic times its population may
not have been Maya, but related, instead, to the peoples of the Ulua Valley to the east. This Ulua Valley, incidentally, is prime agricultural land,
yet it was never the scene of civilization attainments of Maya Classic status. At best, in the Late Classic, it displayed a marginal and reduced variant of Maya Classic culture. Following out this line of argument, I think
it probable that factors of centrality and marginality within the Maya Lowland sphere may have to be taken into account in explaining the beginnings of the Maya florescence. Another geographical factor might have
been locational advantages with reference to sources of outside stimuli.
Perhaps the Central Zone was, in some way, more strategically placed to
assimilate trade and other contacts from Chiapas and the Guatemalan Highlands than was the Southeastern Zone.[6]

On balance, I think the Sanders environmental heterogeneity model
has much to recommend it. Significantly, it is essentially consistent with
the models and hypotheses advanced by Netting (1977), Webster (1977),
Adams (1977), and Ball (1977); and it is not inconsistent with those interpretations which accord diffusion and ideological influences a role in Classic Maya growth.

Netting's model is a historically documented ethnographic one. He
describes the ecological, settlement, and general cultural adjustment of the
Ibo tribe of Nigeria. Living in a tropical forest environment somewhat
similar to the Maya Lowlands, the Ibo practiced a system of "infield-
outfield" cultivation. Household garden plots were maintained for some
crops; others were grown more extensively, at some distance from dwellings and villages, in a swidden-fallow pattern. A variety of crops were
cultivated, including roots, cereals, and trees. Netting suggests convincingly that a change toward increasing sociocultural complexity can be equat-
ed with and causally related to the growth of Ibo populations and their
density. Did the Lowland Maya follow a similar ecological system, and is
the model for a change toward such cultivation intensification applicable?
Netting reviews the arguments that have been made for Maya crop diversification, including root crops and orchards. He also notes the evidence
that has been coming in recently for techniques of intensification, espe-

cially the ridged fields in certain Maya Lowland regions. He concludes that reliance solely on long-fallow milpa cultivation of maize seems most unlikely. He observes that the Maya settlement pattern of ceremonial or politico-religious centers and of continuous dispersed residences is similar to that of the Ibo and that the spacing of households is consistent with infield or kitchen-plot agriculture.

Netting's model has the great value of offering a life situation for comparative analogy with the Lowland Maya. We see an ecological adaptation together with its settlement and sociopolitical systems, and we understand something of their integraton. All of this has particular bearing on Maya Classic Period developments, especially changes between Early and Late Classic. As an adjunct to his Rio Bec regional data paper, Adams offers a model of Maya development. As a part of this diachronic model, he sees a first "florescence," as a climax to population growth, in the Late Preclassic–Protoclassic–Early Classic. A second florescence follows in the Late Classic with, again, population increase and attendant competition and sociopolitical development. This second florescence was made possible by agricultural intensification techniques and crop diversification of the kind Netting is talking about. A related overview model has also been devised by Peter Harrison (1975). Harrison did not participate in the seminar nor contribute his paper to it directly; however, his formulation, which has grown out of field research in southern Quintana Roo, just east of the main Rio Bec sites, is germane to this consideration of Lowland Maya food production and population. Harrison emphasizes "crises" rather than "florescences." It is his opinion that food production remained ahead of population growth from Preclassic times up until A.D. 500, or almost through the Early Classic Period. At that point the Maya began to suffer from food shortages, and this first crisis corresponds, more or less, to the sixth-century stela dedication hiatus. Soon after, though, the situation was improved through agricultural intensification; evidence for this intensification includes not only the ridged fields of the Rio Bec country but the grid patterns in the *bajos* of southern Quintana Roo, which total over 10,000 square kilometers in extent. This *bajo* cultivation is, in effect, a chinampa-type system, similar to that used in the lakes of central Mexico, and its productivity can be very great. It supports Netting's projection of the African Ibo model onto the Maya with even greater force. Harrison's second crisis is the Maya "great collapse" of the ninth century, a crisis again precipitated by population outrunning food production.

I note one omission in both the Adams and Harrison models. This is the indication, in some of the archaeological records at least, that there was an earlier crisis than the one at the end of the Early Classic Period. I have suggested in my Pasión-region data paper that population density began to present serious problems as early as the Late Preclassic, and that the competition arising from this pressure led to serious settlement rearrangements and new political patterns. In keeping with the larger curves of the Adams and Harrison models, the new political institutions of centralization and wider spheres of governance and, perhaps, food-production regulation then allowed for continued growth through most of the Early Classic. Adams (1977), in discussing competition and warfare, alludes to this development, and I think that Ball's Northern Plains Zone data could also be accommodated to this general interpretation. The Protoclassic "decline" in the far north is what I have in mind here; and the somewhat delayed Early Classic revitalization in that region may have been abetted by the spread of southern political patterns in that direction.

The Adams and Harrison models do not explain everything about Classic Maya growth (and decline)—and here I should pause to note that neither author claims that they do and that Adams, quite pointedly, discusses many other factors in his developmental model—but they nevertheless establish for us, along with the contributions of Sanders and Netting, some basic ecological-subsistence-demographic guidelines and restraints and suggest some causal relationships among these systems. By way of caution, Netting (1977) has added (in post-conference commentary): "Intensification [of agriculture] is not an alternative to conflict over resources or to trade—rather I tend to see all three as adaptive responses to the conditions of changing man-land ratios following the pioneering occupation of a new area." And this cautionary comment is a fitting prelude to our next model.

WARFARE

All of the above mentioned authors have alluded to warfare and competition in their models, but Webster (1977) focuses his attention on this institution. He disclaims it as a prime mover in civilizational growth, and, if I understand him correctly, he means by this that it is secondary to the subsistence-demographic complex. It is an "option," given certain demographic conditions. But, given the "circumscribed" nature of the Maya Lowlands, to use Carneiro's term and concept, it seems a very likely option. The archaeological evidence seems to indicate that it was an option often chosen.

Using computations derived from productive capacities of Maya Lowland land areas under long-fallow maize cultivation, plus available archaeological settlement information, Webster concludes that by the Late Preclassic Period there would have been land shortages and no room for further geographical expansion into unfilled territories. New agricultural techniques would have been one possible response to this difficulty, but apparently they were not the solution turned to at this time. Instead, there was expansion at the expense of other populations. The earliest expansion, radiated out of the Central Zone (at least in the south; the Northern Plains may have been another zone of early agressive expansion), where population pressures were greatest. Such expansion was achieved by warfare, and this development fed back into the sociopolitical organization to begin the formation of incipient states. This feedback effect worked both for the original agressors and for those who set up defenses against them. As Webster points out, warfare was not a viable, long-term solution to the problems of food production and overpopulation, but there was a long-term adaptive significance in the rise of sociopolitical complexity. Among some of the more immediate results were, ironically, the depopulation of territories between aggressively expanding and competing political units. Such depopulation would have taken some land out of cultivation, and this process may be reflected in the Protoclassic Period "stabilization" or "decline" that has been noted for some regions. Another result was that the Maya Lowlands did not become "Amazonianized"—that is, they did not end up in a patchwork of more or less equally strong, endlessly competing polities. Some regions had the decided edge. This, I think, was true of the Central Zone and of Tikal, in the Early Classic Period. Later, in the Late Classic, the region was more "Balkanized," splitting into a series of powerful ceremonial centers each with some forty to sixty thousand adherents.

Webster examines the functions of a ceremonial-center elite. He prefers the term "organizational center," rightly arguing that this broader designation more appropriately refers to the broad range of militaristic, governmental, managerial, and ritual activities that must have gone on in these places. He sees the role of the warrior as highly important among those managerial roles acquired by Maya elites, being especially essential in the processes by which a ranked society was transformed into a primitive state. By Late Classic times, warfare had become the firmly established institution of militarism. High-ranked individuals were the focal points for tribal or "national" identification, and their contacts were widened and their prestige increased by their sacred or symbolic identifications with deities. They and their immediate kinsmen were in charge of goods redistribution and trade, adjudicated disputes, and served in other managerial ways. The managerial tasks would include duties related to construction and maintenance of agricultural intensification projects, such as the ridged fields or the *bajo* grids. Webster's discussion of an organizational center, its personnel, and their functions recalls Netting's analysis of Ibo society.

In this brief summary I have not mentioned the archaeological evidences of warfare. I would agree with Webster, however, that "negative evidence is meaningless," especially in the Maya Lowland situation. There are, nevertheless, evidences, both direct and indirect. Scenes of violence, particularly with reference to the humiliation of captives, are common in Maya art, both in sculpture and painting. These, of course, are largely confined to the Late Classic Period. For the Protoclassic, the period at which Webster postulates the first serious warfare, there is the walled organizational center of Becan in the Rio Bec region. There is also a defensework on the outskirts of Tikal, apparently delimiting its immediate sustaining area, that is believed to be of Early Classic date. The more indirect evidence has been mentioned, including changes in territorial settlement-pattern organization. For these, other causes are possible, but the reader is referred back to Webster's detailed arguments, which I find persuasive.

TRADE

Rathje's (1977) model emphasizes long-distance trade as a vital process in Lowland Maya culture growth. He makes no monocausal claims, however, observing that trade is one factor among many, and his model incorporates population growth, food resources, and competition among groups. Indeed, the postulates underlying Rathje's model are much the same as those of the other models. Briefly, in the competition for desirable resources, whether they be arable lands or trade items, larger and more complexly structured social units enjoy an advantage over smaller, less internally segregated units. In the ensuing competition more successful units may incorporate less successful ones, and this incorporation is a process that enlarges the success potential of the successful. While there are limits of growth in both size and internal structuring, the limiting conditions that operate in this regard are more relevant to the fall of a civilization than to its rise.

With regard to the Lowland Maya, Rathje argues, as did other seminar members, that the Central Zone, or the "core area," was the first to cross the developmental threshold to complex society. It did so at the beginning of the Late Preclassic Period. The core area, with its large population, provided the earliest great market potential for large-scale resource procurement, and this procurement system, which was, in effect, long-distance trade, had an important feedback into the sociopolitical development of the core area. Thus, while Rathje does not insist that trade was the prime or only essential mover in the processes of civilization, he sees it, since it involves both exchange and goods production, as an important option—just as warfare is an option—once societies have reached a certain size and density of population. More specifically, if core area development precedes "buffer zone" development—as it appears to do in the Early Classic Period—then organized trade was a very significant process in Maya culture growth, especially in the Late Classic.

Two obvious and very important trade contacts for the Lowland Maya were those of the Salvadoran-Guatemalan Highland Floral Park system and of the Teotihuacan system. The Central Zone "core area," as represented by Tikal and Uaxactun, appears to have been on the outer periphery of Floral Park contacts; but Rathje believes, and I think he is correct, that the Floral Park system had created a market demand in the populous Central Zone for craft items and esoteric knowledge. Shortly after this, Tikal seems to have established itself as the major lowland center for the Teotihuacan, or Teotihuacan-Kaminaljuyu, trading system, a system that was to have a far wider influence on the Maya Lowlands than that of Floral Park. But both of these trading relationships were undoubtedly significant in the growth of Lowland Maya civilization.

IDEOLOGY

No one offered a formal model to explicate the role of ideology in the growth of Maya civilization, but it is difficult to look at the monuments and remains of this civilization without believing that this role must have been an important one. As we examine the record for evidences of population growth, subsistence resources, warfare, and trade, there is a tendency to relegate ideology to an epiphenomenal position, to reject it as a significant causal force or a "prime mover," but, leaving aside for the moment the question of initial or prime cause, there are indications that idea systems played an important part throughout the course of Maya development. Lowe (1977) touches on this subject on Early-to-Middle Preclassic Period levels with his concept of ethnic rivalry and ethnic identification. We have seen that the early Peten "peasants" were in contact with more complex societies that had developed religious iconographies. Beginning with the Late Preclassic an externally influenced but locally reformulated Maya Lowland iconography appears, and this, along with a "literature' in hieroglyphics and a highly involved and evolved calendrical system, flowered during the Classic Periods. This total ideology, rich in symbolism and ritual, must have been crucial in maintaining the entire Maya cultural system as it was directed from its ceremonial or organizational centers. It was also instrumental in bringing the system to decline and termination. All of the contributors to this volume have offered some suggestions as to how this could have come about. Netting, (1977) with his Ibo model, has provided comparative insights from the use of ideolo-

gy, ritual, and symbol by an African elite. He has also reinforced his original remarks with an additional statement (postconference commentary):
"Though warfare was probably a significant factor in the growth of
Maya civilization, the response of channeling work effort and restraining
conflict through the manipulation of sacred symbols and religiously sanctioned social hierarchies still seems to me *the particularly creative strand
in this society*. Ideology, rather than being an epiphenomenon, would
certainly play the central role in such peaceful management of conflict.
The question of the degree to which voluntaristic mechanisms such as the
acceptance of ritual hegemony and the peaceful facilitation of inter and
intraregional trade were more important than military coercion is still
unclear" (italics added).

A major difficulty in all of this is that we do not know—and probably will never know—the nature of the ideas involved. To be sure, ideas,
rituals, and symbols were used to validate the position of a ruler, to prop-
agate his image, or to win allegiance to his cause, but we do not know just
how they accomplished these functions or in what way some ideas were
more efficacious, more successfully adaptive, than others. To go back to
Lowe's example, one wonders what was the nature of "jaguarism" as
opposed to the cult of the "wind god"? The symbols in themselves tell us
little. Undoubtedly they stand for some idea that was, for a time, tran-
scendent, compelling. Are the differences here sheer happenstance? While
the symbols may have been, I do not think that the ideas behind them
were historical accidents. Rather, they must represent significant differences in world views, ideas that had adaptive value. If we knew what these
ideas were, we could, perhaps, see how they interrelated with other systems, how they exerted feedback influences, negatively or positively, on
the whole cultural system of the ancient Maya.

Considering this difficulty, is it worthwhile even to attempt to struggle
with this dimension of civilization, given the archaeological methods and
means available for the study of the Maya past? Should we not, instead, simply
assume that ideological content is a constant, that it is not very important,
and that we should turn our efforts to the more tangible systems that we can
cope with more readily? Some archaeologists appear to think so; I do not. I
realize, however, that it is incumbent upon me, and upon those who think
similarly, to demonstrate how ideology may be "reconstructed" from the
archaeological record. So far, it is fair to say, we have not done so.

THE OVERARCHING MODEL

Lest anyone be misled by this somewhat arrogant subhead, let me
hasten to say that I make no attempt to replace, supplant, or transcend
the models we have been summarizing and discussing. By "overarching" I

mean, instead, a sort of canopy that will cover the models and processes which all of us in the seminar have put forward. It is an attempt, too, to arrive at some sort of consensus, although, as I said at the outset of this summary, I cannot hope to be unbiased in the way I have reviewed and tried to synthesize opinion.

Our model for the rise of Maya civilization is defined much as we defined the model for the collapse of that civilization. "A precise statement of the characteristics and dynamics of a system," the model here proposed is a "qualitative and general one which will be compatible with the known facts and which will suggest leads for more complicated models and, particularly, for models which will be ultimately quantified" (Willey and Shimkin 1973:489). It is viewed as a systemically related set of hypotheses and a research design as much as it is an explanation. Diachronically and developmentally, the model for the rise of Maya civilization precedes and overlaps with that described for the collapse. Again, in briefest form, and in general terms, our model postulates population growth in a previously unoccupied area as the preparatory base for the advance to the civilizational threshold. This threshold was attained through the development of an elite culture by means of intergroup competition and rivalry. The success of the system was stimulated by extraareal cultural contacts through trade and other mechanisms, and this success produced further growth of population and competition between groups. Beyond this point, as we have described in our model for the collapse, internal stresses and external pressures resulted in an increasing rigidity in the system, leading to system failure and collapse. The model as devised here owes much to the form and organization of other model presentations in this volume, especially to the one offered by Rathje.

The model can be broken down by period as follows:

1. At the beginning of the Middle Preclassic Period (ca. 1000 B.C.) populations from the Mexican Gulf Coastal Lowlands, from the Guatemalan-Salvadoran Highlands, or from both of these Mesoamerican subareas entered the Maya Lowlands. This was the first occupation of the territory by a farming people, and it seems quite probable that such peoples had been marginal to more advanced cultures. The immigrants were of Zoquean or Mayan speech or of both. During the Middle Preclassic Period (1000–300 B.C.) these peoples increased in total numbers. Groups multiplied by fissioning. Communities, however, remained small and, probably, essentially autonomous. Trade and perhaps other contacts were maintained with parent populations outside the Maya Lowlands; social and political organization, however, was simple. Culture was generally sim-

ilar throughout, although regional differences are evident in such things as ceramic manufactures.

2. In the Late Preclassic Period (300–50 B.C.) population continued to increase, although population growth rates exhibit some region-to-region differences. The Central Zone of the northeastern Peten reached a Preclassic population peak early in the Late Preclassic Period, as did the Northern Plains Zone of Yucatan. Elsewhere, however, increase continued through the Late Preclassic and, in places, even into the Protoclassic Period. These differentials in population growth rates are attributed primarily to differing environmental potentials for long-term-fallow swidden cultivation of maize. Population pressures led to competition and warfare for agricultural lands. Such intergroup and interregional competition promoted political organization and centralization and the rise of an elite leadership. The sociopolitical focal points were ceremonial or organizational centers. While such centers may have been present in earlier times it was not until the Late Preclassic Period, with its demographic and competitive pressures, that they became marked by a permanent public architecture. It was also during this period that emergent Maya Lowland civilization was assimilating ideologies from more advanced cultures such as the Izapan. The symbolic value of these centers as the seats of elite leadership was commemorated in monumental art. The functions of the centers, and of the resident elite, included military leadership, political governance, economic management, the organization of trade, the direction of craft goods manufactories, and the maintenance and propagation of religious and intellectual authority.

3. In many Maya lowland regions the Protoclassic Period (50 B.C.–A.D. 250) was a time of crisis and political reorganization. Some regions and centers achieved dominance over others. Many former Late Preclassic centers were abandoned as a result of the intensification of competition and increasing incorporation of weaker polities into stronger ones. New ideas and ideologies (and, perhaps, peoples) were introduced into the Maya Lowlands from the outside. The maintenance of foreign trade relations became very important and also highly competitive. Architecture, art, and burials in the ceremonial centers all indicate the further consolidation of an elite-class leadership and a prevalent elite ideology.

4. The Early Classic (A.D. 250–600) saw the crystallization of Maya Lowland civilization in the Central Zone of the northeastern Peten. Architectural, ceramic, sculptural, and other arts flowered. Hieroglyphic inscriptions pertaining to calendrical and, probably, dynastic matters made their appearance. During this period the stela cult spread from the Central Zone to other parts of the Maya Lowlands. Tikal appears as the largest and

probably the most important of the ceremonial centers of the south. Its ideological ascendancy was achieved early and long maintained. The prestige of Tikal was undoubtedly enhanced by its relationships with Teotihuacan and Kaminaljuyu, which involved trade in both utility and luxury goods, dynastic ties, and religious and ideological bonds. It is possible that there was a centralized state, ruled from Tikal, which dominated the Southern Lowlands at this time; certainly the Early Classic Period was an era of stability following one of flux and change.

5. In the last half of the sixth century A.D. the era of Early Classic stability was disrupted. This is the time of the stela hiatus, and the archaeological evidence suggests a breakdown of centralized authority. The most probable causes for this are new increases in population, which placed a strain on Lowland Maya agricultural productivity; the difficulties inherent in sustaining a large-scale political state directed from Tikal and the Central Zone; and, possibly, a cessation of trading and other contacts with the Teotihuacan system. It is, however, possible that the cessation of Teotihuacan contacts came about from the local lowland breakdown rather then the reverse.

6. A new stability was established during the first two centuries (A.D. 600–800) of the Late Classic Period. Stela dedication was resumed; architecture and the arts enjoyed new vigor; old ceremonial centers were revived; new ones sprang up. While Tikal and the other cities of the Central Zone flourished, they were rivaled in size and magnificence by the great centers of the Usumacinta in the west, by Copan in the east, and by Rio Bec, Chenes, and other northern sites. The impression is one of several competing regional polities sharing common cultural bonds but with no single center or region achieving political dominance for any length of time. Increased agricultural production through intensification techniques (ridged fields, *bajo* cultivation, terracing) and greater crop diversification (garden-plot cultivation, root crops, arboriculture) relieved population pressures for a time, making possible this Late Classic florescence. Warfare continued, however, and became institutionalized into militarism.

7. In the last century of the Late Classic Period (A.D. 800–900) a cultural decline set in throughout the south and, to a degree, in the Rio Bec region. It is believed that this was brought about by the population pressures that had been mounting during the two previous prosperous centuries, by food shortages, and by sharpened militaristic competition between regional centers. This was further exacerbated by external pressures in the west from the Mexicanized Putun Maya. There were probably shifts of southern populations northward in this century, and the far northern

regions of the Puuc and Northern Plains flourished somewhat later, until A.D. 1000, the date of the Mexican Toltec entry into the Northern Lowlands.

This model, as cast here, is obviously a very "historical" one. With this historicity stripped away, it places demographic pressure—in its systemic complex with ecology and subsistence productivity—in the position of prime mover or prime cause of the rise of Lowland Maya civilization. This is satisfactory up to a point. Numbers of people and their physical well-being are basic to the maintenance of any society, particularly a large and complex one. But these are self-evident truths—essentially biological conditions. Without these forces and factors, to be sure, nothing would have happened. And yet the forms that they assumed are not, to my mind, really comprehensible from so distant, so superhuman a perspective. Beyond population pressure, a drive for survival through competition represents a second level of causality. Complex social, political, and economic organizations are adaptive mechanisms for survival, but they take many forms. It is at this point that ideas and ideologies enter the picture. When we begin to consider these, and to attempt to achieve understanding on a more human scale, we come to "historical explanation"—something that is derided by some as no explanation at all. Maybe so, but in the study of human events I cannot rid myself of the feeling that this is where the real interest lies.

Notes

1. This summary was prepared in the months following the seminar conference. It was then circulated to all of the other participants during the summer of 1975. Most of them replied with some comments and suggestions for revisions. I have incorporated many of these into a revised text or in the form of footnotes. Others I rejected, either because I felt that they did not affect substantially what I had to say, or because I was in disagreement with them. Again, I emphasize that while what I have written here obviously could not have been done without the work of my colleagues, the interpretive summary is my own.

2. Important revisions to Culbert's (1973a) zonation have been made by Hammond, and the reader is referred to the map, Fig. 1.1, in Adams, ed. 1977 for the details on these. Briefly, Hammond has reduced the area of the Belize Zone considerably by extending the Pasión Zone to the Caribbean Sea and the Central Zone eastward to include much of the western half of Belize (formerly Bristish Honduras). The newly defined Belize Zone is thus essentially the eastern coastal strip and the immediate interior lands of the northern two-thirds of Belize. However, it must be kept in mind that Hammond's discussions in his present paper refer to sites throughout the political domain of present-day Belize.

3. In a postconference commentary M. D. Coe calls special attention to Maya pictorial ceramics as a major cultural trait of the Maya Classic. In his words: "The

iconography, ideology, and textual material given on these ceramics, with the strong development of an underworld cult dedicated to the immortality of the elite, is unique to the Maya and entirely confined to the Classic. It is as characteristic of them as the stela cult and, like that cult, disappears with increasing Mexican influence and the Classic collapse. The 'funerary ceramics cult' has no known Olmec roots. It is *sui generis*, appearing at the beginning of the Early Classic, but reaching its full elaboration in Tepeu 2."

4. M. D. Coe, in another postconference commentary, is now inclined to feel that Zoquean was the original Olmec language, but he adds, "I would still bet, however, that La Venta was Maya-speaking—that is, on the Nacaste time level" (ca. 900-750 B.C., or post-San Lorenzo B).

5. There are good soil data for Belize (British Honduras) (see Wright et al. 1959) although these were not used by Sanders, perhaps because they could not be satisfactorily translated into the fertility scale that he was using for the other regions.

6. With reference to Culbert's criticisms and my comments on these and on his statements, Sanders (postconference commentary) writes:

> I believe both of you are still confusing origins with process. The process I describe of a population colonizing an area, increasing in number, and ultimately saturating the area is a universal and, environmental conditions permitting, should always lead to a large, dense population, agricultural intensification, and social differentiation. What will vary is the date of inception of colonization, and my model does not attempt to explain that—yours of spatial periphery is as good as any.
>
> Assuming sufficient time for the entire Maya Lowlands to achieve population saturation, a second characteristic that will vary is population density—and, I believe, derivatively, locations of centers of political power. This is because the region is not uniform in its capacity to sustain a process of agricultural intensification. The fact that the Copan-Quirigua area is a productive one hence is not an argument contrary to my views— in fact, it supports them since two major Maya centers were located there. Whether the region is as productive as the core is unknown since we have no data one way or the other, but I think that the difference in agricultural potential (in Maya terms) will relate to differences in population density and number of centers (the core clearly has a greater overall population density and more major centers than the Copan area).

3 Pre-Hispanic Maya Agriculture:
A Contemporary Summation

In this attempt to summarize the papers of the present volume the word *contemporary*, in the above title is most appropriate. Knowledge and ideas about ancient Maya agriculture have changed rapidly and drastically in the last few years, and continue to change, so that any review must be dated as a kind of progress report. In addition to the rather surprising new data that have come in from field archaeology, geographers, geologists, palynologists, and botanists are helping the archaeologists revise their thinking about the ways in which the Maya managed their agricultural subsistence in the tropical forest lowlands.

As of this writing, however, and based upon a reading of the assembled papers, it is fair to say that three general conclusions, or at least working premises, have emerged. The first of these is simply that the old idea that the Lowland Maya lived by a swidden (slash-and-burn, milpa) system of maize cultivation alone is fallacious. Peter D. Harrison (1978a)

and B. L. Turner (1978a) make this point very explicit, and all of the other authors allude to it in one way or another. Other farming techniques of
greater productive potential must have been used by the Maya instead of,
or in addition to, the swidden method; and, indeed, there is direct archaeological evidence that this was so.

A second conclusion relates to the first; in fact, in point of investigative procedure, it might be said to precede it. This is that Lowland Maya
populations were much larger than was heretofore believed and, even more
important, that they lived in larger and denser concentrations than long-
fallow swidden cultivation would have been able to support. In other words,
the settlement information that has come in over the past dozen years is
inconsistent with the swidden hypothesis.

A third conclusion, or working premise, is that there was considerable and significant variability in agricultural practices as these were followed throughout the Maya lowlands. No single model can pertain to the
entire area throughout its agricultural history. Differences in agriculture,
obviously, were related to differences in environmental regions and niches,
but it also seems probable that they were influenced by cultural choices.

The possible means of agricultural intensification—that is, the increase
of agricultural production—were, it appears, numerous and varied. Frederick Wiseman (1978) and Turner (1978b) list and discuss these. They
include: short-fallow milpas or swidden, made possible by various techniques of crop rotation, companion planting or inter-cropping, hand weed-
ing, mulching, and fertilizers; multiple annual cropping (as referred to by
Culbert, Magers, and Spencer [1978]); "infield" or kitchen-garden farming; the production of diverse crops, including root crops and tree crops
(especially the ramon nut); terracing; and raised-field farming, either along
active streams or near still water. Of these, only terracing and raised fields
leave appreciable direct archaeological traces; the others must be inferred
from various lines of archaeological, palynological, or ethnohistoric-
ethnographic evidences.

Although not addressing himself to terracing alone in his present
papers, Turner (1974a, 1978b) has done the most work on the subject.
Currently, terraces are known from the ridge lands of the Rio Bec country
in southern Campeche and from somewhat similar terrain in western Belize.
They usually involve a degree of stone construction and appear to have
been built both as silt traps and to protect slopes from erosion. In the Rio
Bec region, where they have been well-studied, it is obvious that they represent a considerable expenditure of effort. They are to be distinguished
from low stone walls which divide the nearby Rio Bec flat country into
what look like demarcated field plots. The presence of these latter, though,

suggests crowding and careful apportionment of agricultural lands, lending credence to the idea that the nearby hillslopes were exploited for terrace farming as a result of community needs. In view of this, and in the light of known heavy Late Classic settlement of the Rio Bec region, it seems probable that agricultural terracing here was largely a Late Classic phenomenon; however, it should be cautioned that this is still speculative. Elsewhere in the Maya lowlands agricultural terraces have been reported from Belize, where they are still said to be extensive on many of the hillslopes; however, these have not been plotted or described in any great detail.

Of all of the techniques of intensification, those involving raised fields and related forms of water control have recently attracted the most attention. Alfred Siemens and Dennis Puleston (1972) first called attention to such fields along the banks of the sluggish Rio Candelaria, on the western edge of the Maya lowlands. Since then these artificially raised garden areas—similar in principle to the Central Mexican lake chinampas—have been reported from along the Rio Hondo in northern Belize. On a more extensive scale claims have been made for their presence in old swamp or *bajo* areas in various places in the Maya Lowlands. Peter Harrison (1978b) estimates that several hundred square kilometers of such fields can be seen from the air in southern Quintana Roo, in the vicinity of the major site of Tzibanche. The evidence in question is seen as series of rectangular grid lines on the air photographs, such lines being assumed to be the separating canals between such raised cultivation plots. Similar phenomena have been reported elsewhere, including the vicinity of the great site of Mirador in the northern Peten and, perhaps, even more significantly in the Bajo de Santa Fe on the edge of Tikal. Are these *bajo* grid lines the remnants of raised-field-cultivation rectangles? Puleston (1978) is highly dubious and thinks it more likely that they are gilgai, natural formations caused by the deep cracking of mud flats. Clearly, on-the-ground exploration is indicated, for if raised-field agriculture was as extensive as the preliminary air photo reports suggest, Maya lowland subsistence must be reviewed in a whole new way. Even in the tropical forests, with problems of insect pests, the food production yield from the chinampa-like plots would have been enormously high. Is Tikal's great size to be attributed to such a subsistence resource?

The matter of the raised fields along some Maya lowland rivers and their putative presence in the *bajos* relates to what Siemens (1978) has had to say here about the karstic landscape which underlies most of this country. He observes that in this landscape there are two kinds of rivers: those that show little fluctuation in water level and those that have an appreciable rise and fall. It is the first type, with its "reservoir effects," that produces conditions favorable for raised fields, as in the instances of the Candelaria and Hondo rivers. Siemens also has something to say about riverine-*bajo* relationships. He points out that the destruction of the *bajos*, or their evolution from lakes to swamps, may not have been the result of silting, as in the original hypothesis, but the result of the downcutting of streams into the karstic beds and the draining, through this stream action, of the Peten lake waters into the Caribbean. This discussion takes us back to a reconsideration of the Cooke-Ricketson hypothesis about *bajo*-lake relationships, which was advanced forty years ago (Ricketson and Ricketson 1937). In a paper published elsewhere, Peter Harrison (1977) has resurrected this hypothesis, in spite of the Cowgill-Hutchinson (1963b) strictures against it—strictures with which Puleston (1978) is still in agreement. In Harrison's (1977) paper, which has the catchy title, "The Rise of the *Bajos* and the Fall of the Maya," Tikal, and many other sites, are seen as dependent upon raised-field cultivation in what were then shallow lakes filled with raised fields or chinampas. With the silting of these *bajos*, as hypothesized by Cooke and Ricketson, such agriculture became less and less profitable, eventually bringing about the crisis that led to the great collapse in the ninth century. This leads me to a question: If the Siemens explanation of the "fall" of the *bajos*, that is, their drainage by the downcutting of streams, in turn related to the karstic uplift, is the correct explanation, would this reconcile the Cowgill-Hutchinson findings with the idea that the *bajos* had once been lakes? Or, to ask the question in another way, is it the presumed silting of the lakes that Cowgill and Hutchinson object to, or is it the presumption that they had been lakes at all?

I should like to make a partial digression at this point to say that there are things in the lowland Maya archaeological past that seem very consonant with a former lacustrine or still-water aquatic environment. These are seen in the imagery and symbolism of much of Maya Classic art. Hammond refers to some of this in his present paper, and both Harrison (1977) and Puleston (1977) develop this theme at some length. Puleston cites the water-lily motif, among many others, and especially the association of the water lily with the maize plant, and of both with the deity Itzamma, whom he is inclined to interpret as a crocodile, the supreme animal of a tropical forest environment. These themes in Maya art do suggest an ambience of shallow lakes, swamps, and, perhaps, canals and lagoons that were made for raised-field agriculture.

Such Maya lowland water management or hydraulic engineering could also have served other purposes. Some years ago J. E. S. Thompson (1974) made the suggestion that the canals of the raised-field systems of the Rio

Candelaria would have made ideal breeding and live-storage places for fish. This would have been an important subsistence supplement, as several of the writers in the present volume have commented. *Aguadas* and reservoirs near major lowland sites were obviously used for potable water storage. At Edzna, in Campeche, Ray Matheny (1978) has mapped and explored reservoirs, canals, and moats that served such purposes and also those of transportation and defense; according to Matheny, similar "waterworks" are known from Uxmal. Matheny points out that the "water complex" at Edzna, which had all of these functions and, perhaps, those of plant cultivation as well, was built into the original city planning and may have had ritual and aesthetic significances as well as these more practical ones. These findings and observations, while taking us away from our central theme of agriculture, do indicate, nevertheless, a depth of tradition on the part of the Maya in the manipulation of subsurface and surface water in which raised field farming would not have been a surprising part.

Another form of agricultural intensification that is referred to in several of the accompanying articles is that of "kitchen-garden" supplementation. Root crops were undoubtedly important in this regard, as Bennet Bronson (1966) indicated a decade ago. Orchard produce must also have been a part of this "infield" farming. It has also been argued by Dennis Puleston (1973) that orchards were considerably more than a mere supplement to maize cultivation; Puleston, again, makes this case very forcefully in the present volume (1978). Maize cultivation, he states, was never important in the old "core area" of the Northeast Peten. Here, instead, the ramon nut was the principal crop from the beginning. Puleston feels that of all the farming techniques available to the Maya—including not only raised fields, terracing, and other intensification measures, but the swidden systems as well—harvesting from the ramon or breadnut tree was the most productive per man- or woman-hour of work, and he cites modern experiments to back his theory up. In this sense ramon-nut harvesting would have been the "line of the least resistance" for the Northeast Peten environmental niche—easier than simple swidden farming and infinitely more productive. Puleston points to the absence of terracing anywhere in the Northeast Peten or Tikal vicinity, a situation making the ramon-nut dependence of the large population concentrations here still more likely. One possible joker in the equation is the recently discovered possibility that the Bajo de Santa Fe, near Tikal, may have been filled with raised fields; as already noted, however, Puleston thinks that this possibility is very slight. Using the presence of chultunes as the archaeological clue to ramon-nut harvesting and storage, Puleston believes ramon-nut dependence was the principal economic mode in the Tikal region as early as the

Late Preclassic and, perhaps, even before. The role of the ramon nut as the major staple for the Northeast Peten has been questioned by W. T. Sanders (1973:341), who, while conceding its value as a supplement, is hesitant to see it as the primary crop. He notes that nut-bearing trees are "notoriously variable in their yields from year to year" and that dependence upon them would therefore be risky. He also observes that the ramon nut, today, is considered rather a second-class food and a poor substitute for maize, and he thinks it likely that such attitudes prevailed in the past. The question remains open, especially in view of the possibility of raised field or chinampa cultivation in the nearby *bajos*. At this point another question occurs to me: If the lowland Maya of the Northeast Peten had such a reliable and easily obtainable food resource as Puleston believes the ramon nut to have been, why did they "collapse"? If Puleston is correct, this "collapse" must have had little or nothing to do with subsistence problems.

The second general conclusion or working premise, that lowland Maya population concentrations were too great for the carrying capacity of swidden maize farming alone, is touched upon by several of the contributors. Don Rice's house-mound counting in the Yaxha-Sacnab is a systematic example (Rice, 1978). He comes up with population estimates that climb from Middle Preclassic beginnings of 25 persons per square kilometer to 210 persons per square kilometer for the Late Classic (A.D. 600–800) climax. These Classic-period estimates, which are conservatively drawn, are well in excess of the carrying capacity of a one-to-four-year swidden fallow system. In Rice's opinion, agricultural intensification measures were taken to sustain this population growth. Another case would be that described by D. T. Vlcek and his coauthors (1978). This concerns the Northern Lowland site of Chunchucmil. At the end of the Late Classic the large architectural center of Chunchucmil covered a square kilometer. Surrounding this were another 6 square kilometers of closely packed structures, with individual small mound groupings separated by boundary walls. Farther out is another 13 square kilometers of less densely packed small structures. An estimate of at least 12,000 persons is given for the inner zone of 6 square kilometers, a population far too large for the surrounding terrain to have supported by swidden farming. In the Chunchucmil example intensive cultivation in the immediate environs seems to be precluded by the nature of the setting and soils, and it is the archaeologists' opinion that foodstuffs must have been imported from elsewhere to sustain the population.

These two examples lead us into a consideration of the third conclusion or working premise, that of variability or variation in agricultural techniques, in time, in space, and by cultural choice. Wiseman (1978) has stated (p. 113) that "no single agricultural technique, either actual or hypothetical, will satisfy the requirements of the demographic, ecological, and palynological data." Viewing the Maya lowlands as a whole throughout its agricultural history it is difficult to dispute this statement. But beyond this point there is considerable difference of opinion as to the course of this variability, especially in the chronological dimension. What might be called the conventional view of Maya lowland agricultural development is that expounded by Sanders (1973) and generally accepted in the papers from the Santa Fe symposium on *The Classic Maya Collapse* (Culbert, ed., 1973). It is again set out in the second Santa Fe symposium on *The Origins of Maya Civilization* (Adams, ed., 1977; see especially the article by Sanders). According to this view, agricultural production steadily increased from Preclassic through Classic times, stimulated by population increases. Whether we follow a Boserup (1965) model or merely hold that there was an interlocking relationship, as yet not fully understood, between population growth and food supply, the assumption is that long-fallow swidden, with maize as the principal crop, was the initial agricultural system in the Maya lowlands. Then, as population grew, it became necessary to augment food production, and the intensification techniques came into existence, being variously and regionally deployed according to environmental conditions. In the Yaxha-Sacnab region Rice's (1978) settlement studies do seem to support this kind of a sequence. In the Middle Preclassic what he designates as the "tall upland vegetation zone" probably would have supported all of the regional population. This is an environmental zone well-suited to maize swidden cultivation, and the interpretation is further supported by the fact that most of the settlement of the period is confined to this zone. Settlement was dispersed through the zone, although even at this early time there are indications of an organizational center. Afterward, toward the end of the Late Preclassic period, with an increase in population, the first subsistence stress is suggested by the first occupation of the "moist slope" environmental zone. While there are no definite evidences of intensification techniques, either through terracing or clues to crop diversification, Rice speculates that maize was probably now supplemented with root crops and that an attempt may have been made to reduce the maize fallow cycle. By Classic times increased populations (as indicated by increased settlement) probably demanded ramon-nut harvesting in addition to the former crops. In Rice's opinion, the situation by this time allowed the population few options. They were exploiting all the agricultural possibilities of their environment, and that environment, in its upland and slope zones, was suffering from erosion as the result of agricultural activities. It is pertinent to note that in this instance there are no indications of raised fields having been constructed in the swampy areas of the lake shores. Whether or not this was a cultural choice or one in some way dictated by particular soil or drainage conditions is uncertain. As I say, Rice's work seems to support the conventional developmental picture although the data for intensification are somewhat equivocal, and the techniques or means used did not include either terracing or raised fields.

In the Rio Bec region, as already noted, Turner (1979) is of the opinion, although he advances it cautiously, that the very definite agricultural terracing found there is probably Late Classic. This implies that earlier farming methods were probably of the swidden type, and this is supportive of the conventional sequence. By and large, though, as of the present writing, the early-swidden-to-later-intensification methods sequence is largely a "logical" reconstruction based on the belief that in a tropical forest environment swidden farming is the simplest and easiest. That is, until population pressure begins to mount, food requirements are best satisfied, with the least expenditure of labor, by annual cutting and burning of the vegetation, planting, and harvesting, followed by a fallow cycle. We have seen that Puleston (1978) has challenged this belief with his ramon-nut theory, at least with reference to Tikal and the Northeast Peten. The conventional developmental model has also been challenged elsewhere and for other reasons.

Norman Hammond (1978) poses such a challenge in his paper by suggesting that a raised field or chinampa technology was brought to the Maya lowlands by the first agricultural settlers, in Middle Preclassic or even Early Preclassic times. Presumably, such immigrants would have moved into the region from Lower Central and South America. By farming this way, little Preclassic communities would have been able to maintain a relatively restricted area of residence and to expend less time and energy going to and from distant fields than would have been demanded under a swidden system. Eventually, with population buildup, more extensive farming would have been necessary. Some of this could have been carried out by enlarging raised fields and increasing their number, but when the population moved into terrain unsuited for this technology, swidden cultivation would have been practiced. Thus the conventional developmental sequence is turned around in this hypothesis. Hammond, as well as Puleston, cites early radiocarbon dates for raised fields in northern Belize, dates that carry the technique back to the second millennium B.C., so that there is at least some—although not very much—chronological evidence to the effect that raised-field intensive farming has a great antiquity in the Maya lowlands.

Other kinds of variability have been discussed in several of the papers. Culbert (1978) and his colleagues, using modern ethnographic data, refer to the possibility that multiple-cropping, or the growing of two or even three harvests per year, may have been practiced in the past, as it is today, in the Poptun region. Were certain regions of favorable soils and rainfall more advantageous than others? Does this apply to the Northeastern Peten, the region that appears to have been the original "core" of the development of Classic Maya civilization? Or were the advantages here to be found in the availability of the ramon tree, following Puleston's suggestion?

Most interesting in regard to this matter of variability is the factor of cultural choice. It is, of course, difficult to explain. Vlcek, Garza, and Kurjack (1978) cannot explain the location of the organizational center of Chunchucmil on the basis of agricultural potential of the immediately surrounding land. Given the settlement evidences there, food to support the resident population must have been brought in from elsewhere, although probably not from a very great distance. In the Chunchucmil case it is a possibility that salt resources and the exploitation of and trade in this commodity were responsible for the city's location. And yet there are no easy answers. In the concluding section of his impressive paper in which he compares Tikal, Angkor, Prambanan, and Anuradhapura, sites of tropical lowland settings in various parts of the world, Bennet Bronson (1978) states that neither favorable agricultural soils, nonagricultural resources, nor sitings for trade-route advantages will explain the location of such cities. He also makes the point that in comparing the Maya and southeast Asian civilizations he feels that the greatest weakness of the former, in the sense of developmental potential, was a logistic one, the ability to move goods, especially bulk goods like foodstuffs, over long distances. Such a weakness or limitation might give more force to the argument that urban development for the Maya would have been more closely tied to, even if not completely confined by, food resource regions. But, as we have seen, there do seem to be exceptions.

Let me close with some personal conclusions. These are over and above the three general conclusions with which I began this summary and with which, I think, most of us are probably in agreement. In addition, it would now be my first speculation that all of the cultivation techniques which have been reviewed here were probably known from the time of the earliest farming settlements in the Maya lowlands. The one possible exception would be terracing, but even of this I am not sure, for silt-trapping, on a small scale, is probably a very old technique. Second, as to the sequence of techniques, I am not sure, nor do I think that anyone else can be at our present state of knowledge. Working the sequence out by securing the right kinds of evidence is going to be very difficult and something that will be with us for a long time. It would be my guess that this developmental sequence will vary from place to place. What is clear is that population size, although perhaps fluctuating downward temporarily during the Protoclassic and, again, at the time of the Classic Hiatus, moved generally upward until the Terminal Late Classic, accompanied by a deployment of agricultural techniques to take advantage of as many possibilities as could be discerned in the light of existing technology. Third, I am in agreement with those who have emphasized the importance of cultural choice or decision making. It is a factor to be reckoned with along with the natural environmental and technological ones. Ideas are a part of any ecological equation dealing with humans. Fourth and finally, let me say that after reading all of these assembled papers I am still convinced—whatever the farming technologies employed by the Lowland Maya—that certain kinds of urban development, indeed those aspects most closely associated in our minds with the formal definition of the word *urban*, the close-spaced residential districts of Teotihuacan or Tenochtitlan, or the ancient Middle East, were not feasible in this tropical forest environment on a preindustrial level. Perhaps this is overstated, and I might be willing to modify it to say certain *degrees* (rather than *kinds*) of urban development, or to change "on a preindustrial level" to "without more effective logistical support"; but I think my meaning is essentially clear. This is not to deny a number of important urban or civilized functions to Tikal; but its 50,000 persons dispersed over 165 square kilometers (Haviland 1969, 1970) makes for not only a quantitatively but a qualitatively different entity than does Teotihuacan's 100,000 to 200,000 residents packed within a zone of 21 square kilometers (Millon 1973). The lowland Maya "ceremonial center," or "vacant city," concept has undoubtedly been overpolarized and overdone, for there can be no denying the many urban qualities of such great centers as Tikal; we are dealing, however, with a continuum in sizes, population densities, and functions. This continuum is, I think, to be viewed in the course of lowland Maya developmental prehistory, and it also has value for comparative projections of the Maya vis-à-vis other Mesoamerican developments. In my opinion, the Classic Maya failure of the ninth century A.D. might be described as a failure to proceed far enough on the ceremonial-center-to-true-city continuum. This is a digression from the strict theme of Lowland Maya agriculture, but the connections and implications are there for any Mesoamericanist to see.

4 Maya Lowland Settlement Patterns:
   A Summary Review

Some Introductory Observations

This is the third of three School of American Research Advanced Seminar volumes on the archaeology of the lowland Maya. In the first two, *The Classic Maya Collapse* (Culbert,ed., 1973) and *The Origins of Maya Civilization* (Adams 1977, ed.), it became clear that many of our assumptions and interpretations revolved around the data of settlement. Land use, population numbers and densities, and sociopolitical and economic structures were mediated through settlement pattern information. This information has been accumulating rapidly over the past three decades. While it is still too scant to bear the weight of the reconstructions that have sometimes been placed upon it, it is obvious that the whole subject is a vital one. This present volume, and the seminar that generated it, are dedicated to a current review of the whole broad and complex subject.

Virtually all the participants in the three Maya seminars have been engaged in field and other archaeological research activity in recent years, and this period has seen notable revisions in our ideas about the Maya past. These revisions—which are still ongoing—are amply documented in these three seminar volumes. There has been considerable overlap of participants in the seminars; three of us—Adams, Sanders and myself—have attended all three. This has provided, although in no planned or explicit way, some continuity to the proceedings. At the same time, sufficient new blood has been fed into these endeavors so that there has been no conformity to any one set of opinions. While this has no doubt precluded the sharpness of focus in the final results that a more single-minded perspective would have offered, it has had the advantage of faithfully reflecting the "state of the art" in contemporary Maya archaeology.

As chairman or moderator of all three of the seminars, I would like to make the following observations, admittedly subjective but nonetheless of some pertinence. I found this one, on settlement patterns, the most difficult in which to develop the discussions. Similarly, it is the most difficult to summarize. The "Classic collapse" and "Maya origins" themes, while standing in danger of overgeneralization and diffuseness, have the advantage of centralizing problems that make for coherence. "Lowland Maya settlement patterns" has no centralizing problem. The data of settlement lead in any direction in the investigation of the Maya past. As a subfield, "settlement" is still an unformalized branch of Maya archaeology. Investigative strategies have been diverse and often quite specialized. Aims have been unstated, implicit, and sometimes not clearly formulated. They have focused variously on population estimates, subsistence adaptations, micropattern details of architectural layouts, or macrosettlement problems of site sizes and hierarchies. All of these are desirable goals, but in pursuing them archaeologists have given precedence to certain sets of data at the expense of others, have followed different field and recording procedures, and have used different vocabularies. These barriers to easy communication became apparent early on in the seminar meetings. The seminar discussions covered much of the same ground as that the papers in this volume. We dealt with general definitions of the subject, with micropatterns and macropatterns of settlement, with the biological interface and subsistence, with demography and population estimates, and with processual models that might help explain the growth and development of Maya settlements. In our treatments of the primary data of settlement, which followed a region-by-region presentation, we were at pains *not* to emphasize terminology or concepts, for we felt we would become bogged down in a methodological arguments. This fear proved to be well founded, for at the close of the descriptive presentations, when we did turn to these matters, we came to the toughest and slowest part of the sessions. While we did not resolve all of our differences, some progress was made and this is reflected in Ashmore's (1981) revised paper on methodological and theoretical considerations.

This summary overview attempts to take account of both the seminar discussions and the accompanying papers. It is best described as my understanding of what my colleagues have said and written, conditioned by my own knowledge and thoughts about the subject.[1] This does not necessarily mean that these colleagues will agree with it, in whole or in part.[2] It may sometimes be difficult to disentangle my opinions from those I am summarizing. As an antidote I can only recommend recourse back to the specific papers. I am, however, the sole author of the summary and take responsibility for it.

The summary is organized into two main parts. The first, "The Data: Forms and Functions," treats the basic information about lowland Maya settlement.[3] Our concern, however, is not only with the formal and static aspects of settlement—the patterns—but with tht functional and behavioral aspects—the settlement systems. Much of this is what Ashmore (1981) has referred to as "placemaking behavior" (constructions for living and the establishment of central places); but evidences of "integrative behavior" (e.g., roadways, walls, and the like) and "resource management behavior" (farming terraces, raised fields, reservoirs, and so forth) are also taken into account.

The second part of the summary deals with "Processual Models" as these have been advanced in three papers to explain the nature of lowland Maya settlement.

This order follows the general organization of the volume but is not a detailed recapitulation of it. For instance, the paper on this historical background of Maya settlement studies and the one on geographical and chronological frameworks are succinct statements in themselves and need no further summarization. Ashmore's method and theory paper is referred to at various places, and the one on volumetric analyses of centers by the Turners and Adams (1981) is discussed under "macropattern" reviews of the data.

Ecological and agricultural themes form a major part of any consideration of lowland Maya settlement. They are dealt with, in varying degrees, in most of the data papers, and they came up constantly in seminar discussions. I have not attempted to treat them under a separate head in this summary, but I do refer to them in numerous contexts of both data descriptions and interpretation. It should be noted, too, that the recent publication *Pre-Hispanic Maya Agriculture* (Harrison and Turner, eds., 1978) has made current findings and interpretations on Maya agriculture and ecology readily available to interested readers and is a book that could well serve as a companion volume to the present one.

The matter of population estimates is referred to in many of the papers and was discussed at some length during the seminar. Numbers of persons per house building or household unit were debated. The average figure of five persons per dwelling unit was considered by some as being too high for the single house or minimal residential unit, and it was suggested that four may be a more representative number. On the other hand, from five to seven seemed generally acceptable for the patio group, or extended household unit. There was also some discussion of floor space and of roofed floor space as potential quantitative criteria for population estimate. Finally, there was a general consensus that house mound counting and agricultural potentials (persons per cultivated hectare) should be used in concert. Beyond this the subject was not developed. I do not want to leave the impression that the conferees were satisfied with or complacent about the methods that have been devised to seek answers to this very important problem, but as a more extensive summarization could add little more, I have not devoted separate space to it in the summary.

The Data: Forms and Functions

RESIDENTIAL UNITS

Ashmore's (1981) *minimal residential unit* is, as the term implies, a basic building block of lowland Maya settlement. It refers to the single, small, structurally isolated building. It may be defined archaeologically by a small earth or rock platform or, sometimes, by nonmounded floor space distinguished only by postholes or plaster-gravel or packed earth surfaces. The house superstructures varied from those with completely perishable wood and thatch walls and roof to those with stone walls and stone masonry vaulted roofs. Living debris (sherds, metates, manos, and other utility implements) are usually found in or near such Maya minimal residential units, and, in some regions, subsurface chultun storage pits are in proximity. Burials were frequently placed under the house floors.

Such minimal residential units are assumed to have served as the residences of a single nuclear or biological family. Residence, of course, comprises a set of activities, but such a primary building is thought to have provided sleeping quarters for the family. Ashmore suggests that these buildings had a minimum of 20 square meters of roofed space.

This minimal constructional unit is found everywhere in the Maya lowlands. At Tikal, the typical Classic minimal residential unit often has interior benches and porch features, a type common in the south. In the north, at Dzibilchaltun, the Classic period house often has two rooms, and the structure tends to be wider in proportion to its length than the southern ones. Kurjack and Garza (1981) describe a Dzibilchaltun house as having a low (20 cm) platform, 8.80 by 7.50 meters. The house structure on the platform was 5.50 by 3.65 meters. Dzibilchaltun houses tended to be apsidal, rather than rectangular, in floor plan.

The chronological range of the minimal residential unit is from Preclassic through Postclassic. Data are relatively few for those earlier or later than the Classic period; it is likely, however, that the common Preclassic house was the characteristic small, oblong, single-room type of the Classic. This type also persisted into the Postclassic; but in addition, there is a Late Postclassic house form of Northern Yucatan known as the "tandem" plan, in reference to its enclosed interior or back room and its semiopen front room.

The single minimal-residential-unit house will sometimes occur in isolation. Don Rice (Rice and Puleston, 1981) observes that they form 15 percent of the total small structures at Tikal and Yaxha. It is my impression that the percentage would not be this great for the Copan Valley. Rice's figure of 50 percent for Uaxactun seems much too high. There has been some difficulty, however, in archaeological recognition of single versus group structures. Thus at Barton Ramie, in the Belize Valley (Willey et al. 1965), surface indications suggest that most of the 262 mounds surveyed were individual structures; excavation, however, showed that some (BR-1) were, but others (BR-123) were group arrangements. The problem takes on importance in residential unit counting and population estimates derived therefrom: the individual house will not accommodate as many people as the group residential unit. Some of our seminar debate about population estimates had its roots in misunderstandings about the definition of the settlement unit to be counted.

The *group residential unit* is next on the scale of rising complexity in Maya dwelling sites. It is, in effect, composed of two or more minimal residential units. From two to six buildings would be an average range for such groups. The functional implications of the group residential unit are those of an extended family household. Two, three, or even more biological families may be represented. However, not all of the buildings of the group may be actual dormitory residences; storehouses, kitchens, and other service buildings could be represented. Sometimes one building of the group may be larger and better constructed than the others, suggesting a "head residence," or, perhaps, even a temple shrine.

There are two subtypes of the group residential unit. The *informal group* is that of "several structures at a single siting with no central ambient space or patio." The *patio group* plan is "several structures with a central ambient space or patio." (See Ashmore, 1981 above.)

The patio group is the most common residence type of the Maya lowlands. It has been designated variously as a "single-plaza residential unit," a "plazuela residence," or a "courtyard residence." They are known from all regions. The "walled farmstead" to which Adams refers in the Rio Bec region, while somehwhat different in form and features, is a comparable unit of residence.

The third unit on the ascending residential scale is what Ashmore has called the *cluster*. While it is true, as Sanders (1981) writes, that disagreements began to appear at this point in the seminar discussions, most of us would agree upon the reality of this aggregate, which is composed of several group residential units. Bullard referred to such "clusters" in his northeast Peten survey, noting that they were composed of 5 to 12 residential groups (Bullard 1960). In seminar discussions Haviland referred to such clusterings at Tikal as "multiplaza" (more than one patio group) residential units, stating that each consisted of 8 or 9 groups clustered together and separated by empty spaces from other such clusters. Quite often clusters have one patio group, or one structure within such a group, that is larger or more imposing than the other constructions of the cluster. This, again, suggests a "head residence," "administrative building," or, perhaps, a shrine.

Implicit in the above would be the function of the cluster as some kind of a kin gathering of residences. A variant of this would be the interpretation that Leventhal (1981) has offered for cluster units on the far peripheries of Copan, where the main household of an important or wealthy person is surrounded by those of servants, retainers, and, possibly, poor relations. Another possibility would be that clusters are aggregates of craft production households where artisans of the same kind (pottters, obsidian workers, and so on) lived in proximity. This clustering, or course, could also have followed kin lines. Such an interpretation, if it could be supported with evidence, would be important, as it would imply a degree of urban-type specialization. To date, there are some indications that individual household units—patio groups—were so specialized in crafts, but there is no firm evidence that crafts are correlated with clusters (see Becker 1973).

To recapitulate, three levels of residential settlement have been described: (1) *minimal residential units;* (2) *group units* (both *informal* and *patio*); and (3) the *cluster* (composed of several group units). These three levels or types, despite some regional variations in form, are found throughout the Maya lowlands; and it is highly likely that they persisted through-out the lowland culture sequence. Minimal and group units are most clearly defined, and there are good reasons to believe that their primary func-tions were to house, respectively, nuclear families and extended families. Clusters are less definitively patterned, but they can be discerned in some densely settled contexts as well as in more thinly settled areas. Their func-tional correlates are more ambiguous than those of the smaller units, but kin significance is possible.

CENTERS

Centers are aggregates and nucleated arrangements of pyramids, big platforms, palaces, and other buildings that were the foci of Maya politi-cal and religious life—"special purpose buildings," in Ashmore's termi-nology. In effect, they are what "old-fashioned" Maya archaeology was all about. Because their functions were probably multiple—and certainly not fully understood by archaeologists—the seminar group preferred the simple designation "center" to the other and more frequently used term, "ceremonial center." "Political," "civic," "organizational" (see Web-ster 1977) are other adjectival possibilities; but "center" alone seemed sim-plest and most noncommittal.

While centers, in one sense, do stand in contrast to residential units, they are by no means unrelated archaeological phenomena. In our descrip-tions of patio groups and clusters, we have mentioned "head residences," possible "administrative buildings," and "shrine" features as being incor-porated in residential units and as suggesting "leadership" or "special pur-pose" functions in small kin units. As such, these buildings would fore-shadow those representative of higher levels of authority in the centers.

Residential units are also found in and around centers. Some of these are of ordinary, modest size; but others are of size and elaborateness to be considered as "palaces," and their attached shrines are big enough to be designated as "temples" or "temple pyramids."

Sanders (1981) argues that many of the temple-palace complexes of such a center as Tikal were the residences and shrines of great lineage lords. It was here that stelae were set up commemorating their power and from here that they ran the affairs of their kinsmen, their servants, and their outlying estates. Eventually, they were buried in lavishly furnished tombs within these structures. Structure 7F-1, the "dower house" of Haviland's (1981) interpretation, was such an architectural complex. To Haviland's way of thinking, this was not a "minor center," even though it was found at a distance of some two kilometers from Tikal's main center. Its functions were not administrative but residential. Here were housed the members of an aristocratic family that had been evicted from central power at Tikal; through a combination of hieroglyphic information and burial data Haviland tells their story of political ups and downs. Although I understand the direction of his argument, I would see the "manorial" role of this complex as "organizational" or "administrative" in the broader sense. Even if removed from central power for a time, the members of the 7F-1 lineage still must have exercised some degree of leadership and controlled a certain amount of wealth to have maintained their aristocratic status. There were probably other nobles in the Tikal polity with much the same sort of status.

As Sanders admits, a number of features of Tikal indicate an overreaching political structure for that center, a structure that appears to have transcended, at times at least, the various lineage heads. Indeed, hieroglyphic research has determined this (Coggins 1979). The Early Classic ruler "Curl-Nose," with his Central Mexican affiliations, seems to have establised such a hegemony; and elements of iconography and ball-court ritual games imply centralized religious beliefs and direction. After the decline of this dynasty the idea of political and religious centralization may have waned for a time (the Maya "hiatus," see Willey 1974) but then it was revived in Late Classic times (see C. Jones 1977). This Tikal "history," from archaeology, leads us away from strictly settlement-pattern concerns; but I mention it here in trying to put the political nature and functions of Maya lowland centers into perspective. Centers were the bases of lineage heads, but the form of government must have varied; and, as Sanders suggests, foreign stimuli probably played a part in these developments and fluctuations.

Some centers were fortified, so we know that their functions were sometimes defensive and military. They were also manufacturing and craft loci, but how organized such activities were, the degrees to which such pursuits were full- or part-time, and the percentage of the population engaged in them are still highly debatable issues. There is similar disagreement about the importance of exchange or trade in the centers; but we will return to these questions further along.

There is a considerable range in Maya center size, from relatively small single-plaza or single-architectural-complex units, covering no more than fifty square meters of ground, to mammoth agglomerations such as Tikal, with major architectural features disposed over several square kilometers. Usually, although not always, architectural adornment, monumental art, and hieroglyphic inscriptions—all features of

Maya elite society—have a positive correlation with center size, linking elaboration with greatness and massiveness. It seems very likely that this range in center size and elegance signified levels of importance in ancient Maya society.

Maya centers vary in architectural styles, and this stylistic variation establishes one of the main sets of criteria for the regional or zonal divisions of the Maya lowlands. While style in building form and ornamentation was not a primary concern of the settlement pattern seminar, there are also regional differences in center layouts, and these are more germane to settlement study. Centers of the southern zones—the Greater Peten, Belize, and the Southeast—tend to follow compact plaza arrangements. Structures are close together, and plazas are often contingent and interconnected. Acropolises, great mass platforms, frequently composed of successive building levels, are typical. In his descriptions of centers in Belize, Hammond (1981) observes that many of them have a dual unit plan, of two separate constructional masses; and he makes the suggestion that the functions of the two units may have been different, the one being elite residential and administrative, the other ritual and ceremonial. Centers in the Rio Bec and northern zones are usually more spread out than those of the south. This is especially true of Late Classic plans. Integrative plazas and acropoli are often lacking. A notable Rio Bec exception to this is Becan, a compactly arranged hilltop group surrounded by a defense wall. Here, however, it is likely that the siting and basic plan were Preclassic and Early Classic. The more characteristic open or dispersed center arrangement for the Rio Bec region in the Late Classic is seen at the Rio Bec site proper and others in that part of southern Campeche. In southern Quintana Roo many centers are of the open, dispersed plan. These tend to be Late Classic, while Early Classic and Middle Classic arrangement is more like that of the compact centers of the Peten. In northern Yucatan, center arrangements tend to be open and of "unplanned" appearance.

The construction of centers and their "special purpose" buildings goes back to the Preclassic. Those of the Middle Preclassic (and possibly even the Early Preclassic) were small, with platforms of modest size, and little has been left by way of superstructural architecture. The first big platform and pyramid centers date to the Late Preclassic. Most of the centers to which we have referred were either built in the Classic period or received their final architectural enlargement at this time. Rebuilding of centers was a characteristic of the lowland Maya. Center construction continued, in those lowland regions still occupied by the Maya, throughout the Postclassic period.

MICROPATTERN PERSPECTIVES

How do centers and the mass of residential units relate to each other in their spatial organization? We can consider this from two perspectives, that of the micropattern and that of the macropattern.

The seminar essayed no formal definitions of these two concepts, although they were employed throughout the discussions and are implicit in all of the papers. There is, however, a set of definitions formulated by K. C. Chang (1968) some years ago that offers useful points of reference. According to Chang (1968:7):

> The cultural and social structure of a settlement we call its "microstructure." The larger cultural and social systems, on the other hand, composed as they are of individual settlements, become "macrostructures." The microstructure is the model for an archaeological community reconstructed on the evidence from an archaeological settlement, whereas the macrostructure is the model for the larger sphere of social/cultural activities (beyond those relevant simply to the community) in which members of the community participate, as well as the sphere of cultural and social influences the community imparts to the outside world during a certain time span.

By "microstructure" and "macrostructure" Chang meant social systems rather than settlement patterns, but the association is clear. Settlement patterns reflect settlement systems and the "microarticulation" and "macroarticulation" of social units.

How do we apply Chang's definitions to the lowland Maya data? What are the limits of the "within," the "community" (microstructure or micropattern) with relation to the "beyond," the larger social order (macrostructure or macropattern) in Maya settlement? Is a cluster arrangement of a dozen or so patio group residences the microsettlement, the self-contained, "within" community? Or do they belong to the same community as several other such clusters all situated within a kilometer radius of a small center? Or are several such cluster-cum-center entities within a five-kilometer radius of a larger center the microstructure, the micropattern? Obviously, there can be no ready answer. We would have to know more about the nature of community activities, the degrees of self-containment on the various settlement levels, to attempt an answer; it is to elucidate these activities and functions that we are studying Maya settlement patterns. But it is necessary to make a beginning in sorting out the data; and to this end, and for this discussion, I am going to set arbitrary limits of a five-to-six-kilometer radius around a major center as a working frame of reference for micropattern or single community analysis. This arbitrary figure is one taken from the few lowland settlement studies available in which centers and their peripheries have been examined.

Tikal, in the Central Zone, is the largest Maya center in the southern lowlands. It is also, from the standpoints of both center and peripheral investigations, one of the best known. Its site core, as this can be defined by plaza, temples, palaces, and other "special purpose" buildings, covers an area of at least four square kilometers or perhaps more, depending on just how the "big architectural" heart of the site is defined. Within the core there are a good many residential units. This would include the palaces and also small patio group and informal group units that must have served as living quarters. Presumably, most or many of the core residents were of elite status, as the quality of their homes would indicate. If we enlarge this core by drawing a six-kilometer radius around Tikal, as Haviland did in his discussions at the seminar, we embrace an area of about 120 square kilometers in which residential quarters have a density that has been translated into a 600 persons per square kilometer estimate. This can be rendered into a total site figure of 72,000 persons, an appreciable concentration even if we cut this down somewhat to adjust for the possibilities of noncontemporaneous occupation of some of the dwelling units.

Within the Tikal six-kilometer radius there are, in addition to the main architectural nucleus, other "special purpose" architectural nuclei of palaces and temples. Haviland and Puleston referred to these, according to size and elaboration, as secondary and tertiary centers, apparently using the terms and concepts in an administrative or subadministrative sense. We have noted the exception, however, which Haviland has made with reference to one of these (probably a tertiary-sized architectural unit), the complex 7F-1, which excavation led him to interpret as the elite residence of a noble (and intermittently royal) family. As I have said, I do not see the distinction here as being as important as does Haviland (1981). If we conceive of Classic Maya social structure as feudal, as suggested by Adams and Smith (1981) and by Sanders (1981), such an elite household must have had functions of economic control and possibly religious leadership for a segment of Tikal society.

There are implications of a hierarchical or feudal structuring in other micropatterns where spatial factors in settlement seem to emphasize it. The Copan Valley is about 12 by 4 kilometers in extent. The main architectural center, near the middle, is confined to something less than a square kilometer in the valley bottom. As one moves out from this big architectural nucleus, there are quite densely settled zones in the valley bottom immediately to the east. Even here, however, there are some residential clusters that include special purpose buildings, such as the relatively high mound in unit CV-43 (Willey, Leventhal, and Fash 1978), with its hieroglyphic throne or bench, which could well have served as a politico-religious "centralizing" element for an immediate cluster of other, and smaller, patio groups. Farther away, in the lower hillslope sectors of the valley, Leventhal (1981) calls attention to residential clusters dominated by central patio groups that incorporate large high mounds that would appear to be special purpose constructions. In these suburbs, such clusterings, with their central constructions, are separated, one from another, by open or thinly settled spaces of 100 meters or more. On the simplest interpretive level, this settlement scene looks like a stage in process of urbanization, with available outlying living space gradually being filled up by expanding populations.

Because of heavy alluviation, the settlement situation around Quirigua is more difficult to appraise than that in the Copan Valley, but Leventhal's summary indicates a similar pattern. The main site nucleus, like that at Copan, is relatively small, but north and east of this are scattered clusterings of patio groups, informal group arrangements, and larger quadrangles, and even a small center with a monument.

Hammond's (1981) description of Nohmul, in northern Belize, is also similar. There is a suburban density of patio groups around the main center, and nearby there is at least one architectural complex of minor center proportions.

In the Rio Bec region most settlement work has been done in the vicinity of Becan. We have mentioned that many residential units here have been referred to as "walled farmsteads" and that these are situated among the extensive hillslope agricultural terraces of the region. Adams (1981) quotes figures of 134 (B. L. Turner 1974) and 162 (P. Thomas 1974) such residential units per square kilometer. Most of these Rio Bec houses are thought to have been built and occupied in the Late Classic, but, even allowing for reductions for noncontemporaneous occupancy, the figure is still impressive. If one multiplies the house count by five persons per unit, the results can compare favorably with the population estimates for Tikal's six-kilometer radius area. In other words, there was an urban-type micropattern around Becan in Late Classic times. Places such as Xpuhil and Chicanna, in their close proximity to the Becan center (about five kilometers), suggest a parallel to Tikal secondary centers; and smaller "*plazuela*" units (see Adams and Smith, 1981), constructions larger than "farmstead" groups but smaller than the secondary centers, may occupy a tertiary position.

According to Harrison (1981), settlement density in parts of southern Quintana Roo must have been as great as that around Becan. For instance, there are stretches of terrain 40 to 50 kilometers in length in which there is no gap between structures greater than 100 meters. Presumably, most of this continuity is maintained by small or residential structures, but there are also many centers of varying sizes. The largest of these is Tzibanche whose architectural core is one square kilometer, and this is surrounded by a zone of dense settlement covering 45 square kilometers.

In the Northern Plains of Yucatan the ruins of Dzibilchaltun are so extensive that it is more than ordinarily difficult to draw a distinction between what should be considered micropattern and macropattern observations. Kurjack (Kurjack and Garza, 1981) has estimated that there was a density of settlement of 2,000 persons per square kilometer within a twenty-square-kilometer area at the heart of the city. Beyond this, settlement is thinner but continues substantially for a much greater distance. In the seminar discussions Sanders was loath to accept such an estimate, offering the alternative explanation that such density of house foundations resulted from some noncontemporaneity of occupation. In his paper, however, he does seem to accept the highly urban nature of Yucatecan settlement, though he remains unconvinced of their urban functions of economic heterogeneity.

Kurjack and Garza (1981) describe the overall pattern at Dzibilchaltun as consisting of numerous concentric zonings, with each of these concentric patterns focusing in upon its own architectural nucleus of temple-palace or "special purpose" buildings. Such nuclei may be confined to a single hectare of ground or cover several hectares. Sometimes these concentric clusterings would be separated from each other by thinly settled or open space; in other instances they appear to have grown together as more and more residences were constructed. The nuclei themselves may be as much as a kilometer apart although sometimes they are closer. Often paved causeways connect the nuclei. These causeways are obvious evidence of planned and sanctioned interaction between these multisettlements within the larger settlement. This diffuseness of the arrangement of big architectural complexes at Dzibilchaltun is reminiscent of the separation of temple-palace components of centers in the Rio Bec and southern Quintana Roo regions. Dzibilchaltun is not the only place in the Northern Plains where it occurs or where the separate components are linked by causeways. Kurjack and Garza cite other examples, inlcuding the public buildings at Labna.

Another aspect of Northern Plains settlement is the use of fortifications circumscribing sites or core portions of sites. Kurjack and Garza observe that seven sites in the Northern Plains, all of Late Classic date, have such a feature. In all of these cases the fortification wall appears to have been superimposed on existing community plans.

By Late Postclassic times sites were built, *de novo*, as planned fortified centers. Mayapan, in the Northern Plains, is the prime example. Freidel notes that within its three-by-two kilometer area it has nine separate special-purpose architectural nuclei; but these are all subsidiary to a main, big plaza and *castillo* pyramid, dedicated to the cult of Kukulcan and representative of the cultural tradition of the elite foreigners who had begun to dominate Yucatecan politics with the Early Postclassic founding of Chichen Itza. Mayapan undoubtedly drew together the strands of administration for a large territory. Before this, in Classic times, polities had been attempting to adapt to a highly competitive environment by constructing fortifications as secondary, or "afterthought," developments; by the period of Late Postclassic Mayapan this had become an accepted way of life.

What can we draw together by way of summarizing generalizations about lowland Maya settlement patterns as these are seen in micropattern perspective?

First, intracommunity ties and organization were obviously strong. The "special purpose" buildings in the centers could have been constructed only through directed community effort in a nonegalitarian society.

Second, the centers were foci of population concentrations. These population densities varied, according to center size and, probably, by region; nevertheless, the data from the largest of the Maya centers—in the Peten, the Rio Bec, the Northern Plains, and probably elsewhere—indicate densities of over 500 persons per square kilometer during the Late Classic period.

Third, within these micropatterns of center and periphery there are usually evidences of minor centers, in addition to the main one, that are also marked by "special purpose" architecture. These minor or lesser centers vary in size, and there are some indications that they might be graded in a hierarchical ranking. The function of these minor or lesser centers remains speculative; however, the hypothesis that they might have been the residential complexes of the heads of important lineages, outranked only by the center's high ruler, is supported by Haviland's excavation of one of them at Tikal. The degree to which power was held by a high nobility in a feudal-type social structure, or was centralized under a transcendant community-wide (or even wider?) authority, remains one of the fascinating problems of lowland Maya settlement study and archaeology.

Fourth, and finally, the several unifying elements of Maya culture—hieroglyphics, calendrics, and trade in exotic items—indicate that its many communities (microstructures) were linked to other communities in macrostructural formations; and this takes us into a consideration of macro-patterns in Maya settlement.

MACROPATTERN PERSPECTIVES

A most basic datum for a consideration of the larger arrangements of lowland Maya settlement would be an accurate knowledge of overall pre-Columbian population distribution. As Sanders (1981) has pointed out, we do not have this and must make do with very limited information. Most of this pertains to the larger Maya centers. "House mound" and small center surveys are still few in number; the best we can do is to follow the logic that total settlement density probably corresponds to major center distributions. There is a heavy clustering of these in the Central Zone of the northeast Peten and adjacent Belize. Much of the terrain here is well drained and includes some of the best agricultural soils of the Maya lowlands; this natural environmental factor may account for the density of settlement (Sanders 1977). Other concentrations of major centers are to be found in the Campeche, Central Yucatecan, and Northern Plains zones. Elsewhere there are fewer concentrations, although there are some impressive centers in the Usumacinta, Pasion, and Motagua drainages.

This is essentially a Classic distributional picture, especially a Late Classic one. For Preclassic times we just do not know. All parts of the lowlands seem to have been occupied at this early time, but we can say very little about population densities. All evidence would indicate that Early and middle Preclassic populations were relatively small and scattered. There was a notable population increase in the Late Preclassic, and this corre-lates with the building of the first large centers. The Protoclassic and Early Classic periods saw a leveling off in population. There also may have been times of stress and disruption. In some places previously active cen-ters of the late Preclassic period were abandoned; in other regions, how-ever, such centers continued and expanded. The first two centuries of the Late Classic, from A.D. 600 to 800, were a time of renewed lowland-wide population growth and of widespread construction activity. Decline set in during the Terminal Classic (A.D. 800–1000). This was experienced first and most severely in the south, slightly later in the Campeche and Central Yucatecan zones, and latest of all in the far north. Early Postclassic occu-pation is little known except for the big Toltec-influenced center in the north, at Chichen Itza. In the Late Postclassic the Northern Plains was still the place of greatest activity. Elsewhere, along the Quintana Roo coast and around the Peten lakes, there were minor population enclaves.

In the previous section, on micropattern perspectives, we focused atten-tion on big centers and their immediately surrounding communities. One of the largest of these, Tikal, had a circumferential settlement of a six-kilometer radius in which population density was estimated at 600 persons per square kilometer. Other comparable major center concentrations were noted for other lowland regions. To what extent can the densities of these major center populations be extrapolated to the Maya lowlands at large? Was there a virtual sea of continuous residential settlement over all reasonably habitable land in the entire lowlands, with this sea dotted by the many "islands," large and small, of the architectural nuclei of the centers? The degree to which this image might approach the truth of the situation will probably not be fully known until infrared and other aerial photographic techniques and surveys have been developed further than they are at present; nevertheless, I think it unlikely that the heavy, Tikal-type settlement densities can be extended to the entire arable lowlands. The data available tend to support this negative opinion. The figures that Rice (Rice and Puleston 1981) cites for his Yaxha-Sacnab survey in the northeastern Peten are substantially lower than the 600 persons per square kilometer figure of the Tikal community. In the intersite area between Tikal and Uaxactun (these centers are eighteen kilometers apart) Puleston's (1974) survey showed intermediate settlement, while still present, to be less than that in the immediate community environs of either center. Elsewhere, as in southern Quintana Roo, while there are long stretches where no residential mound is out of sight of the next, Harrison (1981) also states that there are other stretches where there is no settlement.

The reasons for irregularity in macrosettlement are not always obvious. In some instances, these may have been environmental, with soils inadequate or not well suited for farming, or poorly drained terrain unsuitable for dwellings. In other instances the reasons may have been cultural. To anticipate Sanders's (1981) explanatory model for Maya settlement, he would see the nucleation around major centers as being correlated with "infield" farming or gardening, the raising of root crops or the tending of ramon-nut trees in these interhouse plots. Farther out would be more thinly populated stretches where swidden farmers cultivated maize in "out-fields" or maintained raised-field cultivation sections in nearby *bajos*. And beyond these would be vacant areas that were, in effect, "buffers" or "no-man's-lands" between polities.

What were the territorial sizes of these lowland Maya polities? Were they confined to the community micropattern entity—a major center and a 5- or 6-kilometer radius—or did they range farther afield? Is the presence of a big center simply to be correlated with a rich and populous immediate sustaining area, or does part of the reason for its bigness lie in the fact that it sustained hegemony over a much wider area and over lesser centers? While these are all difficult questions, I think most of us in the seminar felt that the system was a hierarchical ordered one; big centers, that is, drew not only upon an immediate support area but upon a much larger one that included several lesser centers. As some of the present papers indicate, there is a frequent macropattern of large centers spaced at 20 to 30 kilometers and smaller ones rather evenly placed at intermediate distances between the larger ones. This does not prove hierarchical structuring of political orders, but it is highly suggestive of it. Moreover, there are other lines of archaeological information, such as hieroglyphic texts, that support this interpretation.

Bullard (1960) was the first to develop a systematic hierarchical model for Maya lowland settlement and to suggest that the settlement macropattern model could also be read as a table of political organization. His descriptive model of settlement is based on muleback surveys in the northeast Peten. It has drawn comment—and criticism—ever since, but it is of value for its conceptual, if somewhat idealized, clarity. As already mentioned, his lowest hierarchical rung is the residential *cluster* unit, disposed over a 200–300 meter diameter. His *zone* consists of a dozen or so clusters within an area of a square kilometer in which there is also a minor center. The top hierarchical level is the *district,* an area of about 100 square kilometers, which has within it a number of zones and minor centers and one major center. It will be noted that Bullard's district is just about the same size as the Tikal community or microstructure, with its 120-square-kilometer area. Bullard's districts, however, do not seem to have been so thickly and continuously settled as the Tikal community but to have consisted of a number of spatially discrete clusters. Two of the major centers to which he refers are Dos Aguadas and Yaxha. These are of a size, and close enough to the still larger centers of Tikal and Naranjo, that they might have been secondary centers in the orbit of either (see Marcus 1976: fig. 1.14). Thus the difference in the density of settlement described by Bullard for his typical district and for the Tikal district might correspond to a difference in hierarchical ranking.

Bullard's three-level model has been expanded by Hammond (1975b) in an analysis of settlement in northern Belize. Hammond's scheme has nine levels. The first four of these are residential units, in approximate correspondence to minimal residential units, group residential units, and clusters. The next five levels are all centers (ceremonial centers). At the top of the scale are those like Nohmul and Aventura. There are several of these, and they average between 20 and 30 kilometers apart. At varying intermediate distances between them are the lesser centers of Hammond's scale. I doubt if the data of the Dos Aguadas–Yaxha sector and those of northern Belize are substantially as different as these two analyses would seem to indicate. My surmise would be that Bullard, moving rapidly through the heavy Peten bush, was "lumping" in his classification while Hammond, spending somewhat more time in the Nohmul vicinity, was "splitting" in his. One difficulty, of course, is the matter of establishing ranking criteria for centers.

Attempts have been made, and are being made, to set up more systematic and objective procedures for site ranking. One of these has been the application of central place theory and Thiessen polygons to the lowland Maya data (Flanntery 1972; Marcus 1973, 1976; Hammond 1974). This approach dealt with spatial arrangements and began to give some preliminary ideas about sizes of center sustaining areas. The matter of ranking, however, was still done largely by center size, or impressionistic evaluations of size. Joyce Marcus has begun to modify this by bringing hieroglyphic textual information into the ranking evaluations. This information, which may offer clues to the allegiances of smaller centers to larger ones, has been developed by noting that very large centers display only their own emblem glyphs and never those of lesser centers. Ones of secondary rank show their own emblem and that of their nearest big center but do not mention tertiary size centers. The latter will mention, in addition to their own emblem, those of the nearest secondary and primary center. Like the old Bullard model, this is something of an idealization and simplification, and the problem of an initial objective size ranking still remains; but the approach holds great promise, for it would seem to outline something of the way the Maya themselves felt about political and macrostructural affinities. It should be pursued in connection with more objective size rankings of centers.

This more objective approach to size ranking is that of constructional—or qualitatively modified constructional—volumetrics. This is set forth in this book in the article by the Turners and Adams (1981) and further explored by Adams (1981) in his regional paper. A research history of the development of the method can be found in the two papers. Originally, ratings or coefficients were assigned to centers on the presence and number of such constructional and layout features as acropolises and paved courtyards. Other systems based upon numbers of monuments (stelae) at a site were also explored. In the volumetric method there was a quantification of the cubic volume of constructional materials used in building as well as metric consideration of planned plaza and courtyard space. These formulas were modified by qualitative features, including monuments, ornamental decoration, and treatment of spatial relationships among buildings. The summary statement of the method is best expressed by the authors (Turner, Turner, and Adams, 1981) themselves:

> Essentially, a volumetric model represented by a parallelepipedon has been created that can describe the center or any individual structure or group of structures. This parallelepipedon displays two principal components. The first is its face (or graphic two-dimensional area), denoting the value for the architectural/spatial elements of the center. The second component is the depth or third dimension of the graphic parallelepipedon, whose value is equivalent to the center's qualitative cultural elements. The product of these two components gives the center volume measure, whose cube root establishes the hierarchical rating for the center. (p. 77)

There are obvious limitations to the method, as Adams has pointed out. For one thing, as it has been employed to date, there has been no attempt to take chronology into account. Virtually all the sites that have been appraised volumetrically are either Late Classic constructions or have terminal construction phases dating to that time. Possible or probable earlier construction bulk has not been computed separately, for it would be impossible to do so without extensive excavation. Then, too, there are regional differences in architectural styles which complicate comparative weighting of qualitative elements that go into the parallelepipedon model. In spite of the limitations, however, the method should be explored through application. Even a few tentative examinations of its results are of great interest.

Table 9.8, in Adams's (1981) regional paper, lists sites from the Peten and elsewhere on a continuous ranking scale. Tikal has a factor of 85; Naranjo 42; Nohmul 12; and La Muralla 1—to select but a few examples. A number of interesting plottings can be made from these ratings. Centers spaced around Tikal, at distances varying from 15 to 20 kilometers, include places such as San Clemente (rating 5), Nakum (rating 16), and Uaxactun (rating 23). Are all of these Tikal dependencies, or are Uaxactun and Nakum too large to be so considered? Clearly, the method cannot answer such a question; but in this same context of site plotting, little Uolantun, only 4 kilometers from "downtown" Tikal, has a rating of only 1 and must be a dependency of its giant neighbor. Some other regional examinations should include one made in conjunction with Marcus's (1976:fig 1.15) Calakmul hexagon. Calakmul has a rating of 42. It is surrounded by other centers at average distances of 25 to 30 kilometers. Some of these and their ratings are: Naachtun (21), La Muñeca (11), Oxpemul (11), Uxul (9), Altamira (8), and Balakbal (5). And on Marcus's map, very small centers, 5 kilometers or so from Uxul, and perhaps to be interpreted as making up the microstructural community of that center, are plotted in a much smaller hexagon than the large one centering on Calakmul.

What may be a graded universe of sites that may have made up a regional political entity are 12 centers on the Rio Pasion drainage. Here Seibal rates at 23, Altar de Sacrificios at 8, Dos Pilas and Aguateca at 5 each, Cancuen at 3, El Pabellon at 1—to give some idea of the range. A nice polygon of these cannot be drawn, but the riverine location of all these sites, with its implications for communication and transport, may very well have distorted such ideal central-place arrangement.

In the Southeastern Zone, Copan rates at 14, Quirigua at 6. Three smaller centers, La Canteada, Los Higos and El Paraiso (none of which have been rated), lie intermediate between the two big ones. All five of the sites are 20 to 30 kilometers apart, and it is quite possible that their locations mark an exchange and communication route such as Leventhal suggests.

For other zones and regions comparable volumetric ratings are not available, but these deserve some macrosettlement comment. In southern Quintana Roo Harrison (1981) reports on some rather amazing uniformities in center macrodistributions. In spite of topographic variation and, as Harrison says, against all expectations, he finds that his largest centers of Kohunlich, Tzibanche, La Reforma, Margarita Maza de Juarez, Lagartera, and Chichmuul are all about twenty-six kilometers apart. There are centers of secondary rank, between the largest ones, at a spacing of approximately thirteen kilometers. There is, he says, a little variation in this sometimes, but not more than a kilometer or two. All of the sites in question are believed to have been occupied in the Late Classic.

For some regions the macrodensity of settlement is so great that the plotting out of hexagons or major-minor center relationships seems precluded—at least with present data. The Rio Bec region is one of these. We have referred to a Becan community, in micropattern perspective, with its possible secondary centers in close proximity. Also nearby is the Rio Bec site (or sites) proper. The totality of these, in their volumetrics, surpasses Becan; but do these several big architectural nuclei compose one center or a number of centers?

There is a similar complicating density of centers at places in the Northern Plains Zone. We have mentioned in our earlier consideration of Dzibilchaltun that this big site blurred the distinctions between a micropattern and a macropattern perspective. Architectural nuclei within Dzibilchaltun are sometimes linked by causeways, and causeways were also used to link other northern sites on a truly macropattern scale. Kurjack and

Garza (1981) suggest that these causeway patterns may, quite literally, be the on-the-ground diagrams of political coalitions. Quite often such a pattern will demonstrate four tiers of settlement. At one end of the causeway will be a mammoth site, the primary center; at the other end will be another large center, but one secondary in size to the first. Dotted along the causeway, equidistantly spaced, will be centers of tertiary size. Finally, back away from the causeway, at some distances, and on either side, are what appear as residential hamlet groupings. The great Coba-Yaxuna causeway, 100 kilometers in length, integrates such a pattern, with Coba as the largest site, Yaxuna as the secondary, and six tertiary centers along the road in between. Another *sacbe* or causeway also takes off from Coba, but in a different direction, and ends at the tertiary-sized center of Ixil. The Izamal causeway system is another, linking with Ake and with other smaller centers. Still further examples are the Uxmal system and the one connecting Uci and Cansahcab. All of these pre-Columbian systems and polities must have collapsed after the Classic period, for the states extant when the Spanish came into northern Yucatan in the sixteenth century maintained no such causeway features.

Freidel's (1981a) paper attempts to explain the macropattern differences in northern Postclassic settlement as compared to that of the antecedent Classic, as well as to trace the continuities between the two periods. Various processes were at work in the transition, including the abandonment of many Classic centers, the shifts of population to the coasts to participate in coastwise trade, and, above all, a trend toward political centralization, the results of which we have seen in Mayapan. Much of this centralization, however, had broken down just prior to the advent of the Europeans.

The analysis of macropatterns is the most difficult aspect of lowland Maya settlement study. The potential data are vast and most of them still shrouded with jungle growth; those actually surveyed and carefully examined are few. Still, I think we can make some generalizations.

First, the entirety of the Maya lowlands was occupied, at least as far back as the Classic period, if not before. This occupation, though generally heavy, was variable in its density. It is highly unlikely that the dense settlement patterns that immediately surround some major centers can be projected for the entire lowland countryside. Both natural environment and cultural choice probably played parts in this variability of macrosettlement density.

Second, the evidence of settlement, as well as other lines of archaeological evidence, supports the view that ancient Maya society was hierarchically ordered and that this hierarchical structure is reflected in spatial or geographical arrangements. A basic unit of such a macropattern is the maximal micropattern unit, the community, which we have defined as consisting of a main center, surrounding lesser nuclei or petty centers, and the circumambient populations of residents, all within a 5-to-6-kilometer radius of the main center. Beyond this, these communities are linked into macropattern networks. Larger centers and communities are frequently between 30 and 20 kilometers apart; smaller ones are found at varying intervals between these. Sometimes these macropattern arrangements seem to follow a hexagonal lattice plotting; in other instances, though, as with the causeway-connected centers of Northern Yucatan, or the river bank centers of the Pasión, the spacing is more linear.

Third, our control of the data does not yet allow us to generalize further on what we mean by "primary," "secondary," or "tertiary" centers. There is as yet no standard scale; however, with "nearest neighbor" analyses, central-place plottings, volumetric assessments, and various qualitative criteria, archaeologists are trying to arrive at standard ranking scales.

Fourth, in this review of macropatterns we have been aware of the problem of chronology, but at this stage of investigation have been more or less forced to ignore it. Eventually it must be taken into account. It seems highly likely that macropatterns of dominance and site rank changed through time. States and coalitions undoubtedly were formed only to be dissolved and rearranged in the fortunes of war and politics. It may be that, at times, there were superordinate coalitions ruled, as Marcus (1976: 24–28) has suggested, by such centers as Tikal, Calakmul, Copan, and Palenque. All this remains to be discovered and explored.

Processual Models

Processual models to explain, or to show the systemic articulation of lowland Maya settlement patterns with other aspects of Maya culture, were developed by three seminar members. Adams, Sanders, and Freidel set forth their views during a late session of the seminar; afterward, they revised them for inclusion in this volume. All three models have been constructed from ethnographic or historic analogies. These are not, however, analogies drawn from sixteenth and seventeenth ethnohistoric sources on the Maya. While these have their obvious value in aiding archaeological interpretation, particularly in matters of culture content, the essentially "reduced" nature of Colonial period Maya society and culture poses serious problems for the use of these data for the understanding of structure and process. Instead, all three models have been developed through the use of comparative analogies with cultures in full vigor even though these are historically unrelated to the Maya.[4]

Adams, together with his coauthor, the historian Woodruff Smith (Adams and Smith, 1981), proposes a feudal model for an understanding of the workings of Maya Classic society. While medieval Europe is the main source for such a model, it can also be supplemented with data from medieval Japan and various East African states. The characteristics of a feudal-type sociopolitical structure are: diffused political power; authority, status, and wealth based upon ownership of agricultural lands; and a hereditary principle for the passing on of power and lands. It is also essential that the farm lands be worked by people other than the owners, that a surplus be available from these lands, and that this surplus be at the control of the land-owning elite. Neither the surplus nor the elite need be very large; in fact, they are usually relatively small. The diffused authority and power is graded or ranked, and the behavior of these ranks is determined by codes of obligation, to those above and below. There are also carefully defined "horizontal," as well as "vertical," relationships; for instance, the elite intermarries in a way that maintains a social stratification. Trade is weakly developed and maintained mostly for the purpose of providing luxury and exotic items for the elite.

A variety of evidence suggests a good "fit" of this feudal model to the Classic Maya. As Adams points out, the nature of Maya settlement and architecture was one of the first things that prompted the analogy with feudalism. Architecture is graded as to size and elaboration, with major centers and smaller replicas of these on descending minor center levels. There is a parallel to the scale of royal, ducal, and baronial establishments of European feudalism. Maya formal architecture—the temple and palace constructions—constituted the precincts of the elite. The small size of palace rooms suggests to Adams and Smith the mobility of European and other feudal courts, with the king and his nobles and retainers moving from one center to another and maintaining only very temporary residence in these quarters.

These strictly archaeological data are reinforced by Maya and Mesoamerican ethnography and ethnohistory. Aristocratic leadership and elite ownership or control of agricultural lands is the rule, as is the practice of obligatory commitments between individuals as in the feudal model. We know from sixteenth-century Yucatan that towns had chiefs or leaders— *batabs*—and, over a wider area, the supreme ruler or paramount chief was the head of the most important town, and bore the title of *halach uinich*. Similarly, the contemporary hieroglyphic texts of the Classic, insofar as these can be translated, attest to a hereditary aristocracy and to geographically widespread linkages of the members of this aristocracy through marriage and other associations.

Adams makes the observation that the feudal system had great advantages in controlling widely dispersed populations in that the widely distributed elite, although relatively few in number, had local ties and authority and could exercise this more effectively than could the leadership of a more tightly centralized system. While he does not press the argument that the origins of the Maya feudal system are to be found in agricultural ecology, the inference can be made.

Sanders (1981) is somewhat more explicit in this latter regard. As in his earlier papers (1973, 1977), he sees that growth and development of Maya settlement as linked to ecological constraints. In his view, after a Preclassic spread of farming populations throughout the lowlands, increased population and intensification of cultivation techniques made possible the densely settled Maya centers such as Tikal. Terraces and raised fields are techniques for "outfield" intensification of agricultural production; and household garden plots, root crops, and the harvesting of ramon nuts are the "infield" intensification techniques. These "infield" techniques were necessary to allow for dense and concentrated settlement—that of the 600 persons per square kilometer estimated for Tikal. This decision to nucleate, he concedes, was a cultural one, and was taken for reasons of political control. From a purely agricultural adaptive standpoint, very dispersed residence probably would have been the more sensible choice. Actually, by Late Classic times, the Maya were following both: big center nucleations and dispersed farming households.

For Sanders, as for Adams and Smith, the function of the centers was political. In a great center there would be the main residence of the paramount chief, and he would be surrounded by lesser chiefs and nobles. From here, and with the aid of still other elite living in scattered minor centers, they administered their outlying agricultural lands. Quite specifically—and in agreement with Adams and Smith—he does not see the lowland Maya center as an important trading or manufacturing place, in the manner, for instance, of the Mexican Highland city of Teotihuacan. To Sanders, too, the replicative quality of Maya centers, on their graded scale, suggests the feudal model.

For his ethnographic analogues, Sanders turns to the West African Bafut and the East African Baganda, both feudal-type kingdoms. The capital city of the paramount chief or king of Bafut covered an area of 50 square kilometers within which some 20,000 people resided. Their city area was interspersed with "infield" gardens. At the center was the palisaded compound of the ruler. Outside the 50-square-kilometer area were swidden cultivation fields tended by people from the capital plus others who lived farther out. On a larger territorial scale, the kingdom of Bafut was divided into 24 townships, each ruled over by a lesser and semiautonomous chief from his appropriate capital. The reasons for the nucleation in the capital city appear to be administrative and defensive; crafts and trade are reported as weakly developed. The situation of the Baganda was similar.

Sanders sees the parallels with the Classic Maya as striking. This applies not only to settlement arrangements and government but to other features. Both the African and Maya societies placed a strong emphasis on ancestor cults, and the capitals or centers of both served as royal burial places. Both societies apparently share in the institutions of the patrilocal extended family and in the patrilineage. The great emphasis on rank or status goes with access to, or stewardship of, lands. Other functions of the nobility are adjudicative and military.

In concluding, Sanders contrasts this kind of society, with its graded rankings of individuals and its dispersed and graded settlement, its almost total emphasis on agricultural management, and its small attention to manufacture and trade—in effect, a feudal society—with that of the centralized-type state, for which he draws examples from the Old World Middle East and the Mexican Highlands. In this latter type of society all settlement is tightly nucleated, whether in small villages, in larger towns, or in cities of 60,000 or more persons. Associated with such a society are highly developed institutions of manufacturing and trade.

Freidel (1981b) begins by posing questions about population nucleation, or urbanism, and degree of sociopolitical advancement. Is such nucleation necessary for civilization and the state? Did the Maya "make it" or not? He definitely feels that the "Maya made it," but he thinks that they did it without a fully developed urbanism. He argues that the remote origins of dispersed settlement may have been in some ancient "naturally dispersed" pattern, but he does not believe that continuing ecological restraints on the Maya dictated such a settlement form. Rather, it was social invention, a technique of governance that allowed for a semblance of equality in a system that was nonegalitarian. This interpretation is not altogether inconsistent with what both Adams and Sanders have argued. Feudal lords dispersed over the countryside would have been much more effective as governors if they were thought of as rooted parts of the local population rather than as alien administrators sent in by a central authority.

Freidel is more concerned with the production and distribution of goods than is either Adams or Sanders. He concedes that Maya craft production remained on the household level, but he also points out that this is not the same as having individual household autonomy for production and distribution. Both production and distribution must have been tied into a larger integrated system. If so, what kind of a model might be sought or constructed to simulate this? Such a model would have to allow for a high mobility for both goods and information. It would have to ensure the distribution of these through all centers and all levels. And, in his further opinion, it would have to allow for all of this movement to take place under the sanctions of a pervasive ideology or religion. Freidel does not state why he feels that this last qualification is necessary, but I would judge that he feels it consistent with the general cultural traditions of pre-Columbian Mesoamerica, and I would agree.

His model is then created through general comparative analogy. He calls it the *pilgrimage fair model*. Aspects of it are not out of keeping with European feudal societies of the Middle Ages, although, as Freidel makes clear, it is a synthetic construct for which he can point to no specific ethnographic or historic source. The model, in its operation, has two aspects: a regulated circulation of people under religious sanctions (pilgrimages) and a means of integrating groups of people through an exchange of goods and services (fairs). These fairs are periodic markets which articulate local economies with a wider one. They coincide with religious holidays and the pilgrimages. They are scheduled by the elite-maintained calendar so that production and distribution can be maintained in a predictable manner. As such, they would be controlled by the elite who could levy taxes on them. Goods would be channeled from community to community, from major centers to lesser ones. Such a model would not preclude the localized integration of kin or other small groups by goods redistribution; on the contrary, representatives of these groups would attend the fairs.

It is a fascinating model but one that may be hard to test archaeologically. Freidel makes no recommendations along this line, although he does suggest that ethnohistoric and ethnographic research may pick up residual clues indicating that the pilgrimage fair system was once a reality. There are slight hints now, as, for instance, from the island of Cozumel where trading and pilgrimages seem to have been associated. On the other hand, we do know that true markets, rather than "fairs," existed in Yucatan in early colonial times.

Are these three models reconcilable with each other? It seems to me that they are and that much in the feudal sociopolitical system fits the lowland Maya scene. Freidel does not use the term *feudal*, but I see no real inconsistency between the model he proposes and that kind of a social order. To what extent is the feudal social order related to the environmental-ecological situation of the lowlands? The articulation of dispersed and hier-

5. Settlement Patterns seminar, 1977. Photo by David Noble. Courtesy of the School of American Research. (left to right seated: William A. Haviland, Gordon R. Willey, Wendy Ashmore, William T. Sanders, Dennis E. Puleston. left to right, standing: David A. Freidel, Edward B. Kurjack, Norman Hammond, Richard M. Leventhal, R.E.W. Adams, Peter D. Harrison)

archically graded settlement with lowland Maya agriculture seems well demonstrated. At one point Sanders says that center nucleation is a cultural choice; yet from the whole line of his larger argument it is difficult not to see the agricultural economy and its interface with the natural environment as the *deus ex machina* of the model. Nucleation, up to a point, can be achieved through a combination of "infield" and "outfield" farming, but the wider distributions of population over landscape, even if these are not always continuous distributions, are related to farming and the need to exploit large territories whether by swidden, terracing, or raised fields. The secondary and tertiary centers that go along with this distribution are the means and extension of political control. The fundamental difference between Mexican highland settlement and that of the Maya tropical forest, given the agricultural base of the societies of both regions, seems inevitably to be linked to natural environmental setting. Limitations can be transcended only to a degree, and the Maya achievement shows the degree to which this can happen. If this is Sander's argument, I would agree. I think the feudal order was the best compromise that could be worked out between ecological constraints and political choices in this environment.

Freidel, apparently, would not agree with this and would reject environment and ecological adaptation as the causes behind settlement dispersion. In this disagreement, he cites the early compact village at the Cerros site. Such small community compactness does seem to characterize other Maya lowland Early and Middle Preclassic villages, although our excavation sample of these is pitifully small. Later, in the full Late Preclassic, with the rise of big center architecture, there is more community dispersion. I will offer the guess that, with the generally expanding Maya lowland populations of this period, we begin to see some of the first signs of the "feudal order"—the separate architectural nuclei of a center. These nuclei have their roots in the dispersed agricultural activity in the hinterlands, and the lineage heads of the outlying congregated, although with some spatial separations, in the centers.

In support of his pilgrimage fair model, Freidel notes that the Classic Maya symbol system, in its art, calendrics, and hieroglyphics, is the most dense and continuous system of its kind in all Mesoamerica. I think this probably could be extended to the whole New World. The great Peruvian "horizon styles" may be more extensive geographically, as would elements of Olmec art in Mesoamerica, but they lack the continuous density, the pervasiveness of the Maya symbols. I suppose there must have been various mechanisms to bind the Maya symbolic system into a whole—state formations and alliances, interregional dynastic marriages, maybe even conclaves of priestly scholars arriving at recondite resolutions of calendrical-astronomical matters—but Freidel's pilgrimage fairs would have been an ideal addition for sociopolitical and ideological integration. In a scheduled manner, representatives of all levels of society could have been brought together for material and nonmaterial interchanges under benevolent sanctions. It helps explain much; among other things, it helps explain trade.

On reflection, it seems odd that two of these models play down the role of trade as a major dynamic factor in the growth of the Maya system. Neither the Adams and Smith model nor that of Sanders sees it as an important institution in the development of the Maya centers. This is in startling contrast to other views on Maya trade, such as those expounded by Webb (1973) and Rathje (1973f, 1977) at the two previous Maya seminars. To these and other scholars, the institution of trade was the driving force that led to Maya civilization.

My opinion would be that the pro-trade contingent, if they will let me call them that for a moment, was mistaken in seeing trade as the "Operation Bootstrap" that lifted Early Preclassic villagers to more complex social and political levels. I think complex society in the lowlands was achieved without much in the way of trade, at least on the early rungs of the socio-political ascent. Some trade undoubtedly took place from the very beginning, but I would guess the infusion of ideas was more important than the goods that went along with them at this time. Later, trade and manufacturing were obviously important. Adams and Smith and Sanders probably do not pay enough attention to them, although I would agree with them that trade was not a crucial factor in the basic, dispersed, hierarchically graded settlement of the Maya. I would estimate that it became more so in the Late Classic and that some of the population nucleation in such centers as Tikal, Dzibilchaltun, or especially the specialized salt-production center of Chunchucmil in northern Yucatan is to be attributed to trade and craft production. and there is both archaeological and ethnohistoric evidence to show that interregional trade assumed major importance in the Post classic Period.

In looking at the whole institution of trade, I am inclined to think that Sanders's African models cannot be transferred easily to mesoamerica. The importance of trade in the Mexican highlands and elsewhere during the Classic period must have had an effect upon the lowland Maya. Perhaps, for a substantial time—most of the Classic Period—this influence was not strong enough seriously to affect lowland Maya customs with regard to exchange and distribution of goods. By the end of the Classic, though, I think it was beginning to have its effects; and, as has been stated in our earlier Maya seminars (Willey and Shimkin 1973; Willey 1977b), Mexican highland—type trade, and the failure to integrate it fully into the old Maya system, may have contributed to the Classic Maya "collapse" and the settlement rearrangements of the Postclassic. If so, it would not have been the only time that an agrarian feudal order and its nobility were disrupted by the rising institution of trade.

Notes

1. There has been no systematic attempt to cite all pertinent literature in this summary. This has been done in the other seminar papers, and a combined bibliography has been assembled by the editor for the whole volume. Here, I refer to the various papers of the present volume by author's name; and by consulting the

paper so mentioned the reader may follow up appropriate bibliographic references. Only occasionally have I made other citations.

2. I should add that my colleagues did not have the opportunity to see this summary before publication.

3. Sanders, who also wrote his paper after the seminar, has anticipated me somewhat in this data summarization; however, what he has to say is pointed toward the development of a particular explanatory and processual model of Maya settlement growth while I go over the data in a more formally systematic way and at greater length.

4. See Willey (1977c) for a discussion of types of analogy in archaeological interpretation.

5   Towards an Holistic View of Ancient Maya Civilisation*

Maya archaeological research of recent years has been concerned with several lines of investigation not previously emphasised. These have involved ancient subsistence systems and settlement patterns. The prehistoric evidences for these have resulted in drastic revisions in population estimates and, carrying inferences a step further, in revisions of previous thinking about such matters as Classic Maya urban development and regional socio-political organisation. These new directions in Maya research have been supplemented with continued advances in more traditional Maya archaeology, such as hieroglyphic study and interpretation. As a result, there is now emerging a greatly improved picture of the functionings of old Maya society and the interdependences of all its parts. In this sense, the archaeological approach to the Maya is becoming more holistic. [*The Huxley Memorial Lecture 1979, *Man* (N.S.) 15, 249–66.]

137

The Maya ruins of central America properly impressed and mysti-
fied the European explorers of the sixteenth century and have continued
to be a source of wonder since that time. Their archaeological exploration
began in earnest in the nineteenth century with the field investigations of
Stephens and Catherwood, Maudslay, Charnay and the hieroglyphic and
calendric studies of Forstemann and Goodman. By the beginning of the
twentieth century an appreciable corpus of information had been accu-
mulated, including the romantic discovery that most of these ancient cities
had been abandoned at least 500 years before the arrival of the Spanish.
The Maya hieroglyphic writing and a rich and complex art and iconography were conducive to humanistic interests in the field; and these early
interests have since been supplemented with what we have come to think
of as more scientific archaeological concerns. Today the Maya field is one
of the most developed sectors of American archaeological research. The
last three decades have seen almost innumerable new discoveries as well
as some radically new interpretations of the data.

My intent here is to review and appraise some of this current Maya
research and, especially, to show how this research has revealed the integration and coherence of ancient Maya civilisation. That such a coherence
existed in Precolumbian Maya society and culture is not exactly a new
concept. The late Sir Eric Thompson certainly had such a view of the Maya
even if he did not express it in quite this way. What is new is the way
recent research trends have converged to document the Maya holism. In
this I think it can be said that Maya archaeology has benefited more than
it has suffered from the experimental directions—some would say the
excesses—of a 'new archaeology'. Its early humanistic preoccupations have
not been lost in the quantified searches for process. On the other hand, it
will be my thesis that history and process are not antithetical goals in archaeology; rather, they are bound together in close complement that can only
be prised apart at a loss to each.

In this brief presentation I shall not attempt the impossible task of
synthesising all Maya archaeology. Much of standard Maya prehistory
will be taken for granted or alluded to only incidentally. Thus, I will not
be primarily concerned with new discoveries bearing on Maya early origins, such as those made by Norman Hammond (1977a) in Belize, nor
the findings of very early hieroglyphic texts by John Graham (1977a,b) in
Pacific Guatemala. Nor will I devote special attention, *per se*, to the complexities of central Mexican-Maya relationships or to the numerous new
writings on that fascinating subject, the 'collapse' of Maya civilisation.
The emphasis will rest, instead, on the internal workings and developments of ancient Maya society and culture and, particularly, on the func-

tionings of Maya subsystems as these intermeshed with one another. I will focus on four major subsystems or themes in old Maya life, especially as these have been elucidated and reconstructed by recent archaeological research.

The first is *subsistence*. Obviously it is basic, but this is not the same thing as saying that it is the 'prime cause' or 'only explanation' of the Maya way of life. The second theme is that of *settlement patterns*. We shall see how settlement patterns or the settlement subsystems are closely linked to both the subsistence theme and to other subsystems. The third is *socio-political organisation*. This subsumes social organisation, politico-religious structure, militaristic activities, and trade. Such a subsystem of Maya culture obviously rests on a higher level of inference than the two previous themes. It rests on inferences drawn from them as well as from other conventional archaeological data resources, from burials, crafts, architecture, art, and hieroglyphics. The fourth is *ideology*, world-view. It, too, must derive from inferences, fortunately supplemented now by information from hieroglyphic texts. One of the most fascinating developments of recent research has been the archaeologist's increasing ability to disclose some of the articulations that linked ideology with the material world.

From an examination of these themes a strong case can be made for the essential unity, the holism, of past Maya civilisation. This view does not deny the rich diversity, expressed both regionally and chronologically, of ancient Maya life. Such a diversity is seen stylistically and in the themes under consideration. At the same time, as David Freidel (1979; 1980b) has pointed out in two recent articles, Lowland Maya culture presents an amazing continuity in both space and time, a continuity established early on, and subsequently maintained over several centuries, by an intercommunicative network among its parts.

By way of final introductory comment, I should explain that I am dealing with the 'Lowland Maya area', the territory of the Peten Department of Guatemala, adjacent portions of Mexican Chiapas and Tabasco, the whole of the Yucatan Peninsula, the present state of Belize, and a small western fringe of Honduras. It was occupied in the Precolumbian past by peoples of Mayan speech, and parts of it are still so occupied today. The Mayans of the highlands of Guatemala, Chiapas, and Salvador, while related to those of the Lowlands, were in many ways quite different from those of the Classic Maya civilisation of the Lowlands and are not directly considered here. The conventional chronology is given in table I.

TABLE I. Mesoamerican chronology chart.

Preclassic				Classic			Postclassic		Colonial period
		B.C.	A.D.						
Early	Mid	Late	Proto	Early	Late	Terminal	Early	Late	
2000	1000	300	0	250	600	800	1000	1250	1520

Subsistence

The Maya, like virtually all native Mesoamericans, were agricultural-ists, and their primary food dependence was on domesticated maize. The history of its domestication goes back several millennia in Mesoamerica, and for the Maya Lowlands we can be sure that it was grown as early as the beginning of the Early Preclassic Period, or at about 2000 B.C. In historic times the Maya grew maize by a slash-and-burn, *milpas*, or swidden meth-od of shifting fields and long-fallow periods; and archaeologists have pro-jected this method back into the past. While there is little doubt that swidden must have considerable antiquity in the Maya Lowlands, there have always been questions as to whether or not it was the only system employed in ancient times and as to whether maize was the only important food sta-ple. Back as early as 1937, O. G. Ricketson, Jr. (Ricketson & Ricketson 1937) felt that there were too many residential mounds in the vicinity of Uaxactun to be compatible with a sole reliance on long-fallow swidden cultivation and that more intensive modes of farming must have been employed. In his view annual or short-fallow cropping of the same fields must have been used. Other archaeologists tended to be sceptical, and no immediate attempts were made to follow up this line of inquiry. But some decades later the question was reopened in the same way as attention had been drawn to it in the first place. Settlement pattern studies, carried out in the 1950's and 1960's, indicated too many residential structures, and by implication too many former inhabitants, to have been supported by maize swidden farming alone.

But the difficult question remained. What had been the alternatives to, or significant supplementations of, the swidden method? Archaeolo-gists set about trying to resolve this in various ways. The possibility of supplementary crops was one of the first things explored. Here the evi-dences were largely inferential rather than directly archaeological. Bennet Bronson (1966) made a case for root crop cultivation by the Maya. Mod-ern distributional, early historical, lexical, and botanical data supported his idea of the utilisation of the sweet potato (*Ipomoea batatas*) and man-ioc (*Manihot esculenta*), dating back, perhaps, as early as Preclassic times in the Maya Lowlands. Manioc has a high caloric value per unit of land so cultivated, and the Maya farmer could have augmented his maize *milpas* significantly in small 'kitchen gardens' or by 'infield' cropping. Both David Harris (1973; 1978) and Robert Netting (1977) have enlarged upon the value of such supplementary cropping in tropical forest environments. With reference to the Maya this pertains not only to root-crops but to tree-crops or orchards. In this connexion, Dennis Puleston (1968) had called attention to the possible role of the *ramon* nut, or bread-nut, in the ancient Maya diet. *Ramon* trees grow in profusion in the immediate vicinity of Tikal and other major ruins of the Peten. The nut is a nutritious edible often used as food by the Maya today. Had it been in the past? Puleston developed his argument for the bread-nut as an economically important staple in ancient times by investigating the subsurface storage pits, or *chultuns*, found around Precolumbian Maya house sites at Tikal. These pits were shown, through experiment, to be especially effective for long-time storage of bread-nuts whereas maize could not be so similarly stored in them. As the *chultuns* dated back to the Late Preclassic, if not before (Puleston 1971), the use of the bread-nut might also be projected back to this period. In Puleston's further opinion, *ramon* harvests were more than a supplement to maize; they were, at least at some sites and in some times, the Maya staff of life. In addition to these arguments for 'kitchen-garden' crops and orchard crops, other investigators (Lange 1971; Pohl 1974) have called attention to the importance of marine foods and land animals in the ancient Maya diet. From all this, the overall picture that was beginning to emerge was that of a Maya subsistence economy of considerable diversification rather than one wholly dependent upon the swidden cultivation of maize; but the breakthroughs that were to change the old picture were the direct archaeological discoveries that suggest intensive agricultural methods.

These discoveries of intensive farming methods pertain to large-scale terracing and to hydraulic cultivation with artifically raised or constructed fields. While a few agricultural terraces had been reported from the Maya Lowlands in earlier surveys, credit for the discovery and description of extensive terrace systems goes to B. L. Turner II (1974; 1979). These were found in the Rio Bec region of the central Yucatan Peninsula, an undulating limestone country with heavy seasonal rainfall. The soils here are good although thin and subject to erosion. Hundreds of thousands of stone-walled terraces can be seen on the Rio Bec hillslopes, strung out over an area of 10,000 sq. km. The terraces were obviously effective in checking erosion; they would have required a very substantial labour expenditure to construct and to maintain; but if they were properly maintained, annual, or very short-fallow, cropping would have been possible. Residential units are found scattered through the terraces areas in great numbers, and there are several major centres or cities in the Rio Bec zone. It is generally believed that the terrace systems of the Rio Bec date largely to the Late Classic Period although dating information is still very limited. Similar terraces are also known from the Central zone of the Peten and from Belize.

Not all Lowland Maya terrain was suited to terracing, however, and in many of these regions raised field cultivation was practised. This method would appear to be a highly intensive form of agricultural production. It is both a means of drainage and of plant irrigation that is carried out in lands that are perennially or seasonally wet, as along sluggish river courses, in shallow lakes or ponds, or in swamps. Muck, vegetation, and soil is piled up, usually in rectangular ridges or plots separated from one another by canals. Raised fields are known from elsewhere in Precolumbian America, especially in South America (Parsons & Denevan 1967); and the method was also practised by the Aztecs with their construction of *chinampas,* or 'floating gardens', in old Lake Texcoco (Coe 1967). In the Maya Lowlands artificial raised fields were first reported along the slow-flowing Rio Candelaria in southern Campeche (Siemens & Puleston 1972). Subsequently, others were discovered along the Rio Hondo, in northern Belize. Here, in the course of their exploration, a wooden retaining post was found *in situ* in the mud, and a radiocarbon date on this post is approximately 1100 B.C. (uncorrected), suggesting a respectable antiquity for the raised field system in the Maya Lowlands (Puleston 1977). Still more recent reports refer to vast tracts of such raised fields in *bajos,* the extensive seasonal swamps that are found throughout much of the Maya Lowlands. First detected in aerial photographs, they appear as series of raised rectangles carefully defined by grid-like canals. They have since been explored on the ground in southern Quintana Roo where Peter Harrison (1978b) states there are many sq. km. of such patterns.

As a result of all of these studies, and especially those of the terraces and the raised field systems, archaeologists now conceive of the old Maya Lowland subsistence economy not as a precarious slash-and-burn agricultural struggle in a hostile tropical forest environment but as a highly sophisticated undertaking which maximised natural resources, emphasised variability in crops and planting, and devoted a huge labour investment in a programme of large-scale agricultural intensification. The recently published collection of essays, *Pre-Hispanic Maya agriculture* (Harrison & Turner, eds., 1978), may be taken as a gauge of the complexity of the subject and the very recent advances that have been made in it. To be sure, the history, or prehistory, of Maya subsistence remains to be worked out in detail. Was the earliest settlement and agricultural exploitation of the lowlands dependent upon swidden methods, with the more labour intensive and sophisticated intensification methods adopted only as population increased and land filled up? Or were some intensive farming methods, notably that of raised fields, very important in early times, perhaps with the first agricultural settlers of the area, with the less productive swidden technique coming later (Willey 1978a)? These questions cannot be answered yet, but what is certain is that the Precolumbian Maya had a subsistence economy fully commensurate with the settlement densities and cultural achievements of that society. Civilisation can grow and thrive in a tropical forest environment, at least under certain conditions, and it did so in the Maya Lowlands.

Settlement Patterns

From the foregoing the close relationship between subsistence and settlement pattern in Maya archeaology is abundantly clear. Two main questions arise in any consideration of Maya settlement patterns. What were the sizes and densities of the populations involved? And what are the actual patterns involved? Earlier Maya population estimates were always based on agricultural production estimates—the single exception being Ricketson's projection from house mound figures. While volume of maize production per unit of land is a perfectably respectable basis for demographic estimates, in the Maya case the initial assumption of primary dependence upon swidden cultivation set up a closed circular argument of low agricultural production equals low population figures. Settlement surveys broke this circle, and house mound or residential unit counting became the primary method for population estimates. Such population figures can now be computed from a number of surveys, including one conducted in the environs of the major centre of Tikal (Carr & Hazard 1961; Haviland 1966a, b; 1969; 1970, 1972). Two critical or possibly deranging factors come into these estimates. One is the population figure assigned to the individual counted residential unit. This, in turn, is conditioned by what is considered as a single residence. Individual buildings have often been considered as housing from four to five persons—the husband, wife and children of the nuclear family. The Maya, however, more frequently lived in small patio-type residential arrangements for extended families. If these patio-groups are taken as the counting unit then a figure of somewhere between seven and ten persons per unit is thought to be more reasonable. The second complicating factor is the dating of the residential unit. In the recent settlement pattern surveys at Tikal and elsewhere (Willey *et al.* 1965; Tourtellot 1970; Kurjack 1974; Willey & Leventhal 1979) this has been taken into account; still, it is often difficult to demonstrate exact contemporaneity when archaeological phases can rarely be shaved as less than 100 years in duration.

In spite of the problems, progress in settlement-population estimates has been made. Tikal, which is the largest centre or city in the southern Lowlands, has a 'downtown' nucleus of temples and palaces that covers 4 sq. km. In and around this core are many residential mounds. By drawing a 6-km. radius around the centre, a distance settled upon by archaeologists on the location of an outer defence wall and upon a general density of small mounds, W. A. Haviland (1980) has estimated a Late Classic Period population of 72,000 persons for an area of approximately 120 sq. km., or a figure of 600 persons per sq. km. In the Rio Bec region R. E. W. Adams (1981) projects a figure of about 500 persons per sq. km. in and around such centres as Becan, Rio Bec, and Xpuhil; and in the far northern Lowlands, around Dzibilchaltun, E. B. Kurjack (Kurjack & Garza 1980) estimates that there were as many as 2,000 persons per sq. km. living in the vicinity of that centre during its Late Classic height. These figures and densities have brought about a reappraisal in our thinking about ancient Maya urbanism. A strong trend towards, if not an achievement of, the urban condition is certainly indicated. It should be made clear, of course, that such densities and figures as these cannot be projected over the Maya Lowlands as a whole. For one thing, not only are large tracts of the Lowlands unsuited for residential sitings because of terrains and drainage, but we have been describing nucleated population centres—or cities. Other stretches of land were undoubtedly given over largely to agriculture, and many communities were much less densely settled. For instance, D. S. Rice's (Rice & Puleston 1981) house mound counts in the vicinity of the two smaller centres or cities of Yaxha and Sacnab can be translated into population estimates of 200 to 500 persons per sq. km. Thus, as far as overall Lowland Maya area population estimates are concerned, any attempt at even an approximate figure is premature until we have more settlement data. Obviously, it was somewhere in the millions. Viewed chronologically, our settlement samples at hand indicate a general population growth throughout the Preclassic Periods, a stabilisation or lessened growth in the Protoclassic and Early Classic, an upsurge again in the Late Classic, and a marked decline in the Terminal Classic and Postclassic; but within the framework of this broad statement it must be noted that there are some significant regional differences.

What of the patterns, the settlement arrangements, themselves? The several articles of a symposium volume (Ashmore, ed., 1981) are addressed to this question, and we have already had some indications of settlement form in reviewing population estimates. We have referred to single houses. These are marked, for the archaeologist, by low rectangular or apsidal platforms of earth and stone which served as bases for small, usually one or two-room, buildings constructed variously of poles-and-thatch, stone masonry, or combinations of these. Such constructions may occur singly or, more often, in the patio-groups to which we have referred. These patio-groups may be considered as the basic 'building block' of Maya settlement study. They consisted most usually of from two to six structures. Some of these were residences, others kitchens or storage places. Patio-groups are, in turn, often found in clusters of from five to twelve. In such clusters one patio-group, usually in a central location in the cluster, is larger than the others and has one mound or building that is more imposing than any of the others in that patio-group or in the cluster. Where these have been excavated it has been found that this 'most imposing' building, frequently situated on the east side of its patio-group, had the functions of a shrine, a little temple, or, perhaps, an administrative office. There is an excellent example of such a cluster and building in the Copan Valley, on the outskirts of the great Copan centre. Here a cluster of five patio-groups has a principal group with a principal building. In this case the structure in question was on a platform mound about 4.00 m. high, and it had three rooms. In the central room, which faced out over the patio, was an elaborate stone bench or throne carved with an hieroglyphic inscription. While the other buildings of the patio-group and the cluster gave abundant evidences of domestic functions, this particular building did not, and its form and features suggest special functions (Willey *et al.* 1978).

These special patio-groups and buildings of residential clusters in a sense replicate the form and presumed functions of the Lowland Maya centres. In the centres, patio-arrangements, or, more properly, courtyard arrangements, consist of much larger structures, of pyramids topped by temples and adjoining multi-roomed palaces on high platforms. To a degree, a distinction between residential units and the public buildings of the centres appears to be one of scale, and there is a gradation from one to another.

I have mentioned the question of urbanism in connexion with population estimates. It is an old problem in Maya studies (see Becker 1979). The reaction of the first Europeans who visited the great Maya ruins was to call them ancient abandoned cities. Later, this view was challenged by those who looked upon them as ritual or ceremonial centres, precincts for the priests and rulers but largely unoccupied by the masses except on special occasions. As we have seen, the intensive settlement studies in and around them has swung opinion back towards the first interpretation. Sites such as Tikal and Dzibilchaltun, while serving as places of worship and festival centres, had large residential populations in the immediate vicinity of the temples and palaces. The social makeup of these populations, however, is still a matter for argument. While this anticipates our next theme, that of socio-political organisation, it is a fairly low-level archaeological inference to assume that some of the centre dwellers were members of an elite who lived in the palaces and finer residential units. At the opposite end of the social scale, some centre residents were probably farmers who walked out to maize fields and also cultivated household garden plots. Others may have been engaged in production and trade. It is the nature, size, and importance of this segment, of what might be thought of as an emergent 'middle class', that is most debatable and open to future archaeological investigation to determine such things as full-time craft specialisation or professionalisation in trade.

There are some indications that an increase in the pattern of urban-type settlement characterised Maya development in the Late Classic Period. As an example, our Copan Valley cluster with the little temple building is situated about a kilometre from the main centre of Copan public buildings and monuments. In this location it is one of several such clusters of patio-groups, with each cluster separated from its neighbour by only relatively short distances of open ground. Indeed, in some instances the clusters merge one with another so that it is difficult so to identify them. Then, as one moves farther out into the valley, clusterings appear farther apart from each other. Are we observing steps in a process of urbanisation? C. F. Baudez's current excavations and surveys in the Copan Valley should throw light on this question by disclosing the settlement patterns of earlier periods. At Tikal, also, such clusterings of patio-groups are visible in places although in others there is little in the way of intervening space between them (Haviland 1966a, b; 1981); and the same can be said for Dzibilchaltun (Kurjack & Garza 1981).

Another important aspect of Lowland Maya settlement is that of macro-patterns, of the disposition over the landscape of centres and residences in the large. Centres or cities are of varying sizes, and they are located geographically in ways that suggest a hierarchically-structured organisation. Again, this moves us towards socio-political inferences, but the descriptive data of settlement are extremely interesting in themselves. Allowing for regional variation, as well as for great gaps in information, there are indications that the greatest centres—those with multiple courtyard arrangements of temples and palaces, with ball-courts, sculptured monuments and hieroglyphic inscriptions, as well as large circumambient residential populations—tend to be about 20 to 30 km. apart. In regions where riverine transport was feasible these distances tend to be somewhat greater. Smaller centres are evenly spaced at intermediate distances between these larger ones; and still smaller ones may be arranged as satellites around the latter. Residential house mound clusters are usually found in greatest numbers immediately in and around centres; but these are often found, although not so densely distributed, through the intervening territories between centres. This settlement disposition has encouraged attempts at systematic centre ranking, including the application of Central-Place theory and Thiessen Polygon networks (Flannery 1972; Hammond 1972; 1974; Marcus 1973; 1976). While the results may both profit and suffer from the limitations of such methods, such applications are worth pursuing further. It is also of interest to note that in northern Yucatan the Maya themselves offered on-the-ground diagrams of centre hierarchies by connecting their cities and towns with raised roadways, some extending for many kilometres. Such arrangements often show as many as four tiers of settlement sizes (Kurjack & Garza 1981). The largest centre will be at one end of the causeway; at the other end will be a centre of secondary size; dotted along the causeway, more or less equidistantly spaced, will be tertiary size sites; and, finally, back away from the immediate sides of the roadway are clusters of residential mounds. The great Cobá-Yaxuná causeway is an example of such settlement integration. It is 100 km. long, with Cobá at one end, Yaxuná at the other, and six lesser centres located in between.

Socio-political Organisation

The close articulation between settlement patterns and socio-political organisation has been referred to in the foregoing and is obviously implicit in much that we have said about settlement. But to approach the matter very systematically, and to begin at the micro-pattern end of the settlement scale, there is ethnohistoric and ethnographic evidence to link the single house or minimal residential unit with the nuclear family and the larger patio-group unit to the extended family, all in a kin system that was essentially patrilineal and patrilocal. The social correlate of the next largest settlement unit, the cluster of patio-groups, is more uncertain although it seems most likely that it had kin significance. Certainly the presence of the 'most imposing' building, the temple, shrine, or office, in the clusters suggests a locus for small group authority that is compatible with lineage organisation.

As we go up the settlement scale, the gradation in size and elaboration from the 'most imposing' building in the residential cluster to the temple or palace of the centre suggests that the political and religious power of the Maya Lowland centres was originally rooted in family lineage authority. Such an interpretation is reinforced by the developmental perspective on the rise of centres that comes from archaeological excavation. As an example, the earliest occupation at the major site of Altar de Sacrificios consisted of a small cluster of Middle Preclassic Period patio-group residences. At the end of the Middle Preclassic Period one of these patio-groups had been rebuilt so that it was noticeably larger than the rest. A few centuries later, at the close of the Late Preclassic Period, successive rebuilding of this same patio-group unit had transformed it into a temple-palace architectural complex of what could be considered Maya centre proportions. That is, the temple pyramid of the complex was now 10 m. high, terraced, with an elaborate stairway, and decorated with stucco reliefs. This architectural transition, which continued into the Classic Period with further enlargements and elaborations of the same building complex, were accompanied by other changes in the culture, including a steadily increasing import of exotic trade goods, the local production of fine pottery and other products, and the burial of high status individuals under circumstances indicating the rise of an elite class. With the Classic Period came hieroglyphic texts authenticating the rulers of the centre (Willey 1973a). From these data a reasonable case can be made for a ruling lineage arising from an earlier dominant patio-group household.

The hierarchical scaling of centres or cities, to which we have already referred, may well be an expression of the relative importance and power of noble Lowland Maya lineages. Various processes could have achieved this. Lesser members of great royal lineages of major centres could have been vested with the authority to found outlying secondary or tertiary centres; or old centres and their ruling families could have been assimilated, in lesser positions, under more powerful kings. We have spoken of geographic locational theory as a means of plotting spheres of political influence. This has been abetted by turning to Maya history as recorded in the hieroglyphic texts found in the centres. In this, Maya archaeology may be said to occupy a shadow line between history and prehistory. There have been some positive developments in the translating of Maya hieroglyphic writing in the last twenty years. Most authorities now concede a degree of phoneticism in the hieroglyphic system and agree that the famed Landa 'alphabet' of the sixteenth century has a role in deciphering earlier inscriptions (see Knorozov 1968; Lounsbury 1974a; Kubler 1974; Kelley 1976). To be sure, there are still discouraging differences of opinion among experts on how certain texts may be read, and the end is by no means in sight; nevertheless, the identification of emblem glyphs for cities (Berlin 1958), of name glyphs for rulers, and of glyph signs for classes of events, such as a ruler's accession to a throne (Proskouriakoff 1963, 1964), have made possible a framework of history and the recognition of individuals within that framework as far back as the fourth century A.D. Joyce Marcus (1976) has made an imaginative foray into this kind of limited history derived from the partial translation of the hieroglyphs to give us some hints of ancient political structures. She has found evidence to suggest that at major centres, such as Tikal, the only emblem glyph shown on the monuments is the emblem of that city. Centres of secondary importance will also display the Tikal emblem glyph in addition to their own, while those of a tertiary order will enter the Tikal glyph, the glyph of their nearest secondary centre, and their own in their monumental texts. Given the present state of knowledge of many lesser centres and their inscriptions, this formulation may be a little too neat to be true; but it is a research step in the right direction, especially as it may be combined with locational analysis and objective studies measuring the volumetric constructional sizes of the centres (Turner *et al.* 1981).

While the territorial sizes of the former Maya chiefdoms or states and their capitals still remain speculative, we know from the hieroglyphic texts that dynastic marriages, alliances, and wars were common among centres. A dynastic history of Tikal, for example, can now be sketched from its hieroglyphic texts. We know of a fourth century ruler, one 'Jaguar-Paw'. He appears on the scene as the head of an old aristocratic royal lineage. After his death in A.D. 378, he was succeeded by a foreigner, 'Curl-Snout', who is shown garbed and ornamented in the style of Teotihuacan, that distant and great, but completely non-Mayan, city of Central Mexico. Whether or not this new ruler was actually from Teotihuacan is uncertain, but he brought with him the prestige of that city, and he married the daughter or a female relative of 'Jaguar-Paw'. This tantalising glimpse, afforded by hieroglyphics and art, may be projected against the more general archaeological background of Tikal during the fourth and fifth centuries A.D. This was a period in which we see evidences of trade contact with Teotihuacan and Central Mexico. For instance, Central Mexican green obsidian was being brought into Tikal several decades before 'Curl-Snout's' arrival; and this commerce, as well as trade in other items, increased during 'Curl-Snout's' reign. From all this we are beginning to understand something of processes involved in state development and in commerce. This Tikal example of dynastic history is but one of several from the Maya Lowlands. Hieroglyphic and iconographic research at Yaxchilan (Proskouriakoff 1963–4), Palenque (Lounsbury 1974b; Mathews & Schele

1974), Copan (Pahl 1976), and Quirigua (Kelley 1962; Sharer 1978), as well as at other sites, has given us a general insight into ancient Maya politics. It is possible, although by no means certain, that Tikal was a capital of a southern Lowland state of considerable size in the Early Classic Period. There are indications that the ruling house of this 'Tikal state' founded new dynasties at Quirigua and Copan (Sharer 1978) and that royal women from Tikal married into the ruling lineages of other cities (Marcus 1976). It also seems highly possible that Tikal, or a Tikal alliance, conquered and dominated the rival centre of Becan in the Rio Bec region to the north (Webster 1977). We know that Tikal's power declined for a time at the end of the Early Classic Period (Willey 1974; Coggins 1979) and that there were a number of competing city-states during the Late Classic Period.

This story of the rise and fall, of the undulating fortunes, the wars, the alliances, and royal intermarriages, of the Maya cities is threaded through with the dialectic of centralisation, decentralisation, new centralisation, and so on. Such a process is undoubtedly a world-wide phenomenon and as old as the first state formations of human history, but it may throw some light on the way in which the first Maya great cities arose. In my opinion it is linked to the rise of family lineage organisations in the Preclassic Period. At several Maya cities there are hints that more than a single powerful lineage were involved in Late Preclassic politics. At Tikal the great number of Late Preclassic and early Early Classic temple-palace complexes might be interpreted as the seats of cooperating and competing lineages. There are suggestions of the same thing in the Early Classic Period at Quirigua and Copan. At Tikal the accession of 'Curl-Snout' to the throne was accompanied by new central constructions that outstripped in size and magnificence the earlier ones. Do we have here a foreign ruler who imposed on old Maya noble lineages and a more weakly developed institution of kingship the fully state type centralisation that was already known at Teotihuacan?

This is not an attempt to explain the process by diffusion but, rather, to see diffusion and its effects in a proper developmental context. 'Curl-Snout' was succeeded by his son, 'Stormy Sky', under whose reign the processes of centralisation continued and Tikal rose to the zenith of its Early Classic Power. After his death there seem to have been dissensions within the city, with rival claimants to the throne; but later, in the Late Classic Period, there was a revival of centralised royal authority under the individual whom we call 'Ruler A' and who ruled with a conspicuous display of symbols and a lineage identification with 'Curl-Snout' and 'Stormy Sky'. This one view of the trials and tribulations of one Lowland Maya dynasty can undoubtedly be applied to others. The Maya state, or series of petty states, were the power bases of competing aristocratic lineages who were constantly embroiled in the processes of state formation (Cowgill 1979). The tides of fortune ebbed and flowed, but no single polity appears ever to have been able to bring off a truly imperial formation in the Lowland culture sphere.

Our view of the Maya as warlike, and constantly engaged in internecine warfare, is a revision of the recent decades of research. The earlier view of them as pacific, serene, and theocratically directed has been modified by the hieroglyphic and iconographic studies detailing dynastic squabbles; and this line of investigation has been followed by David Webster's (1974; 1975; 1976; 1977; 1978; 1979) writings about Lowland Maya fortified sites and the role of defence, militarism, and conquest in the development of Maya civilisation. Webster argues that the Maya state arose, at least in important part, in response to these factors; and G. L. Cowgill (1979) is of the opinion that the endemic Lowland Maya inter-city warfare, as competing polities struggled for overall control, was a crucial factor in the Classic Maya decline.

Warfare is one means of establishing relations with one's neighbours and compeers; trade is another. How important was trade, especially long-distance trade, in the rise and growth of Lowland Maya civilisation? W. L. Rathje (1971; 1972; 1973; 1977) and M. C. Webb (1973) have both advanced hypotheses about trade which answer this question in the affirmative. Some specifics of their hypotheses and arguments, such as the development of a Maya elite class from egalitarian beginnings through the control and distribution of scarce commodities, seem unfounded; but the entirety of their case cannot be brushed aside. Certainly, as we have seen, there is evidence of trade in obsidian, as well as in jade and other exotic goods, in the Maya centres, as at Tikal. How were these and other products handled in the Maya economic system? In government-controlled markets as in Postclassic Central Mexico? In a redistributive manner? The archaeological record has not yet come up with answers to these questions. In opposition to the Rathje and Webb opinions are those of R. E. W. Adams (Adams & Smith 1981) and W. T. Sanders (1981). Both of these scholars opt for a feudal model in their attempts to explain Lowland Maya society. According to this view, the Maya centres were essentially political nodes in a system designed for the control of peasant agricultural production by an elite class. The primary, secondary, and tertiary ranks of the centres correspond, in this interpretation, to the seats of kings, dukes, barons, in effect a ranked nobility linked together by a code of allegiances and obligations, as well as being linked through lineages and intermarriages. Or, on the African scene, these centres and sub-centres would be the establishments of paramount chiefs, chiefs, and sub-chiefs. Consistent with this model, manufacturing within the centres would have been at a relative minimum, and trade was largely limited to exotics for the upper classes. The archaeological resolution of such an argument—the Maya centres as emergent cities with craftsmen and traders, or the centres as points in a feudal network of agrarian control—is not an easy one; but the problem is a major one in current Maya research. In my own point of view, I think it difficult to isolate trade as a primary causal factor in Lowland Maya civilisational growth; yet it seems reasonably certain that the institution of trade was important in a systemic way, with a positive 'feedback' into Maya society and culture as a whole. I am inclined to favour the feudal model for the Preclassic and Classic Periods; but in the Terminal Classic and Postclassic profound changes were underway throughout Mesoamerica as a whole and in the Maya Lowlands, and interregional trade was a significant element in these changes. If such trade had not been a key factor in the rise of Maya civilisation, I think it may have been a crucial one in its decline or at least its drastic reorganisation.

Ideology

I do not place the theme of ideology last in order of presentation because I feel it is inevitably epiphenomenal to the more material or mundane concerns of subsistence, settlement pattern and socio-political organisation. In a recent Huxley lecture Gerardo Reichel-Dolmatoff (1976) showed convincingly that ideology—religion, world view, cosmology, or however one may wish to describe it—has a formative role in cultural development and is linked to all phases of it. Although he was dealing with a simpler society, his arguments are germane to the Maya scene. Still, as archaeologists, we have a tradition of reasoning from the material to the non-material, and I have followed this strategy in dealing with other matters before turning to the ideological dimension of Maya culture.

I have explained something of the historical or humanistic background of Maya culture history in recounting the advances in hieroglyphic and iconographic research at Tikal, and this background allows us to move in the ideological direction. It will be recalled that 'Curl-Snout', the fourth century ruler with the foreign or Teotihuacan heritage, had effected what looked like a political centralisation of that city. C. C. Coggins (1979) has pointed out that it was during 'Curl-Snout's' reign tht major calendrical changes were effected at Tikal. For the first time dates were celebrated in a Mexican manner. Stelae were erected and dedicated on *katun* (approximate twenty-year period) endings rather than on the specific dates of the births or deaths of rulers. The implications of this might well be that the new ruler was not only following his Mexican heritage but that he was concerned to synthesise this heritage with that of the old Lowland Maya aristocracy, with the Long Count system of dating. And it also suggests, that in his attempts to forge a more inclusive and more centralised state he was emphasising more popular calendrical functions, such as the mass celebration of religious holidays. His successor, 'Stormy Sky', continued with these calendrical innovations, and they did not go out of vogue in the 'time of troubles' between 'Stormy Sky' and 'Ruler A'. Here, I think, is an example of a close articulation of ideology and socio-political organisation seen wholly in the archaeological record. It could be argued that in this case ideology was employed in an epiphenomenal way, as an adaptive strategy in the wake of power politics. Perhaps so, but there is another example in which the articulations or the interrelationships between the world of things and the world of ideas seems more fundamental.

This ingenious interpretation of the role of Maya religion has relied upon art and iconography rather than hieroglyphic texts. It was developed by the late Dennis Puleston (1977) in the wake of his own researches into the Lowland Maya artificial raised field systems. As we have seen, such agricultural features have a respectable antiquity, and this and their physical extent in the Maya Lowlands suggested an importance in Maya life—and Maya thought. With this in mind, Puleston turned to Classic Maya art and iconography and examined it with a new perspective. Contrary to previous opinion, he found that its subsistence themes were not confined to representations of the rain gods or *Chacs*; but they also included another kind of aquatic symbolism in abundance. These were depictions of fish, water-birds, turtles, snails, crocodiles, and, above all, the water-lily—all creatures or plants that are especially at home in sluggish riverine, pond, or swampland (*bajos*) settings. Such settings, it will be remembered, are the environments of the raised field and canal systems of the Lowland Maya. The water-lily—which is a part of the Maya glyph sign for the first of the twenty day names—is both a symbol for abundance in Maya mythology and one that is frequently associated with maize symbols. This same lily is closely associated with Itzam Na, the crocodilian or dragon-like creator god and generally conceded to be the major deity of the Mayas. In Maya cosmology the earth was conceived of as Itzam Na floating in a pond. On an altar at Copan, a crocodile, presumably representing Itzam Na, is shown with water-lilies tied to his wrists; fish nibble at these lilies; and maize sprouts from the god-monster's temples. In his study, Reichel-Dolmatoff (1976) offered a very explicit diagram of how the myths and cosmology of a people can be an accurate summation of the ecological balance upon which their lives depend. The Maya representation of the crocodile, the lilies, the fish, and the maize plants appeals to us as a poetic, artistic, and religious realisation of the ecological system which was one of the main underpinnings of their existence.

Concluding Comment

These four themes—subsistence, settlement patterns, socio-political organisation, and ideology—are interlinked systemically. We see this in our understanding of their functionings as subsystems of Lowland Maya culture, and the point is driven home in the interrelationships of the data as we investigate them archaeologically. An imbalance in the subsistence-settlement equation model led to the search for and discovery of data that resulted in a drastic revision of the model. A more intensive look at patterns of Lowland settlement has led to a reappraisal of the nature and functions of the great Maya centres or cities. Debate still goes on here, posing what we might call a normative urban model against one of a feudal order, but out of it should come a better understanding of ancient Maya society. Our quasi-historical information from the hieroglyphs, together with analyses of art, iconography, and calendrics, has thrown important new light on political organisation; and, at the same time, these things have opened a small window onto Maya ideology of the Precolumbian past. From another perspective we see a closure of the systemic circle with ideology linking to the subsistence and ecological settings of the raised cultivation fields.

As I noted at the outset, I have not been concerned primarily with many of the standard landmarks of Lowland Maya culture history; and yet these have been brought into the discussion in passing. Indeed, looked at from this perspective the 'wave' of Teotihuacan influence into the Maya Lowlands, traditionally dealt with in terms of obsidian cores and blades or tripod cylinder jars, now takes on the aspect of 'Curl-Snout' and his fourth-century followers as they bullied, fought, cajoled, traded, or married their way into one of the best families of Tikal. I think that this systemic, this holistic view of Maya, through its consideration of many factors and the interrelationships among them will lead us to an increasingly better perception as to what happened to Classic Maya civilisation in the ninth and tenth centuries, a subject I have not attempted to pursue here.

For me, one of the most interesting things to come out of these recent decades of Maya research is that ideologies and images of the mind are not random creations out of nothing, spinning along in independence from other aspects of life. They are designs which articulate—through whatever screens of fantasy—with a real and material world; and as the many and complex subsystems of a past culture and society become better known in all of their parts these articulations will be perceived with greater clarity. I see no very useful nor meaningful line separating 'science' and 'humanism' in archaeology. Instead, there is a challenge to understand the dialectic that exists between the tangible creations of the material world and the more abstract creations of the mind. To do this, archaeology, too, must be holistic.

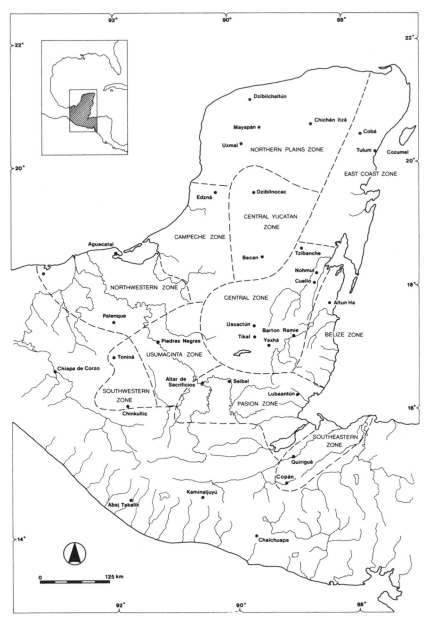

Map of the Maya area. (From *Lowland Maya Settlement Patterns,* ed. Wendy Ashmore [Albuquerque: University of New Mexico Press, School of American Research Advanced Seminar Series, 1981.]

156

6   The Postclassic of the Maya Lowlands:
A Preliminary Overview

This paper was written in the summer months of 1981, and it stands essentially as it was written then. Three members of our Santa Fe symposium group, Arlen F. Chase, Diane Z. Chase, and Prudence M. Rice, have been kind enough to point out to me some errors of fact or emphasis and some omissions of data, and I have benefited from their criticisms by making minor changes in the original text; however, the main theses of the presentation—its chronological and cultural unit organization and its interpretations of the configurations of cultural development through time and in space—remain the same. My original assignment, as I understood the wishes of the symposium organizers, was to prepare a preliminary summary of the available data and archaeological interpretations bearing upon the subject of the Lowland Maya Postclassic Period and cultures. This preview was then to be circulated to the other members of the symposium group some time prior to the preparation of their own individual

and more specialized papers, using my summary structure as a kind of
background frame of reference and, indeed, as a "target," against which
to project their own various and several disagreements. Thus, as I have
indicated in my introductory remarks which follow, I was endeavoring to
present what might best be described as a "conventional" or "tradition-
al" view of the Lowland Maya Postclassic (and the presumably anteced-
ent Terminal Late Classic). At the time I wrote, I was reasonably convinced
of this kind of a presentation and interpretation of the data. As a result of
my reading of the other symposium papers, together with our week-long
discussions at Santa Fe, I would now modify my original views some-
what both as to the timing and to the nature and quality of events charac-
terizing the Postclassic. For one thing, I would agree with the symposium
consensus that there was a considerable chronological overlap (at least a
century, if not more) between cultures which have heretofore been con-
sidered as belonging to the Terminal Classic Period and those traditional-
ly thought of as being Early Postclassic. Most particularly, this applies to
the Puuc sites and culture of the Northern Lowlands and what is usually
referred to as "Toltec" Chichen Itza. G.R.W. December 1982.

The purpose of this paper is a preliminary, general, and brief survey of the archaeology of the Maya Lowlands during what is generally known as the Postclassic Period (A.D. 1000–1520). It was written to provide a base of departure for the more specialized papers which follow, and it was also designed to serve as a starting point for the seminar discussions on the subject.

At the risk of overpersonalizing, let me say that it is probably fitting for me to be the one to draw up such a preliminary statement. Along with most Maya archaeologists of my generation, my attention has been direct-ed largely to the Preclassic and Classic Periods. When I have approached the subject of the Postclassic it has been, so to speak, from "below," from the end of a waning Classic and from the "abyss" of the "collapse." My terms here are selected intentionally to reflect a bias about the Postclassic, and I will confess at the outset that I am still not altogether disabused of this frame of mind. At the same time, I set about learning as much as I could about the Postclassic Period Maya of the Lowlands, and this is an attempt at an objective summary and evaluation.[1]

The archaeology of the Postclassic Period of the Maya Lowlands has not been completely ignored. After all, one of the earliest large-scale Maya excavation programs was at Chichen Itza (Morris, Charlot, and Morris, 1931; Ruppert, 1935); and in recent years investigations of a comparable scale have been carried out at Mayapan (Pollock, *et al.*, 1962). More recent-

6. Postclassic seminar, 1982. Photo by David Noble. Courtesy of the School of American Research (left to right, seated: David A. Freidel, W. Wyllys Andrews V, Diane Chase, Prudence Rice, Jeremy Sabloff. Left to right, standing: Fernando Robles C., Arlen F. Chase, Joseph W. Ball, David Pendergast, Anthony P. Andrews, Arthur G. Miller.

ly there has been a spate of work on Postclassic sites and problems, much of which will be referred to further along and which provides much of the basic data for this volume. Nevertheless, as will be apparent to the reader, research on the Lowland Maya Postclassic centuries is only now becoming of major concern, and these seminar proceedings should serve as a stimulus for a continuation of this interest.

My plan is to survey the Maya Lowlands on the three major horizons of the Terminal Classic, the Early Postclassic, and the Late Postclassic. In doing this for each time horizon I will proceed by regions, or "zones" as these have been called in a recent cultural-geographical breakdown of the Maya Lowlands (Hammond and Ashmore, 1981, see map Fig. 2.1, reproduced on page 156). Following this horizonal treatment

I will recapitulate, very briefly, by presenting salient points of the main data from a diachronic perspective within each zone. In this data survey emphasis will be upon site presence, upon architecture, monuments, residential units, and general settlement pattern. Such information will be related, especially for relative dating purposes, to ceramics. As I see my task, I am to attempt to draw together, in a preliminary single article, the form and substance of the Postclassic occupation (as well as its Terminal Classic immediate antecedents) of the Maya Lowlands.

The Terminal Classic

Any closeup examination of the Postclassic must begin with the antecedent Terminal Classic Period (A.D. 800–1000). These last two centuries of the first millennium A.D. were obviously a time of radical culture change in the Maya Lowlands. They were also a time of change and unrest in much of Mesoamerica. In the southern Lowlands the ninth century saw the decline and abandonment of the great Maya cities—the so-called collapse. Farther to the north events were somewhat different, but change was also in the making.

Let us begin with the Central Zone (see map p. 156 for this and all other zonal locations), the heartland of Classic Maya development in the Lowlands. The ninth century corresponds to the Tepeu 3 ceramic phase and horizon in this zone. After A.D. 810 (9.19.0.0.0) major construction and stelae dedication virtually ceased at the major sites. In addition, there is good settlement evidence for a marked population drop, at least in and around some of the great centers. Thus, Culbert (1973b) estimates that the Tepeu 3 or Eznab population at Tikal was only one-tenth the size of its pre-A.D. 800 maximum. On the other hand, Arlen Chase (1979) states that "the central Peten appears to have been heavily populated during the Termi nal Classic Period." Chase may be referring mainly to the Lake Peten Itza- Tayasal vicinity, but there is some additional support for his views in the surveys which Anabel Ford (personal communication) has carried out in the region between Tikal and Yaxha as well as in the Barton Ramie data from the Belize Valley (Willey, *et al.*, 1965), where the Spanish Lookout phase subsumes both the Tepeu 2 and 3 horizons and where residential mound occupation may have remained more or less constant for this dura tion. In an appraisal of the Barton Ramie data (Willey, 1973b), with this point in mind, I was unable to come to any definite conclusions about it; but, suffice it to say, the problem of Tepeu 3 or ninth century population estimates for the Central Zone is still with us and is of high importance for it relates directly to the nature of the "collapse."

The ceramics of the Tepeu 3 horizon in the Central Zone derive out of the Maya Peten tradition of Tepeu 1 and 2, implying a resident continuity (Gifford, 1976; Chase, 1979; Rice and Rice, 1980). On this, Chase has made the point that the distinctions between Tepeu 2 and 3 ceramics are often difficult to make. One such distinction has been the presence of foreign fine-paste wares in Tepeu 3 contexts, but as Chase rightly cautions such styles may occur differentially at Maya sites and cannot be used uniformly as criteria for the Tepeu 3 time horizon.

For a long time the latter half of the Terminal Classic Period in the Central Zone, the century of A.D. 900–1000, was poorly known or its occupations not recognized. Prudence Rice (1979) once referred to a hiatus separating the end of Tepeu 3 ceramics from those of the Postclassic Isla phase at Topoxte, but is now inclined to doubt this (personal communication). Moreover, the Rice's (1979 Ms.) have recently made new excavations at Macanche Island, in Lake Macanche, also in the Peten Lakes district, which have established a sequence of ceramic types that appear to span the presumed hiatus. They refer to an unnamed early facet of what they designate as the Early Postclassic Period, but which probably falls in the tenth century. This unnamed facet consists of three unslipped types which, they say, would be at home in earlier Tepeu 3 contexts, thus suggesting some resident continuity from Terminal Classic to Early Postclassic. These types are found along with those of later recognized groups, such as those designated as Pozo, Trapeche, and Paxcaman. The early facet complex shows few trade ties to other regions or zones. There is no associated architecture of consequence. A reasonable interpretation would be that of a "post-collapse" population, which stayed on in the locality and, perhaps, was joined by immigrants from elsewhere. Chase's (1979) Lake Peten-Itza data may have a bearing on this Macanche possibility of a Terminal Classic-to-Postclassic continuity. He emphasizes the significance of the aforementioned Trapeche ceramic group as being earlier than and definitely transitional to Paxcaman group ceramics, and, as being at least partially contemporaneous with pottery known as the Augustine group. Augustine ceramics were considered by Bullard (1973) to be the earliest part of the New Town phase at Barton Ramie and, thus, to span the Classic-to-Postclassic transition at that site.

To sum up briefly to this point, there was a clear cessation of large center architectural and related activity in the Central Zone in the ninth century. There was some population continuity of residence although we do not yet know just how large this was in relation to previous Classic population figures. For the tenth century evidence is both scant and uncertain, but it would appear there was some minimal continuity of residence, at least.

Moving toward and into the Belize Zone, we look at some other locations of Terminal Classic activity. At Benque Viejo, the largest ceremonial center in the near vicinity of Barton Ramie, building activity was largely over by A.D. 800 although there was some elite use of the site for another 50 years (see Thompson, 1940a; MacKie, 1961). Whether or not the terminal Benque Viejo IV ceramic phase continued on into the tenth century is unknown. A series of caves in southern and central Belize—Actun Balam (Pendergast, 1969), Rio Frio Cave E (Pendergast, 1970), Actun Polbilche (Pendergast, 1974) and the Eduardo Quiroz Cave (Pendergast, 1964)—were all used by the Maya at the end of the Classic. Ceramics correlating with Tepeu 3 were found in the first two while the latter two showed both Tepeu 3 horizon and Early Postclassic materials. These finds suggest, perhaps, that religious and ritual activities may have been shifted to caves at a time when the old Classic ceremonial centers were being abandoned (Collea, 1981 MS.)

In northern Belize, near but not on the coast, Altun Ha (Pendergast, 1967, 1979), which had been very active in the Early Classic, showed a constructional decline in the Late Classic, continuing into the Terminal Classic, and then stopping altogether. The cessation here was accompanied by the desecration of earlier tombs and buildings. This, apparently, was done by a population that continued to live on the site. There was then some modest construction in the Postclassic, probably both Early and Late. At San Jose, also in the north but further inland, there is good evidence of Terminal Classic activity (Thompson, 1939). This is a small-sized ceremonial center which was occupied from Preclassic times through the Terminal Classic. Its San Jose IV phase (*ca.* A.D. 800–900) is on the Tepeu 3 time level, during which there was some constructional activity; but this activity also continues through San Jose V (*ca.* A.D. 900–1000). This constructional activity is unusual for the Terminal Classic, especially its latter half. While there is no radiocarbon dating for San Jose, Thompson's ceramic analyses of the phases would appear to support the chronological placements. Terminal Classic vigor is shown even more strongly at Lamanai. This is a major center, much larger than San Jose, located somewhat north of the latitude of the latter site and Altun Ha but about equidistant between the two of them (Pendergast, 1981). Two of its major building complexes were initiated in the Terminal Classic, and construction continued on these until well into the Postclassic Period. Located on a large lagoon connected to the Caribbean by the New River, Lamanai was well sited for trade, and the evidences for this have been found abundantly at the center. Moving still farther north, the substantial center and occupation area of Colha also gives evidence of a vigorous continuity of constructional and other elite activities through the Tepeu 3 horizon (Adams and Valdez, 1980; Hester, *et al.*, 1980). Then, however, at about A.D. 900, the Terminal Classic occupation was ended violently, an event seen in the archaeological record in what are interpreted as mass pit-burials of the elite. There is an Early Postclassic occupation at Colha, but it is not accompanied by large-scale building. In far northern Belize, Nohmul, on the Rio Hondo is a major center which was largely constructed in Preclassic and Classic times; however, there are some indications of Late Classic-to-Early Postclassic building continuity and use in some of its structures (Hammond, 1974; personal communication, A. F. and D. Z. Chase).

We see, then, that in northern Belize the story is somewhat different. Terminal Classic elite activity continued well into that period. Acts of violence appear to have terminated this activity at some sites; at others, such as Lamanai, the entire Terminal Classic Period seems to have been an active one, with evidences of continuity into the Early Postclassic.

To continue with our zonal survey of the Terminal Classic, the Pasíon Zone lies to the south of the Central and Belize Zones and includes the southernmost part of Belize and the Pasíon drainage of the Peten. There are some major centers in southern Belize. The one most thoroughly reported upon is Lubaantun (Hammond, 1975a), and, because of its Tepeu 2–3 occupation, it is also the most germane to our Terminal Classic survey. Hammond places the last major building activity at the site at about A.D. 850; after that the site ceased to exist as a major center. The two largest centers on the Pasíon are Altar de Sacrificios and Seibal. Altar, which lies at the confluence of the Chixoy-Salinas-Usumacinta system with the Pasíon, has a long history extending into Tepeu 2–3 times. Its Boca phase is essentially contemporaneous with Tepeu 3 and the earlier half of the Terminal Classic Period. It was not a time of either important building (Smith, 1972) or stelae dedication (J. Graham, 1972) although there was a considerable resident population at the site (Adams, 1971; Willey, 1973a, b). However, it should be pointed out that Altar is situated on what amounts to a small riverine-swamp island. This island was thoroughly surveyed, and our settlement data in support of the above statement derive from this. We do not know much about the lower Pasíon Valley (presumably the support area for Altar de Sacrificios) settlement pattern changes through time. The Jimba phase succeeds the Boca at Altar, and its estimated dating is A.D. 900–1000. There was no public building during the phase although the site continued to be occupied. It has been speculated that the Jimba phase represents the invasion of an alien people (Sabloff and Willey,

1967), perhaps Putun or Chontal Maya from the Tabasco Gulf Coast (Willey, 1973a, b). The ceramics of the Jimba phase are fine paste wares, the Terminal Classic Fine Oranges and Fine Greys (Adams, 1971). The phase is also marked by the appearance of fine paste figurines which break with the Classic Maya figurine tradition in presenting images of a non-typical Maya physical type. In discussing fine paste wares and figurines, it should be noted that these began to appear during the Boca phase; however, they were then a minority addition to the total ceramic complex. In the Jimba phase virtually all pottery is fine paste. After the close of the Jimba phase (*ca.* A.D. 1000) Altar de Sacrificios was abandoned.

Seibal had a quite different history from Altar de Sacrificios. There is a long sequence of occupation here, but some of the most impressive buildings and stelae date to the Terminal Classic Period (Willey et al., 1975). This latest phase at Seibal is contemporaneous with Tepeu 3, is in a Peten ceramic tradition, but the assemblage is heavily laced with Fine Orange/Fine Gray increments. The several stelae which date to the phase—from 10. 1.0.0.0 to 10.3.0.0.0—are in a style of portraiture that suggests "foreign," probably Chontal-Putun, influences (Thompson, 1970). Shortly thereafter, however, at about A.D. 930, this major center was abandoned. The extensive settlement pattern surveys made in a five kilometer radius around Seibal have not yet been fully analyzed nor published (Tourtellot, 1970); however, if house mound occupation continued beyond A.D. 930 it would appear to have been of a very minor nature.

The Southeast Zone is the Motagua-Chamelecon region of Guatemala and western Honduras. The two main sites here are Quirigua, in the Motagua flood plain, and Copan, on an upper Motagua tributary in the hill-and-valley country toward the South. Quirigua (Jones and Sharer, 1980) was a vigorous center in the Late Classic. Major construction was going on as late as 9.19.0.0.0 (A.D. 810) and for a few years thereafter. Subsequently, there is little in the way of a building record and no more stelae dedications. The site, however, continued to be occupied throughout the Terminal Classic and into the Early Postclassic, before being finally abandoned at about A.D. 1250.

Copan also had a brilliant Late Classic development, and the center drew upon large outlying residential populations in the Copan Valley (Willey and Leventhal, 1979). Shortly after A.D. 800 it ceased to be an important city. Some Early Postclassic ceramic markers, such as Nicoya polychromes and Plumbate ware, have been found in superficial levels of the main center or in occasional tombs there (Longyear, 1952), so it is likely that there was some scattered occupation or use of the main site; nevertheless, it is fair to say that the old Maya Classic culture, and most of the population that went with it, had been dissipated by the beginning of the Terminal Classic Period.

The western part of the Maya Lowlands has been defined in terms of three zones: the Usumacinta, along the middle course of that stream and including the major site of Piedras Negras; the Southwestern Zone, lying to the west, and including Tonina and Chinkultic; and the Northwestern Zone, of the Lower Usumacinta drainage and including Palenque. Piedras Negras, the best-studied site in the Usumacinta Zone, probably erected its last dated monument in 9.18.5.0.0 (A.D. 795) although it is possible that such activity continued for another katun-and-a-half at this center. The Chacalhaaz ceramic phase at Piedras Negras corresponds to the Tepeu 2 horizon and tradition. Subsequently, the short-lived Tamay phase, sherds of which are found superficially in post-architectural levels, breaks clearly with the Peten Tepeu tradition and is represented by fine paste wares. Most of these fine paste wares however, are not the Fine Orange and Fine Gray types seen in the Terminal Classic phases of Altar de Sacrificios or Seibal, but, instead, relate to the north, to Tabasco, Campeche, and Yucatan. A few scattered Fine Orange and Fine Gray sherds, which would be at home in the late phases of Altar and Seibal, have been found at Piedras Negras, but it is believed that these postdate Tamay (Rands, 1973b). Stelae dedication at other Usumacinta Zone sites waned or died at about the same time as it did at Piedras Negras: Bonampak (9.18.10.0.0 or A.D. 800), La Mar (9.18.15.0.0 or A.D. 805), El Cayo (9.19.0.0.0 or A.D. 810), and Yaxchilan (between 9.19.0.0.0 and 10.0.10.0.0 or between A.D. 810 and 840) (see Rands, 1973a for a summation of these datings and Proskouriakoff, 1950, 1960, 1964 and Ruppert, Thompson, and Proskouriakoff, 1955). In sum, the Usumacinta Zone major centers appear to have given up about a century before those of the Pasion drainage.

At Toniná, in the Southwestern Zone, elite activity trailed off more gradually than in the Usumacinta Zone. Becquelin (1979 Ms.) reports a decline in monuments after A.D. 805; however, some continued to be erected until A.D. 909 (10.4.0.0.0). At that date or shortly after, Toniná suffered a brutal desecration and destruction of monuments and sculptures, and the site appears to have been abandoned for a time. There is, however, a scattered Early Postclassic occupation of the site; but in this period the most important center of the Ocosingo Valley was Chamun and not Toniná. At Chinkultic (Ball, 1980) there was continuity of elite architecture and stelae dedication from Late Classic into Terminal Classic in the Yobnajab phase (A.D. 700–900). The late facet of this phase shows Altar Fine Orange and related Fine Gray pottery. The succeeding Tepancuapan phase (A.D. 900–1250?) has ceramic continuity out of Yobnajab, with fine paste wares present in its early facet. There is also some constructional continuity into this latter, essentially Early Postclassic phase.

The Northwestern Zone is the lower Usumacinta and environs and includes such sites as Palenque, Jonuta, Trinidad, and others, known from the surveys of Rands (1967a, b, 1973b, 1979) and Berlin (1953, 1956). The zone lies largely outside of the Peten ceramic traditions, and it is, without much question, the original hearth of the fine paste wares which date here to well back into the Classic Period. The later and better known Altar and Balancan Fine Oranges, which are Tepeu 3 time markers on the Pasíon and upper Usumacinta, have their derivations here in the Northwestern Zone. At Palenque an Early Balunte phase, which has continued Classic-type constructional activities, correlates chronologically with the latter part of Tepeu 2. The ceramics are largely fine paste but do not include Balancan or Altar types. The subsequent Late Balunte phase, estimated to the first half of the ninth century, is the time of constructional decline and cessation. Some Balancan sherds appear at this time. After what may have been a short period of abandonment, there is a reoccupation which has been dated as Early Postclassic although it may have been confined largely to the end of the Terminal Classic Period (ca. A.D. 900–1000). At Jonuta Initial Series dates are missing, but some sculptures there have been placed stylistically by Proskouriakoff in an A.D. 750–810 time range; and these, interestingly, show non-Classic Maya elements (Thompson, 1970). The site, however, is best known from the subsequent Jonuta horizon which is dated at about 9.19.0.0.0 to 10.5.0.0.0 or from A.D. 810 to 928, in effect to the early half of the Terminal Classic. The Jonuta horizon ceramics are in fine paste wares and include Balancan Fine Orange and related Fine Grays. The end of the horizon is, apparently, coeval with the late reoccupation at Palenque.

The Northwestern Zone must be of particular interest in any consideration of the Terminal Classic Period for it was apparently the homeland of the Chontal or Putun Maya (Thompson, 1970) who have been considered by some to have been the instigators of the Classic "collapse" in the southern Lowlands (see Willey and Shimkin, 1973, for a summary of such views). This question is a complex one, and direct Chontal or Putun invasion of the Pasíon Valley, via the Usumacinta (see Sabloff and Willey, 1967), is not the only possibility, or certainly no more than a part of it. It is also reasonably certain that Chontal or Putun influences began to impinge on the Late Classic cultures of northern Yucatan toward the close of the eighth century A.D., resulting in the synthesis of the Puuc florescence of the Terminal Classic (Ball, 1974); and it may have been from this latter base that Chontal-Putun invaders moved southward in the Terminal Classic Period to such a center as Seibal (Thompson, 1970; Willey, 1973a; Sabloff, 1975; Ball, 1974).

The Campeche and Central Yucatan Zones lie to the northeast of the lower Usumacinta country. Some surveys have been conducted along the Campeche coast, extending from the edge of the Northwestern Zone around the Laguna de Terminos as far north as the city of Campeche (Eaton, 1978; Ball, 1978). This reconnaissance indicates major site construction activities through the Terminal Classic and probably into the Early Postclassic. Fine Orange and Fine Gray ceramics, comparable to those of the Jonuta horizon, are present in the ceramic complexes.

The Central Yucatan zone is known for the Rio Bec–Chenes architectural tradition of the Late Classic Period (Potter, 1977). The best known sequence is that established at Becan by Ball (1977c) where the Rio Bec style buildings date from the Bejuco phase (A.D. 600–750). This is followed by a short Chintok phase (A.D. 750–830) during which constructional activity declines and ends. The story at the nearby site of Chicanna is similar, with the last structure there dating to the end of Chintok (Eaton, 1974). At both sites, however, there is evidence of an immediately subsequent "squatter-type" occupation, that of the Xcocom phase (A.D. 830–1100), spanning the Terminal Classic and extending into the Early Postclassic. In Ball's (1974) opinion, Xcocom ceramics show a synthesis of older resident traditions with the introduction of new modes brought by an invasion or migration of peoples from the north. This interpretation relates to our foregoing comments about Chontal-Putun infiltrations into northern Yucatan and the subsequent movements of these peoples and cultural traditions to the south during the Terminal Classic. New ceramic types in the Xcocom assemblages include Balancan Fine Orange. An interesting observation in connection with the Xcocom culture is that while the populations of this phase occupied the old Bejuco and Chintok temples and palaces as residences, they did not continue to maintain and use the extensive system of agricultural terraces which had been an important feature of Late Classic life in the Becan-Chicanna vicinity.

The Northern Plains Zone covers the northwestern and central portions of the Yucatan Peninsula. Here, quite unlike the events of the Maya Lowlands in most of the south, the Terminal Classic Period was a time of vigorous ceremonial center construction and maintenance. In the local regional chronology this is referred to as the Pure Florescent Period (Andrews IV, 1965; Ball, 1974). At Puuc sites, such as Uxmal, this corresponds to the Cehpech (R. E. Smith, 1971) ceramic phase. Ball (1974) has argued, and I think rightly so, that Puuc and Pure Florescent architectural adornment is strongly "Mexicanized" (see also Sharp, 1981). He would further link this to the Chontal-Putun incursions into northern Yucatan beginning in the latter part of the eighth century. Ball (1974) sees the founding of Chichen Itza in A.D. 780–800 as a "first-coming" of a Chontal-Putun group known as the Itza. They were responsible for the Pure Florescent or Puuc style buildings at that site during the Terminal Classic Period. And they are to be distinguished from a "second-coming" of Itzas to Chichen, perhaps also Chontal-Putun, who were responsible for the Early Postclassic Toltec phase of the site's history.

The sequence at Dzibilchaltun, in far northern Yucatan (Andrews IV and Andrews V 1980), parallels that at Chichen Itza in part. The Pure Florescent or Terminal Classic Period, which lasted from A.D. 800/830 to 1000, was one of considerable architectural activity and this in the Puuc style. The ceramics of the Copo 2 phase are contemporaneous. They show resident continuity out of the earlier Copo 1 (A.D. 600–800) styles but with the addition of new types, including Fine Oranges and Fine Grays and Thin Slate ware. Copo 2 pottery is coeval with, and related to, Smith's (1971) Cehpech complex. Unlike Chichen Itza, Dzibilchaltun has no building activity in the immediately following Modified Florescent or Early Postclassic Period. The site was, however, occupied at this time, and this occupation is referred to as the Zipche 1 ceramic phase which is coordinate in time with Smith's (1971) Sotuta complex. The period of Zipche 1 (A.D. 1000–1125/50) is, of course, the time of Chichen Itza's great Toltec Early Postclassic growth. In Zipche 2 (A.D. 1125/50–1200) there was a modest building revival at Dzibilchaltun which then continued on into the Late Postclassic.

Ball (1974) has stated that the Terminal Classic (Pure Florescent) Period in the Northern Lowlands Zone was a time of prosperity and peace. On the first score there seems to be no argument. As he has said elsewhere, Puuc architecture represents the apogee of Lowland Maya great building construction—perhaps of all Mesoamerican architectural achievement. Cities such as Uxmal, Kabah, Sayil, and Chichen Itza of the Pure Florescent Period are without rivals. On the second score, that of peace, I would be less certain. Webster (1978) has described three smaller places— Chaccob, Cuca, and Dzonot Ake—which are walled, probably for defense, and which appear to date from the Terminal Classic. On a more general interpretive level, it seems at least likely that in a period of growth of populations there would have been increasing rivalry among centers. Moreover, this was also, as has been argued, a period of Chontal-Putun infiltration which suggests another source of unrest. Finally, that the Terminal Classic in the Northern Plains was brought to an end by the "second coming" of the Itza at Chichen, and the very militaristic overtones of this event, is a further suggestion that the political climate of the period may have been a warlike one.

We are left with the remainder of northern Yucatan, the East Coast Zone, which consists largely of the state of Quintana Roo. The zone was well occupied in the Classic Period, with Coba the largest city of that time; however, Coba was abandoned prior to the Terminal Classic. But a number of lesser sites show continued Terminal Classic occupation and building; among these are: Tancah (Sanders, 1960; Miller, 1977), Xelha (Andrews IV and A. P. Andrews, 1975), Calderitas (Sanders, 1960), El Diez (Sanders 1960), and others (Parry, 1981 Ms.). Architectural features in some of these sites relate them, in a marginal way, to what was going on in Puuc centers farther to the west. The off-coastal island of Cozumel enjoyed a marked population increase during the Terminal Classic, and this was accompanied with architectural construction (Freidel, 1976; Fogel, 1981 Ms.).

Can these statements about the Maya Lowland Terminal Classic Period, already synoptic to a high degree, be further reduced in any kind of a meaningful summary? I believe there are some general observations that can be made and will attempt to synthesize along such lines.

First, there is what we have known for a long time. This is that there was a decline and eventual cessation of elite politico-religious activities in the ninth century A.D. and this occurred over a large part of the Lowlands. The decline begins to be manifest at about A.D. 800—or at the beginning of what we have called the Terminal Classic Period. There is some regional and site-to-site variation in the speed of this decline, but complete or near-complete cessation of elite activities occurs by the end of the century. This decline-and-cessation is seen in the Central Zone, the southern and central portions of the Belize Zone, the Pasíon Zone, the Southeastern Zone, the Usumacinta Zone, and the Central Yucatan Zone. It is less pronounced in the Southwestern, Northwestern, and Campeche Zones.

Second, it appears that the succeeding tenth century, or the last half of the Terminal Classic Period, represents the very nadir of elite activity, and perhaps overall population decline, in those zones where the decline-and-cessation phenomenon was most pronounced. This is true even for Seibal, that rare exception in the Central Zone, where major building and stelae activity continued vigorously throughout the ninth century but where the site was abandoned immediately after that.

Third, the phenomenon of the ninth century decline and cessation of Classic elite activity did not occur in the Northern Plains Zone, in the East Coast Zone, and at certain sites in the northern part of the Belize Zone.

In the north, if anything, some of the most brilliant center construction took place during the Terminal Classic Period.

Fourth, while facts of decline and cessation in elite architectural and stelae dedicatory activities are there for all to see, events in the wider socio-economic sphere are less clear. How great were population losses? To what extent did large non-elite populations continue to occupy small centers and outlying hinterlands? This old problem in Lowland Maya settlement archaeology is still with us.

Fifth, the "Pure Florescence" of the Northern Lowlands contains within it, as expressed in architectural styles, sculpture, and iconography, as well as in ceramic traditions, "foreign" or "Mexicanoid" elements, suggesting that the continued vigor of the north during the ninth and tenth centuries owed something to "foreign" inspiration. That this inspiration may have come from invaders is a possibility, and such "invaders" have sometimes been identified as Chontal or Putun Maya; however, it is quite possible that more than a single group of "invaders" was involved. The new or alien influences are seen most clearly in the Northern Plains. They are present in northern Belize but less strong in the East Coast Zone. Presumably, the original homeland of these "foreigners" was the southern Gulf Coast of Mexico, in the Northwestern Zone. Neither here, however, nor in the adjacent Campeche coastal region, do you have the same architectural expressions as those found in the Northern Plains Pure Florescent sites of the Puuc tradition.

The Early Postclassic

The foregoing on the Terminal Classic Period has not only laid down a foundation for our consideration of the Early Postclassic but has anticipated it to a degree in referring to actual Early Postclassic sites and occupations. As a result, we can move somewhat more swiftly over the ground on this Early Postclassic time level; however, any examination of this period must bring us to Chichen Itza so let us change our geographical order in presentation and begin at that great site of the Northern Plains Zone.

The Toltec horizon at Chichen Itza is generally accepted as the beginning of the Postclassic Period, with a round date for its inception of A.D. 1000 (Thompson, 1941b). This horizon, and this Early Postclassic rebuilding of the site, has also been referred to by some as a "second Mexicanization" of the city or, as noted in our discussions of the Pure Florescent Period, a "second coming" of the Itza.

The Chichen I Period (A.D. 750–1000) refers to a Puuc-related city of the Pure Florescent Period (Tozzer, 1957). The ceramics of the period are in the tradition of the Thin and Medium Slatewares; Balancan and Altar Fine Orange types occur as trade (Brainerd, 1958). This is, in effect, the Cehpech (R. E. Smith, 1971) ceramic complex.

The Chichen II and III Periods subsume Tozzer's Toltec-Maya architectural Stages A and B. The period extends from A.D. 1000 to 1250, or the Early Postclassic Period. Tozzer's distinctions between the periods II and III are made in terms of specific buildings at the site and architectural styles and features of these buildings, supported to some extent by architectural stratigraphy. For the purposes of our survey the subdivisions within the period are not of great importance. Significant, perhaps, is the fact that these Toltec-Maya buildings were constructed immediately after Period I; there was no destruction, although there was some abandonment, of earlier buildings. There is some continuity in constructional techniques and even architectural styles between the earlier Puuc-related buildings of Period I and the Toltec-Maya buildings of Periods II–III. There are also some innovations: pyramidal temples without plinths, frequent use of columns, larger rooms supported by columns, gallery-patio arrangements making use of columns, and I-shaped, Tula-related, ball-courts. The ornamental iconography of the Toltec-Maya buildings is heavily Mexican or Toltec. The associated ceramics (Sotuta phase) remain in the Slateware tradition, and trade wares include Silho or X-Fine Orange and Tohil Plumbate. Except for trade types, the pottery is distinctly local and not that of Tula proper or Central Mexican Toltec assemblages. Tozzer's Chichen IV Period belongs to the Late Postclassic and pertains to a "squatter-type" occupation of the site or to its later use as a pilgrimmage and sacrificial center.

Attempts to correlate Chichen archaeology with the legendary history of the Books of Chilam Balam (Roys, 1933) are the source of considerable controversy (see Thompson, 1941; Tozzer, 1957; Roys in Pollock *et al.*, 1962). Are the Itzas to be identified with the Pure Florescent Period founders of the city in A.D. 780–800? Or did they arrive in A.D. 987 and found the Toltec-Maya city on the location of the earlier one? Were the Chontal-Putun involved on both occasions? To what extent were Tula Toltecs a part of the conquest of A.D. 987? Or are the Itzas to be identified with a group who first saw Chichen in the 12th century probably after its abandonment and who, from their base at Mayapan, used the earlier city only as a sacred pilgrimmage center? As far as the specifics of history go, I am more inclined to accept the last interpretation about the Itza (Geselowitz, 1981 Ms.). In wider archaeological perspective, and in the context of our seminar, I think that the important point is that the Maya of the Northern Plains had long been under Mexican influences, both ideologically and commercially, and that these were probably mediated through the Chontal-Putun.

One of the problems and complexities of the Early Postclassic Period in the northern Maya Lowlands is what appears to be a lack of other large sites in the Chichen Maya-Toltec tradition. That is, Chichen Itza is not only a paramount city of the period; it is the only great city. There are, of course, some indications in the archaeological record, as well as in the legendary historical or ethnohistorical record, that former Terminal Classic Period sites, such as the great Puuc center of Uxmal, continued to be occupied and continued to play a part in the political history of the area. But there was no significant building at these places. On the face of it, it would appear that the power establishment at Chichen Itza thoroughly reduced the rest of the northern Yucatan Peninsula to a subordinate political status. Perhaps significantly, in connection with coastal trade or with salt production, there are substantial occupations of Early Postclassic date at a number of coastal sites in the Northern Plains and East Coast Zones. Eaton (1978) refers to some of these, including Emal and Xcopte, both located on salt lagoons; and he notes that "materials collected from Xcopte suggest occupation by foreigners, possibly those called Itza, who appear to have had control of the salt beds." (Eaton, 1978, p. 64). Other Early Postclassic coastal sites are Vista Alegre and Chiquila, first noted by Sanders (1960), and about which Eaton (Ibid., p. 65) says: "Their large structures suggest a relatively rich economy which may have been based more on commerce than on agricultural produce and salt collection. They are not located close to any known salt beds."

In the interior, away from the coasts, there was a continued occupancy at several sites but no notable Early Postclassic construction. The Zipche 1 phase occupation, already mentioned in the Terminal Classic discussions of Dzibilchaltun, would be an example. In the interior of the East Coast Zone, El Diez, Monte Bravo, and Santa Maria all show Early Postclassic ceramics (Parry, 1981 Ms.). A search of the literature showed little Early Postclassic evidences on Cozumel (Fogel, 1981 Ms.), and Connor (1975) notes a decrease in ceramic remains from the Terminal Classic into Early Postclassic. Freidel (1976) does, however, date one group of structures to the Early Postclassic Period, and Robles (personal communication) says that the period is well-represented on the island.

Our Early Postclassic survey of other Lowland Maya Zones can move more rapidly. Campeche Zone sites—the Islas Jaina, Piedras, and Uaymil—continued to be used during the period although it is doubtful if it was a time of major construction. To the west and south, in the Northwestern Zone, there is little that can be identified as Early Postclassic, and the same is true for the Usumacinta Zone. In the far Southwestern Zone we have already referred to the establishment of an Early Postclassic center in the Ocosingo Valley following the fall of Tonina; and at Chinkultic there was some ceramic and constructional continuity from the Terminal Classic into the Early Postclassic Tepancuapan phase.

In the Central Yucatan Zone we have mentined Terminal Classic-to-Early Postclassic ceramic continuity in the Xcocom phase (A.D. 830–1100); but this has been described as "squatter" activity on earlier Rio Bec–Chenes centers.

The Pasion Zone shows no evidence of elite class activity for the Early Postclassic although Gair Tourtellot (personal communication) reports a scatter of sherds for the period on the peripheries of Seibal.

In the Southeastern Zone Copan had no history of consequence in the Early Postclassic. At Quirigua, occupation, as indicated by ceramics, continued after the cessation of major building and stelae dedications, and this occupation lasted through the Early Postclassic.

In the northern sites of the Belize Zone there is considerable evidence of Early Postclassic building. Terminal Classic-to-Early Classic continuity of ceremonial center construction has already been alluded to at Lamanai and Altun Ha; and to these we can add the site of Cerros, a major Late Preclassic center, abandoned during the Classic, and then rebuilt in the Early Postclassic (David Freidel, personal communication 1981). At Colha there is also some modest Early Postclassic construction which followed the Terminal Classic destruction of that site. At this point it seems worth noting that, just as in the Terminal Classic, northern Belize shows Early Postclassic building activity, unlike the rest of the southern Maya Lowlands. With regard to Early Postclassic ceramics in northern Belize, A. F. and D. Z. Chase inform me (personal communication) that these relate to Payil Red, a variety of Tulum Red, and so link to the East Coast.

This brings us back to the Central Zone. Prudence Rice (1979) would place the New Town late facet, at Barton Ramie, in the Early Postclassic. The Barton Ramie data are ceramic and come from house mound occupations. Prudence Rice (personal communication) has called my attention to temple assemblages and large structures at Muralla de Leon and Zacpeten, in the Peten lakes country so some elite activity was going on in some places; however, neither its volume nor its elaboration is very impressive when compared to Late Classic standards for the Central Zone. The Islas phase ceramics from the eastern Peten lakes country is seen by Prudence Rice as contemporaneous with New Town pottery. In the western Peten lakes country the Trapeche and Augustine pottery groups pertain to the Early Postclassic, and both of these groups show some continuity, or at least chronological overlap, with Paxcaman and Topoxte group wares. Both of the later groups continue on through the subsequent Late Post-classic Period (see Chase, 1979; P. Rice, 1979, Rice and Rice, 1979 Ms. I am also indebted to the Chases and the Rices for personal communications on these points).

The available archaeological site reports which I have consulted in the preparation of this overview offered little as to the presence or absence of Early Postclassic public or ceremonial architecture. Bullard's (1970) Topoxte Island report seemed to indicate that all of the major building at that site dates as Late Postclassic; however, Prudence Rice has pointed out to me (personal communication) that Bullard's excavations were on the main island only. New settlement and architectural data on the Peten Postclassic as a whole have been presented by D. S. Rice in the present volume—data not available to me at the time of the writing of this paper. Even in the light of this new information, which I will not attempt to incorporate here, I am still of the opinion that elite architectural activity in the zone in Postclassic times was not impressive.

What are the Early Postclassic generalizations?

First, the establishment of a Toltec-related presence, by whatever means or processes, at Chichen Itza at about A.D. 1000 is the marker event for the inception of the period. Following this, there can be little doubt but that Chichen then became the power center of the northen Maya Lowlands for approximately the next 200 years.

Second, this Toltec presence at Chichen climaxed a gradual cultural "Mexicanization" of parts of the Maya Lowlands which had begun and continued throughout the preceding Terminal Classic Period. This "Mexicanization" of the Maya is believed to have been mediated through the Chontal or Putun Maya who may, or may not, have been the group responsible for the Toltec establishment at Chichen. This generalization relates to, or is essentially the same as, the one made in our Terminal Classic Period summary.

Third, during the Early Postclassic Period there is a scarcity of major sites and major site activity throughout the northern lowlands. It is assumed that this relates to Chichen Itza's dominance. The only exceptions—although these are not major sites in an architectural sense—are several coastal locations which may have served as salt-collecting or fishing stations or trading ports.

Fourth, elsewhere in the Maya Lowlands activity and occupation was spotty or non-existent during the Early Postclassic Period. To be sure, there was some continued occupation and even public building activity. We have noted this in Belize, at Nohmul and Lamanai, as well as Colha. Some coastal sites were occupied in the Northwestern Zone; there was some activity in the Southwestern Zone; at Quirigua, in the Southeastern Zone, occupation but not major building continued; little seems to have been going on in the Pasion and Usumacinta Zones. In the Central Zone, we have referred to residential site occupations on the upper Belize river and around the Peten lakes. Thre was also some—but to my mind modest—elite activity in the lake country.

Fifth, the close of the Early Postclassic Period occurs with the dissolution or withdrawal of the Toltec presence, and its power, at Chichen Itza. This occurred sometime during the first half of the 13th century.

The Late Postclassic

Mayapan (Pollack *et al.*, 1962), in the Northern Lowlands Zone, is the principal Late Postclassic center of the Maya Lowlands. A scattering of Terminal Classic sherds (Cehpech phase) come from the lowest levels of the site; and an even smaller number of Early Postclassic (Sotuta phase) sherds have been recorded there; but no architectural remains date to either of these periods. Site construction of any scale begins at Mayapan in the brief Hocaba phase (A.D. 1250–1300) and continues in the succeeding Tases phase (A.D. 1300–1450). This Tases phase ceramic complex represents what has come to be thought of as the Mayapan ceramic horizon (see R. F. Smith, 1971, for Mayapan pottery analyses).

Ceramic continuity from the Early Postclassic Sotuta phase of Chichen Itza to Late Postclassic Mayapan is minimal. Only one style, Peto Cream Ware, which occurs at Chichen late in the Sotuta phase, is found in the Hocaba phase at Mayapan. It is of interest, however, to note that the Hocaba phase complex is present at Chichen where it occurs in contexts suggesting a "squatter" occupation after the abandonment of the Early Postclassic public buildings.

The Tases phase pottery of Mayapan is characterized by a distinctive Mayapan Red Ware and by unslipped modelled effigy-censers. The Tases phase is completely post-Plumbate in time and also postdates the Fine Orange marker-type Silho; however, a few sherds of Matillas Fine Orange (formerly V-Fine Orange) are found as foreign increments in the assemblage.

Mayapan is a walled city of concentrated residential settlement clustered around a ceremonial or civic center. Population for the 4.2 sq. km. found within the wall is estimated at 11–12,000 persons, and to this might be added another couple of thousand who lived in residential units immediately outside of the wall. The form of the wall, with its parapet-like feature, suggests a defensive function (Webster, 1976, 1978). Richard Ebright (1981 Ms.) has emphasized the discontinuities and dissimilarities between Mayapan and Chichen Itza architecture. The Mayapan dry, slab-and-block masonry is in strong contrast to the finished and elegant stucco-and-veneer styles of Early Postclassic Chichen. Shrines and oratories, which are a common feature of Mayapan, are not found at Chichen; and ball-courts and sweat-houses, well known at Chichen, are missing at Mayapan. The typical Mayapan residential unit has what is known as the "tandem front-back room plan." The front room is open along most of its length, with wooden posts or stone columns supporting the lintel. A low, wide bench lines the rear and the two ends of this front room. The closed rear room, entered by a central doorway, has no benches although sometimes it may have a small altar abutting the center of its back wall. With this use of columns and the presence of an altar or shrine, this residential unit has a generic similarity to the Mayapan shrines and oratories. This Mayapan "tandem" house plan and this tradition of Mayapan architecture has no known antecedents (Freidel, 1981a). There are, of course, a few well-known continuities between Chichen and Mayapan architecture: the Mayapan central "Castillo," with its resemblances to the building of the same name at Chichen Itza; a serpent-columned temple that suggests Chichen's "High Priest' Grave"; and a round structure that is something of a homologue in the Chichen Itza Caracol. But even in these examples there are differences between those at Chichen and their much cruder Mayapan counterparts.

To return to the questions of archaeology and legendary history that were raised in our comments of Chichen Itza, were both cities built by the Itzas? Thompson (1945, 1966), Brainerd (1958), and others have believed that they were. Roys (in Pollock, et al., 1962) thinks otherwise. In his opinion, the Toltecs erected Chichen and ruled there until they were expelled ca. A.D. 1200. The Itza then occupied the city, as "squatters" early in the 13th century. This, presumably, was after their expulsion from Chakanputun, an interpretation that would identify the Itza as Putun Maya. The Itza then founded Mayapan in 1263. They did this, however, in conjunction with the Cocom, and the latter gradually rose to prominence in the city's affairs. Richard Ebright sees a confirmation of this legendary historical and ethnohistorical data in the archaeology. The Hocaba phase "squatter" occupation of Chichen is to be correlated with the Itza's arrival and short stay at that site early in the 13th century. The Hocaba phase founding of the city of Mayapan corresponds reasonably well with Itza founding and cominance there; the subsequent Tases phase sees the supremacy of the Cocom element in the city. Mayapan was abandoned sometime in the middle of the 15th century. This occurred, according to the legendary historical sources, in an atmosphere of tribal rivalries and civil war.

Archaeological knowledge of the Late Postclassic in the Northern Plains and East Coast Zones is still spotty. In early historic times there was a concentration of population in the northwest interior of the Yucatan Peninsula (Freidel, 1981a). This is the general region of Mayapan, and it seems likely that there were other Late Postclassic centers here. At Dzibilchaltun, which is 40 km. north of Mayapan, there was a modest-sized resident population during the period. Some public or ceremonial building continued from Early Postclassic times, and hieroglyphic medallion texts in one building appear to date from A.D., 1392 to 1431, contemporary with the Tases phase occupation at Mayapan. Dzibilchaltun Late Postclassic ceramics, designated as the Chechem phase, include such Mayapan diagnostics as Peto Cream and Mayapan Red. Dzibilchaltun continued to be occupied after the fall of Mayapan and was an active site up until Colonial times (Andrews IV and Andrews V, 1980).

Another Late Postclassic population concentration was along the East Coast of Quintana Roo. We have already noted that there were some sites there in Early Postclassic times, but the later period shows an increase in size and numbers of locations. Sanders (1960) surveyed a number of these. Beginning at the northeast, there is Vista Alegre, also referred to in the Early Postclassic discussion and a site which appears as a sizable town in early Spanish accounts (see Lothrop, 1924). Others include Ichpaatun, Xelha, Tulum (see Lathrop, 1924), and Tancah, to name only a few. The walled city or town of Tulum is linked closely to Mayapan in its architecture and ceramics. The Late Postclassic also saw population and site increase on Cozumel Island (Sabloff and Rathje, eds., 1975; Sabloff, 1977), which has been interpreted as an important link in a Maya coastwise trading system of the period. Such a system was undoubtedly tied to the Mayapan polity, but it also may have enjoyed a kind of semi-independent status as an "international port-of-trade" enclave. The "internationalism" of this system seems further supported by a style of mural painting found at Tulum and as far south as Santa Rita (Gann, 1900) in Belize. The style resembles the Mixteca-Puebla codices of the Late Postclassic (Robertson, 1970).

A more recently discovered Late Postclassic site concentration has been reported upon by Harrison (1979, 1981) in the interior of southern Quintana Roo. Harrison refers to this Late Postclassic culture as the Lobil phase, drawing upon a sample of eighty-one sites. It is characterized by rough stone constructions, in general in keeping with the stone masonry styles and techniques of Mayapan. These constructions, in some cases, have been built over earlier, Classic Period elite buildings; in other instances they are ground-level, residential-appearing low platforms. Associated ceramics link to Tases phase censers and redwares of Mayapan. Harrison states that his survey seems to indicate that Lobil style architectural remains extend from south-central Campeche, across all of southern Quintana Roo, and into northern Belize in the vicinity of Chetumal Bay. All of this, preliminary and tentative as it may be, implies a sizable Late Postclassic population for a large part of the Maya Lowlands lying well to the south of northern Yucatan.

To continue the Late Postclassic survey toward the south, we have evidence of only "squatter-type" occupation of the major sites of the Central Yucatan Zone. Becan is an example, where Mayapan-like effigy-censers are found occasionally and superficially (Ball, 1974, 1977c). This, of course, leaves out of account what has just been said about the Lobil phase distribution which is reported as extending as far west as south-central Campeche, and this could be considered within the Central Yucatan zone. Ball (1978) has stated that the archaeological record along the coast of the Campeche Zone is somewhat disappointing for the Late Postclassic in view of early ethnohistoric accounts about that region. North of Champoton he found very little. There is a ceramic complex at Champoton (Ruz, 1969) which dates to the Late Postclassic on the basis of Matillas Fine Orange and Peto Cream sherds; and both Aguacatal (Xicalango) (Ruz, 1969; Matheny, 1970) and Tixchel (Ruz, 1969) are reported as having pottery collections of the period.

This edges us over into the coast of the Northwestern Zone where the site of Juarez, west of the Grijalva delta, was an impressive politico-religious center with a large residential population (Berlin, 1956; Jaeckel, 1981 Ms.). Much more large-scale digging needs to be done in a site like Juarcz to reveal its full history and dating; but, even on the basis of the information we have at present, there seems little doubt but that the Spanish accounts of important towns or cities along this section of the Gulf Coast do have some archaeological support. And, following these accounts, it seems certain that these towns were important coastal trading centers with ties into the system referred to from the east coast of Quintana Roo.

Farther inland in the Northwestern Zone, and on up the Usumacinta River into the Usumacinta Zone, there is no substantial Late Postclassic occupation recorded. Still further, in the Southwestern Zone, the Tepancuapan phase at the Chinkultic site and vicinity, which has been referred to under the Early Postclassic, may extend, on the basis of some ceramic finds, into Late Postclassic times although this is uncertain (Ball, 1980).

Switching back to the east, and to northern Belize, we can resume with the Late Postclassic evidences from the site of Santa Rita. The site had an earlier history, was abandoned, and then reoccupied and built over in the Late Postclassic. Constructions of this date, although relatively modest in size, contain the well-known murals which Robertson (1970) has designated as being in a Late Precolumbian Mesoamerican "international style." Diane Chase (1981) has also reported upon recent excavations into Late Postclassic platforms at the site. Also in northern Belize, the sites of Aventura, Chowacol, Cerros, and El Posito have Late Postclassic ceramics. A bit farther south, we come, again, to Lamanai which, it will be recalled, showed impressive public construction through the Terminal Classic and into the Early Postclassic. According to Pendergast (1981), there were also some small building projects at the site which date to the Late Postclassic or 14th and 15th centuries. Late Postclassic identifications rest upon pottery which is close to Mayapan Red Ware and Mayapan effigy-censers, and this raises a problem for the radiocarbon dates from Lamanai suggest a date of A.D. 1140, or a century or so before such styles appeared at Mayapan. Following up on this, Pendergast has suggested that the Mayapan Tases complex, which appears with some suddeness in northern Yucatan, may have had its origins in northern Belize. In southern Belize there is virtually nothing that can be placed as Late Postclassic. The exception is the site of Wild Cane Cay, off the coast, where a number of burials of this date have been found. The island also shows occupation up into Colonial times (Rice, 1974).

For the Pasion and Southeastern Zones there are no substantial data on the Late Postclassic.

In the Central Zone we have the Late Postclassic sites of the Isla phase from the Peten lakes district. There is a small, but clearly elite-style, architectural complex on Topoxte Island which is situated in Lake Yaxha (Bullard, 1970). The complex, which measures about 175 by 100 m., consists of temple and palace-type buildings arranged around courtyards. There are earlier constructional levels on the island and these date back to Classic and even Preclassic times. Late Postclassic buildings have been constructed over earlier Classic ones. There are a number of stelae and altars at the site. The sculptured ones are left from Classic times, but the plain ones (probably once painted and stuccoed) pertain to the Late Postclassic center. The Late Postclassic temples at Topoxte have wide doorways divided by columns, and, in general, resemble the Postclassic architecture of the Northern Plains and East Coast Zones. On the matter of relationships, however, Bullard (1970, p. 276) offers the caution:

> In sum, the visible architectural remains of the Isla Phase display a
> number of features which are characteristic of the Postclassic Period.
> Probably most indicative are the building plans using columns and

the stairway 'balustrades' with the vertical upper zones, as well as the concentrated settlement pattern and the island location. Certain architectural details—the slot-like basal moldings and the absence of medial moldings are two examples cited—appear to be local features on the basis of the little we know about Postclassic Maya architecture. Certainly, the resemblances between the Topoxte buildings and the known Postclassic buildings in Yucatan and Quintana Roo are not of such an order to support a belief that the Isla Phase represents a direct colonization from either of those areas.

The pottery of the Topoxte site is largely of the Topoxte pottery group, although some few sherds of Paxcaman wares were also present (Bullard, 1970). There seems to be a geographic division in the lakes district between Topoxte pottery, which is common in the east, and Paxcaman group pottery which is characteristic of the western lakes (P. Rice, 1979 and personal communication; A. F. Chase, 1979; A. F. and D. Z. Chase, personal communication; Rice and Rice, 1979 Ms.). Paxcaman has the somewhat earlier inception of the two, probably beginning in the Early Postclassic; Topoxte beginnings may not go back that far. In the eastern lakes country, at Macanche and Zacpeten, the Trapeche ceramic group, which had Early Postclassic beginnings, also continues into the Late Postclassic (P. Rice, personal communiction). While Isla phase and contemporaneous Late Postclassic Peten ceramic complexes probably had roots in the Peten Tepeu tradition, and in the Tepeu 3 phase of the Terminal Classic, there are, at the same time, elements within the Isla complex, such as the effigy censer forms, that imply contacts with the northern Lowlands, especially with the Tases horizon of Mayapan.

These ceramic similarities between the Peten lakes Isla phase and the Late Postclassic northern Lowlands may relate to legendary history and especially to the supposed arrival of the Itza in the Peten at an 8 Ahau katun ending (Thompson, 1951). Certainly, the Itza were in the lakes region in early historic times.[2] Was their 8 Ahau arrival in A.D. 1201 or 1458? My own guess would be the latter date. The date of 1458, obviously, would be too late for an introduction of Mayapan-derived ceramic traits which are so definitely associated with the Topoxte ceramic group (Chase and Chase, personal communication). Thus, it seems likely that there were introductions into the Peten lake country from the north, either by the processes of diffusion or migration, substantially in advance of a mid-fifteenth century arrival of the Itza.

Let us conclude this section with some Late Postclassic generalizations.

First, the key site of the period is Mayapan in the Northern Plains Zone. Mayapan retains some "Mexican" elements and some architectural resemblances to Chichen Itza; however, it is the position taken here that these resemblances have been overstressed. Mayapan culture is a new synthesis and an essentially Lowland Maya one. Its ceramic complex, especially that of its principal Tases phase, is quite different from that of Early Postclassic Chichen Itza; and it has been suggested that it may have origins in northern Belize.

Second, during the Late Postclassic Period there are many sites along the coast, especially the Quintana Roo coast. This follows a pattern observed in Early Postclassic coastal settlement except that in the later period it is much more pronounced.

Third, elsewhere in the Maya Lowlands there are sites along the Campeche and Northwestern Zone coasts, in the southern interior of the East Coast Zone, in the adjacent Central Yucatan Zone, in northern Belize, and around the Peten lakes in the Central Zone. There is some elite architectural construction associated with some of these Late Postclassic cultures. One has the impression, from architectural similarities and from related ceramic complexes, that a synthesis of a new, widespread Maya Lowland culture may have been in the making.

Fourth, it has been noted by many observers that the Late Postclassic of the Maya Lowlands was heavily oriented toward sea coast trade and traffic. This is expressed in site locations, in the presence of trade materials, and in early historic accounts.

Zonal Recapitulation

The foregoing treatment of the three time periods—Terminal Classic, Early Postclassic, and Late Postclassic—has been deliberately "horizontal" or synchronic in an attempt to relate what was going on, or seemed to be going on, at similar times throughout the Maya Lowlands. It might be well to summarize or recapitulate now on the "vertical" or diachronic dimension and to do this by the zonal subdivisions to which we have been referring.

The Central Zone. The Terminal Classic saw the relatively swift ninth century abandonment of the major centers. This abandonment is clearly registered in the decline and cessation of elite architectural and intellectual activities. There were either large-scale population losses or drastic population dispersals in many localities; however, in some places small sites or residential areas continued to be occupied. For the tenth century, or the latter half of the period, there is very little information.

The Early Postclassic sees occupation in some localities, especially around the Peten lakes. There was some elite activity, evidenced by temple assemblages and stelae; however, this was on a smaller scale than previous Classic building. In the Late Postclassic we have the integration of the Islas phase, with small ceremonial or civic centers in the lake district.

The Southeastern Zone. There was rapid decline here in the Terminal Classic. Copan ceased to be a center; Quirigua continued as an occupied place into the Early Postclassic although without stelae dedication or major building. The record stops after this.

The Pasíon Zone. The record is mixed for the Terminal Classic: Altar de Sacrificios declined; Seibal enjoyed a century of elite activity. Subsequently, the record trails off in this period, with no Postclassic occupation of consequence.

The Usumacinta Zone. Terminal Classic decline in this zone was swift and conclusive, occurring early on in the ninth century. There is no Postclassic record.

The Southwestern Zone. Elite activity continued through the ninth century of the Terminal Classic. At Chinkultic, on the southern border of the zone and near the Chiapas highlands, some occupation continued through the period and into the Early Postclassic and, perhaps, Late Postclassic Periods. At other sites in the Ocosingo Valley there was elite building activity in the Postclassic.

The Northwestern Zone. Palenque suffered a ninth century "collapse." At Jonuta and other sites a Jonuta Horizon occupation continued well into the Terminal Classic Period, but the record fades after this. There is little in the zone that can be identified to the Early Postclassic. For the Late Postclassic, however, both archaeology and ethnohistory attest to impressive trading centers.

The Campeche Zone. Most information here comes from the coast where there was major building of sites through the Terminal Classic into the Early Postclassic. The Late Postclassic sees a tapering off of activities and site occupations. In the southeastern interior of the zone there is a substantial Late Postclassic occupation (Lobil phase), with the building over of old Classic sites in a rough masonry style.

The Central Yucatan Zone. Rio Bec–Chenes centers were abandoned in the ninth century. Some show "squatter" occupation evidences throughout the remainder of the Terminal Classic and into the Early Postclassic. There is little direct information on the Late Postclassic, but there are some "squatter-type" evidences at some sites.

The Belize Zone. Activities in major centers of the southern part of the zone cut off in the ninth century; however, some cave sites may have been used as shrines or sacred places well into the Terminal Classic. In the northern part of the zone some sites show "times of troubles" toward the end of the ninth century; but there are also indications of continued building and activity in centers through the Terminal Classic, into the Early Postclassic, and on into the Late Postclassic. Near the coast there are Late Postclassic sites which appear to have been trading centers.

The Northern Plains Zone. The Terminal Classic Period in the Northern Plains Zone marked an apogee of architectural development and is referred to as the Pure Florescent Period. There were many regional centers of magnificence. While essentially local in inspiration, both the architecture and art of the period shows a degree of alien influence of a "Mexican" quality, often associated with the Chontal of Putun Maya. The founding of Toltec-Maya Chichen Itza at about A.D. 1000 is coincident with a drastic change in settlement. Most old great centers are reduced to apparent impotence. The only outlying sites in the Early Postclassic are coastal locations—trading towns, salt works, or fishing stations.

In the Late Postclassic Chichen Itza is abandoned; the Toltec presence disappears; Mayapan becomes the main city of the northern Lowlands. There are some other smaller centers in the interior of the Yucatan Peninsula; some others exist on the coast although the northwest peninsular coast seems largely uninhabited. Mayapan dominance or hegemony continues until the mid-15th century. After that power appears to have become more decentralized.

The East Coast Zone. The East Coast Zone in the Terminal Classic appears to be somewhat marginal to the Northern Plains, but it, too, participates in the developments of the Pure Florescent era. It also follows suit in the Early Postclassic, being largely denuded of major centers in the interior although there are some important towns along the Quintana Roo coast. In the Late Postclassic there is something of a boom in small trading cities or towns along this coast, including the island of Cozumel. Ceramics and architecture of these several towns relate to Mayapan. Most or many of these places appear to continue up to the time of the Spanish Conquest.

Some Concluding Comments

As I said at the outset, my paper has been an attempt to record, however briefly, the facts of settlement and cultural activity throughout the Maya Lowlands from A.D. 800 until the Spanish *entradas*. I think I have done this with relative objectivity although, as I also stated, I carry, like all archaeologists, some preconceptions and biases. Let me, in these concluding remarks, offer some observations, more subjective and interpretive than the data survey which has just been recounted.

My experience in Maya archaeology would suggest to me that the

Lowland Maya lived in a condition of political instability. This was inter-mittent and recurrent. A waxing-and-waning of Lowland Maya political orders can be traced back to the upswing of the Late Preclassic, with the founding of the first great centers or cities. This was followed by a Proto-classic retrenchment and the abandoning of many of these centers (Willey, 1977a). There was an Early Classic resurgence in some places; but, again, there was a notable drop-off in constructional activity and stelae dedica-tion during the sixth century "hiatus" (Willey, 1974). In the Late Classic there was an undeniable growth spurt as witnessed by the revival of many centers, the construction of new ones, and a proliferation of stelae dedi-cations—all this being accompanied by every indication of overall popu-lation increase for the Lowlands. Then came the decline and "collapse" of the Terminal Classic. Finally, in the Postclassic, there is the rise, domi-nance, and then abandonment of Chichen Itza, the subsequent rise of Mayapan, followed by its desertion prior to the arrival of the Spaniards. In stating all of this I have tended to generalize, to see surges, declines, and resurgences as area-wide phenomena. Recently, David Freidel (1983) has questioned some of this synchronization and geographical inclusive-ness. It is Freidel's argument that Lowland Maya polities were always in a state of flux, with ephemeral states and chiefdoms struggling side by side, approaching centralization and then back-sliding toward local petty autonomies. Without attempting to argue out the validity of wide-scale geographic synchronizations of these phenomena, I think that we are in agreement about the theme of Lowland Maya political instability, and it is a theme to be considered in our evaluations of the Postclassic. If this impression of Lowland Maya political instability is correct, where does cause lie? Is it in the difficulties encountered in establishing and maintaining cen-tralized control of agricultural production in a tropical lowland setting (Sanders and Price, 1968; Sanders, 1977, 1981)? Were there natural resource weaknesses that disadvantaged the Maya? And did such factors keep any one Lowland Maya polity from rising and maintaining full state-hood dominance over the others? Were the Maya unusually vulnerable to "foreign" penetration and if so, why?

The drift of these questions leads us to another observation and set of questions about the importance of "foreign" or "external" agents as causative factors in Maya Lowland development and change. Some decades ago it was the fashion to give considerable weight to "external" influences. More recently, *in situ* forces have been seen as the more important, per-haps righting the balance. But whichever emphasis one prefers, the facts of Lowland Maya involvement with peoples and cultures of other Meso-american regions must be given some interpretive consideration in any analysis of either history or process. The "Mexicanization" of the Terminal Classic Period, the establishment of Toltec Chichen, and the trading contacts of the Late Postclassic, all of which we have been reviewing in this overview, have a long history of predecessors in the Lowland Maya archaeological record. "External" contacts go back to the very beginning of this record, with the appearances of the earliest Lowland Maya pottery (Hammond and others, 1979). Later there are clues to Olmec relationships to the Maya Lowlands (*e.g.*, Willey, 1978b, pp. 97–98); and in the Late Preclassic we have ample evidence of ideological contacts between the Chiapas-Guatemalan Highlands and Pacific slopes and the Maya Lowlands (M. D. Coe, 1977; Quirarte, 1977; J. Graham, 1979). These contacts, revealed in hieroglyphics, iconography, and calendrics, leave the general impression that much of the basic content of Maya elite Lowland culture was assimilated from these "external" sources. Subsequently, in the Classic Period, we know that there was continued communication between major Lowland Maya cities, such as Tikal, and Kaminaljuyu of the Guatemalan Highlands; and this communication network also involved Teotihuacan in Central Mexico. Raw materials and manufactured goods were exchanged as well as ideas. In politics and dynastic matters it is possible that Lowland Maya political centralization and state formation of the Early Classic were stimulated by and linked to the policies of Kaminaljuyu and Teotihuacan. And from there the story can be continued into the "Mexicanoid" and "Veracruzoid" impingements of the Late Classic and Terminal Classic (Proskouriakoff, 1951: Parsons, 1969; Sabloff and Willey, 1967).

I think we have to view Lowland Maya culture history against the background of these two interrelated contitions—political instability and "foreign" involvements—to understand the events of the Terminal Classic and Postclassic Periods. Surely the southern "collapse" of the ninth century must have been related in some way to the amazing florescence of the north at the same time; and both of these developments, in my opinion, are rooted in the circumstances of inherent political instability and vulnerability or susceptibility to alien influences. Admittedly, we do not yet understand the processes of these developments. A single explanation, such as military invasion and conquest, seems too simple an answer; and the facts and findings of archaeology do not back it up although it may have taken place in certain instances. Trading cut-offs and disruptions may have a better general applicability, but it is not altogether satisfactory. If such brought about the downfall of the south, what of the north? Why did the cities there flourish at the same time that the south faded? Was it because the northern Lowlands were bolstered by an actual alien presence—

the Putun Maya who, in turn, had assimilated Mexican ideas and behavior? Had the north, in this manner, through more gradual exposure to "foreign" values and institutions, accommodated or adjusted to them, become more immunized against them, as it were, in contrast to the more protected south?

The establishment of Chichen Itza as the great center of the Early Postclassic Period was a capping or a climax to the Terminal Classic build-up of Lowland Maya "Mexicanization." Almost certainly, this was a power maneuver involving military force. Whoever or whatever the nature of the contending parties at this time, the event inaugurated a new socio-economic and politico-religious regime in the northern Maya Lowlands that was to persist for two centuries, dominating the north and keeping the south in shadows.

The subsequent Late Postclassic society of the northern Lowlands was also linked to greater Mesoamerica and to Mexico, although in a different way. It now became a part, more I think than it ever had before, of a commercial and trading network, one which had its essential direction from Central Mexico and one which was especially mediated through coastwise traffic. There was, in a sense, a Maya "resurgence" in the Late Postclassic, but what was its nature? It was not a resurgence along the lines of the Classic achievements—measured in grandeur of architecture, stelae dedications, and the hieroglyphic texts speaking of the hallowed and aristocratic lineage ancestors. The times had changed; there were other and different values. Charles Erasmus (1968) argued this some time ago. Recently, Ronald Nigh (1981), in a review, has stated:

> We also find annoying the persistence of naive ideas of the "Classic" Maya and their "collapse," a natural result of the fixation on large stone monuments. It is still forgotten that Maya history did not end with the abandonment of such monuments, and that when the Spanish arrived on the scene that most of the Maya area was densely populated by a thriving commercial and agricultural society. The Spanish describe the Chontal of Tabasco as dominated by a commercial class who lived in large houses in towns and owned many slaves to work their cacao plantations and drive their long-distance trading canoes. It seems that the abandonment of stone monument construction, as well as variations in agricultural intensity, could be more convincingly explained by analysis of the relations among the slave class, the priests and the merchants, in the context of an evolving pan-American economic system, where the social field conditioned the allocation of labor, resources, and power within Maya society (p. 709).

I tend to agree with Erasmus and Nigh's argument in favor of an "upward collapse," in one sense, although I would disagree about the naivete of relying upon stone monuments as an archaeological gauge for socio-political integration. There was a "Classic Period" in the Maya Lowlands, defined very clearly, as we have done so, by calendrical dates, big architecture, and carved monuments. It was a reality, but this kind of life faded away, in some places rather rapidly, or was severely modified. In an effort to "make a case for the Postclassic" it is not necessary to deny the record. But what kind of "case" can we make for the Postclassic that will best help us to understand it and to put it in larger Maya and Mesoamerican perspective?

The Postclassic, and particularly the "resurgent" Late Postclassic, has been described as a society representing a set of values built around the wide distribution of consumer goods and the ethos of the wealthy mercantilist and trader (Rathje, 1975; Sabloff and Rathje, 1975; Nigh, Ibid.). But in the context of the Maya Lowlands, and particularly within that context as conditioned by its tradition of political instability and vulnerability to alien incursions, what did this mean? Trade and mercantilism, at least when organized on a scale like that of the Mesoamerican Late Postclassic, are extractive strategies, techniques of imperialism and colonialism that are, in last analysis, imposed by the strong on the weak. The much vaunted wider distribution of consumer goods is a process that benefits the imperialistic, extractive state, not the society under its commercial jurisdiction. It is in the imperialist state that the goods and benefits may, to a degree, trickle downwards in the social strata (Barroll, 1981). In the exploited domain only the upper class retains any of this wealth generated by trade. In the present situation I think we can be sure that the Late Postclassic Lowland Maya were not the imperialist power at the head of the trade chain. That power lay, first, perhaps, along the Gulf Coast, but, eventually, in Central Mexico where all great Mesoamerican power had resided since the Early Classic preeminence of Teotihuacan. In the evolution of the state and of the institutions of trade there had, indeed, been an "upward collapse"; however, the Toltecs and Aztecs of Central Mexico participated in the "upwardness"; the Lowland Maya enjoyed the "collapse."

Because of this, I regard the Lowland Maya Late Postclassic society as a reduced, shrunken, impoverished version of its former Classic condition, brought to this status by its successive confrontations with the rising Mexican states and empires, culminating with the Aztecs. This reduction is reflected—and here I unashamedly turn to the monuments—in the shoddiness of Mayapan architecture and in the curiously "warped" and dwarflike temples of Tulum and Cozumel. Situated at the far end of an extractive commercial chain, led by parvenu merchants who were allied with their Mexican exploiters, their former glories were remembered only in legends and prophecies, in the civilized rhetoric of their remnant priestly class who, with aristocratic and intellectual disdain, recounted the comings and goings of their various vulgar conquerors (Brotherston, 1979).

Notes

1. In preparing this paper I am indebted to the students of my Harvard graduate seminar held during the Spring of 1981. Our theme was the "Lowland Maya Postclassic Period," and seminar papers and discussions were all addressed to it. Participants were Fred Valdez, Jr., Beth A. Collea, Paul Jaeckel, James Parry, Michael N. Geselowitz, Richard H. Ebright, and Heidy Fogel. The titles of their papers are included in the bibliography and are on file in the Peabody Museum (Tozzer) Library at Harvard University.

2. The location of the Itza in early historic times was at a site referred to as Tayasal (Thompson, 1951). There is some dispute as to whether this place was located in or around Late Peten–Itza (Jones, Rice, and Rice, 1981) or at the location of the Topoxte ruin on that island in Lake Yaxha (Chase, 1976).

7 Changing Conceptions of Lowland Maya Culture History

The culture historical framework for Lowland Maya culture history has undergone constant change since the inception of systematic research one hundred years ago. While some changes have been accretive and modifying, others have been more radical, especially within the last thirty years. These include new understandings of Maya Highland–Lowland interactions, Maya linkages to other parts of Mesoamerica, Maya-Olmec relationships, Preclassic-to-Classic configurations of development, and the long-time problem of southern Lowland–northern Lowland relationships. Above all, the reemergence of problems whose solutions had been taken for granted suggests the need for caution as the Lowland Maya space-time cultural-relationship structure is used as the basis for processual inquiry.

Since the inception of serious archaeological research in the Maya Lowlands, our conceptions of the area's culture history have undergone almost constant change. One culture historical model after another has been significantly modified or replaced. At times these changes seem to have come about through the gradually accumulating weight of the evidence; at other times single discoveries have resulted in rapid and radical revisions of the old structure. In this paper I would like to review and examine these changes.

By culture historical models, or structures, I mean the way we conceive of formal cultural content, the ways we arrange it in time or in space, and the ways we construe the relationships of one body of data to another—in effect, what might be referred to as "traditional archaeology." I think that it will be easier to follow the main lines of development in the field by so placing my emphasis. I do not mean to imply that interest in cultural process is secondary to, or must necessarily come after, culture historical structure. Those of us in Maya archaeology have certainly seen, over the course of the past twenty years, how processual inquiry has often led to a restructuring of what had appeared to be an immutable data base. History and process are not easily separated, and I will not try to do so here.

Because I am interested in the chronicle of changing ideas about the Maya past, I will try to adhere to a chronological presentation insofar as this is possible; but, as will be evident as I go along, this becomes increasingly difficult as we come up in time and, especially, into the confluence of new discoveries, approaches, and ideas that has characterized Maya archaeology since the 1950s.

There are other histories of Maya archaeology (Willey and Sabloff 1980; Bernal 1980), including a good, very recent one of article length (Hammond 1983), which provide fuller and more conventional historical contexts. The intent here is a more limited and specialized one of depicting a series of "cross-sections" of the archaeological continuum that will reveal what archaeologists knew, or thought they knew, at various points in time; why they thought that way; and why they, or at least the collective discipline, frequently changed their minds.

Initial Conceptions

At the very beginning of interest in the Maya past, it might be said that there were two competing culture historical models. Both had been advanced as early as the sixteenth century, with the European discoveries of the New World, and both were carried on into the nineteenth century. Both were very general and wholly speculative. One of them might be called the "mysterious appearance" model, the attempt to explain the jungle-shrouded ruins of the Maya by recourse to wanderers from far-off places, such as Hindustan, Mesopotamia, Egypt, China, or from any place in the Old World where the phenomena of civilization were already known. Given the available evidence at that time—the stone temples, palaces, and pyramids found in the Central American rain forests, with no visible antecedents and little or no knowledge about them on the part of the living inhabitants of the area—the hypothesis had a certain logic; but, as we might say now, the hypothesis did not "test out" positively. In spite of the fact that it still has some adherents, the model is a "dead duck."

The second early model for Maya culture history held that the wonders found in the Central American jungles were not the work of Egyptians or other strangers from overseas but were, instead, the creations of native Americans, perhaps the ancestors of the Maya Indians who still inhabited parts of the territory in question. According to this reasoning, civilization had arisen here through the processes of in situ cultural evolution, by a series of stages beginning at some dim date in the past with simple hunting tribes. A number of individuals in the field thought this way. One of the most influential was John Lloyd Stephens, who set down his thoughts in 1841, after an expedition through Mayaland. The model was fairly general and it would be a long time before sufficient archaeological data were amassed to verify it; but it served at the time, continued to serve with archaeologists such as Maudslay, and is one of the concepts still with us today.

Early Research Conceptions

Systematic Lowland Maya archaeological research began in the 1880s, with the field explorations of Maudslay (1889–1902), Maler (1901, 1903, 1908), and Charnay (1888) and with the hieroglyphic and calendrical studies of Förstemann (1906) and Goodman (1897). These researches gave the first substance to the culture historical picture. A correlation of Mayan and Christian calendars indicated that the great ruined cities of the southern Lowlands had been built, and enjoyed their heyday, in the period of A.D. 400–900, with an apparent abandonment thereafter, later to be known as the "Classic Maya Collapse."

Some regionalism was plotted out. Architectural styles of the northern Lowlands were seen as different from those of the south; hieroglyphic texts and Initial Series dates, common to the south, were found to be rare or absent in the north. Maudslay, usually cautious about going beyond basic data reporting, observed that the north reached its cultural florescence later than the south, basing this on early ethnohistoric and native accounts that Maya cities were still in use in this part of the area when the

Spaniards reached it, in the sixteenth century (Maudslay 1892). This voiced for the first time, or at least foreshadowed, the concept of the differentiation between an "Old Empire" of the south and a "New Empire" of the north, opening an argument that is still going on. Seler (1902–23) and Schellhas (1904) observed that deity representations were similar in the Maya area, Oaxaca, the Gulf Coast, and Central Mexico, so that it was clear that Lowland Maya civilization had not grown up in isolation. "Mesoamerica," as a culture-area-with-time-depth, was beginning to be formulated as a working concept, although it would not be so formally designated and recognized until much later.

Thus, by the second decade of the twentieth century, the culture historical model for the Lowland Maya, and for its larger Mexican-Central American setting, had a certain complexity. In situ development of the civilization was taken for granted in scholarly circles, but the question had not received any more attention. Most Mayanists looked upon Lowland Maya civilization as the "donor civilization," the one that had been the ancestor of the related cultures of Oaxaca, Central Mexico, and other parts of Mesoamerica (Joyce 1914; Spinden 1928).

The Discovery of the Preclassic

The first specific information on earlier origins came from research in the Valley of Mexico, where Manuel Gamio found another style of pottery beneath that of the Teotihuacan civilization (Gamio 1913). Herbert J. Spinden referred to this newly discovered style as the "Archaic" and came up with what has come to be known as the "Archaic Hypothesis" (Spinden 1915, 1917; Willey 1981a). According to Spinden's hypothesis, early American agriculture and pottery were first developed in the Valley of Mexico, long before the rise of such civilizations as the Maya or the Toltec, and from there they were carried or diffused to both North and South America. It was a bold idea, the first really large-scale historico-evolutionary concept to be projected in Americanist studies. With his emphasis on an agriculture-pottery base, a definition that could be construed as an "American Neolithic," Spinden anticipated V. Gordon Childe. The weakest part of his Archaic hypothesis was his insistence on its monogenetic beginnings in the Valley of Mexico. Also, Gamio and Spinden had glimpsed only the uppermost levels of the Archaic, or Preclassic; we know now that as a period it has a much greater depth and cultural complexity. Still, Gamio's discovery and Spinden's idea gave, for the first time, some reality to the in situ evolutionary concept of New World civilizations.

The Preclassic search in the Maya Lowlands began with G. C. Vaillant (1927; Merwin and Vaillant 1932). His study of the Holmul tomb collections convinced him that there were Maya Lowland ceramics equally as old as Spinden's Central Mexican Archaic; moreover, the early Holmul assemblages included types not present in Central Mexico but with relationships, instead, that ran southward into Central America, beyond the Maya frontiers (Vaillant 1934; Lothrop 1927). In a word, the Archaic, or Preclassic, was being geographically extended; its center, or centers, of origin were seen as a moot point. In 1927 Vaillant, on a visit to the Carnegie Institution's excavations at Uaxactun, sank some test pits below the Classic plaza floors of that site, revealing deep deposits of Preclassic ceramics. These later became known as the Chicanel (Late Preclassic) and Mamom (Middle Preclassic) ceramic phases of the southern Maya Lowlands (R. E. Smith 1936a, b).

These Preclassic discoveries not only deepened the Maya culture historical structure (as well as the entire Mesoamerican chronological structure) but they also cast doubt on another aspect of these structures as they had been previously conceived. The old construct of Lowland Maya civilization as a "mother culture," one earlier than and responsible for other Mesoamerican civilizations, was called into question. Might not the various civilizations of Mesoamerica have arisen, in their respective regions, more or less contemporaneously, from a Preclassic base? It was not long before it was shown that an interpretation like this was closer to the facts.

Maya Highland-Lowland Connections: A First View

A further expansion in knowledge of the Preclassic Period ensued from the investigations begun by A. V. Kidder (1940), in the Guatemalan Highlands in the vicinity of Kaminaljuyu. There the Preclassic ceramic phases indicated that there had been strong ties between Highland and Lowland Maya (R. E. Smith 1940). Both Kidder and J. E. S. Thompson (1940b), the latter the leading Mayanist of his time, saw the highlanders as having been the donors in these Highland-Lowland cultural contacts. This was a reversal of previous attitudes, which had placed the Lowland Maya in the role of the originators of civilization for Mesoamerica, but it was also a reflection of the theoretical orientation of the times. When questions of origins were raised, it always seemed safest to turn to "outside influences." Far-off lands beyond the seas were no longer to be so designated, but there was still a predisposition to "look elsewhere," rather than to attempt to conceive of specific localized processes of cultural evolution. Also, in the 1930s and 1940s there was a disinclination to see culture contacts between two regions or cultures as a two-way street, as an interactive process which provided growth stimuli for each; instead, the relationship was always visualized as that of donor-to-receiver or, by implication, of higher-to-lower.

The Guatemalan Highland discoveries of the 1930s had another importance in addition to enlarging the Preclassic picture and demonstrating Highland-Lowland contacts on that chronological level. They finally resolved the time relationships between Lowland Mayan and other Mesoamerican civilizations. Kidder's Kaminaljuyu excavations produced excellent grave-lot associations of Classic Teotihuacan-style tripod vessels and Tzakol polychrome bowls of the Lowland Maya Early Classic genre (Kidder and Jennings 1937; Kidder 1940). This was clear proof of what had been suspected in the wake of the first Mesoamerican Preclassic discoveries. In a word, the great regional civilizations of Mesoamerica, including that of the Lowland Maya, were essentially contemporaneous; the Lowland Maya was not the progenitor of the others. Further work in the 1930s, such as that of G. C. Vaillant (1938), in Central Mexico, and Alfonso Caso (1938), in Oaxaca, fully confirmed this major culture historical renovation.

Chronological-Developmental Schemes ca. 1940

By 1940, in the wake of the Preclassic discoveries and the several cultural and relative chronological correlations that had been made in the Guatemalan Highlands and elsewhere, a culture historical structure that was something more than guesswork was beginning to take shape. This structure was formalized in a chart published in the landmark volume *The Maya and Their Neighbors* (C. L. Hay and others, eds., 1940, 484–85). Although it appeared in A. L. Kroeber's summary paper to the volume, the chart was the work of Vaillant. At the bottom, the chart has a "Pre-Ceremonial Period" (a name soon to be realized as inappropriate), dating prior to the Maya Initial Series date of 8.14.0.0.0 (ca. A.D. 300). The period was designed to include all of the "Archaic," Preclassic, or Formative complexes then known for the Maya area and for Mesoamerican. A "Full Maya Period" follows, from 8.14.0.0.0 to 9.15.0.0.0 (ca. A.D. 700), succeeded by a "Maya Great Period," lasting until 10.3.0.0.0 (ca. A.D. 900). A final "Mexican Influence Period" then carried the sequence up to the Spanish conquest. The orientation of the chronology is obviously toward the Maya Lowlands, the area of the theme of the book and at that time the only place where some sort of deep, absolute chronological control was possible, but the format had some meaning for other parts of Mesoamerica.

Vaillant was to repeat this culture historical scheme, with a different terminology, in his book *Aztecs of Mexico*, published the following year

(Vaillant 1941). This time his chronological chart (1941:26–27) reserves an "Early Cultures" bracket for anticipated preceramic discoveries, and the Preclassic is referred to as the "Middle Period," at that time guess-dated as 200 B.C. to A.D. 300. A period of "Independent Civilizations" follows, from A.D. 300 to 1000, with early and late divisions. The final precolumbian period is called the "Mixteca-Puebla," a reference to the dominant culture of much of Central Mexico between A.D. 1000 and 1520. As is obvious, what we now recognize as the standard Preclassic, Classic, and Postclassic chronology was in place by the early 1940s. Thompson (1943, 1945), in two summary articles on the Maya, offered a variant of this sequence with a Lowland Maya orientation, designating four periods as "Formative," "Initial Series," "Mexican," and "Mexican Absorption," the last two being subdivisions of the present Postclassic.

Although both Vaillant and Thompson faulted Spinden for sequence errors and oversimplification of the "Archaic" idea, their schemes share an evolutionary perspective. Mesoamerica and the Maya area had native cultural beginnings, passed through a stage of early farming and pottery making, achieved a stage of civilization, and continued on through later civilizations until interrupted by the European conquest. For this reason, I think it is fair to refer to all of these schemes as "chronological-developmental," in that they pertain to both chronological periods and developmental stages. There is obviously an ambiguity in this usage, which neither Vaillant nor Thompson attempted to resolve, in using the terms "period" and "stage" interchangeably and only incidentally or implicitly referring to cultural processes that might have determined their stages or brought them into being. In this light, their formulations may be contrasted to the more directly and openly evolutionary scheme which Pedro Armillas (1948) essayed a few years later, a scheme in which his "Formative," "Florescent," and "Militaristic" divisions are much more stages than periods, with special emphasis given to the processes believed to have been involved in their formation.

Before we leave these early chronological-developmental schemes, two matters should be commented upon. One of these concerns the previously referred to Old and New Empire concepts, as these had been applied to developments in the southern and northern Maya Lowlands (see Morley 1946). In his 1945 paper Thompson put forward the idea that the Puuc, Chenes, and Rio Bec sites and buildings of the northern Lowlands were largely contemporaneous with the Late Classic (Tepeu) Period in the southern Lowlands. This was a change from Morley's position, which had seen the northern architectural florescence as occurring later. The Thompson view was to prevail for some time; we shall return to it again.

The second point concerns evidences of social and cultural complexity in the Preclassic Period. Although Vaillant, Thompson, and Armillas had also made some brief references to this point, it tended to be slurred over. Archaeological indications of such complexity—pyramid mounds or monumental sculptures—were thought to be very rare or extremely late within the Preclassic Period, harbingers, in effect, of the following period. But Robert Wauchope focused attention on this question, in a paper that presented Preclassic, or Formative, complexity as very substantial. It was his thesis that the Formative, as then known, could be divided into an earlier and simpler "Village Formative" and a later and more complex "Urban Formative" (Wauchope 1950). But perhaps the main thing that drove home the point of Formative, or Preclassic, complexity, well in advance of the onset of the Classic Period Mesoamerican civilizations, was the discovery (or rediscovery) and eventual dating of the Olmec sites.

Maya Origins: Olmec and Related Matters

At just about the time Vaillant and Thompson were tidying up the Mesoamerican archaeological scene with their chronological-developmental schemes, M. W. Stirling was beginning his explorations in southern Veracruz and neighboring lowland Tabasco, which were to introduce complications into their seemingly neat pictures. Olmec sculptures had been discovered and commented on in print as early as the 1860s, and they continued to attract occasional attention up into the 1930s (Stirling 1968); but archaeologists had never systematically investigated this unique art style or the sites where it had been found.

Stirling began his Olmec fieldwork in 1938; shortly afterward, he and his associates uncovered a stela at the site of Tres Zapotes, in Veracruz, that bore a bar-and-dot inscription which they interpreted as being in the Maya Long Count system, dating from the seventh *baktun*, or a few years before the beginning of the Christian era (Stirling 1940). Thompson (1941a) immediately challenged this interpretation, refusing to see the Tres Zapotes date as being in the same system as the Maya dates and denying any great antiquity for the monument.

So began a debate that was to continue for more than a decade. Early on there were ceramic indications that Tres Zapotes had Preclassic Period levels, and Vaillant so placed it on his 1941 time chart; but there was considerable resistance in some quarters to admitting that Olmec large mounds and monuments dated so early. This was especially true with reference to the monumental site of La Venta, in Tabasco. Indeed, even Drucker (1952), one of Stirling's associates, who published the first monograph on La Venta, was inclined to think that the great Olmec art of the site pertained to the Early Classic Period. By all rights, so some reasoned, such sophisticated art and monumental florescence should belong to the same period and stage as comparable art and architecture in other regions of Mesoamerica—namely, to the Classic period—as was then believed to obtain for the Maya Lowlands or Teotihuacan.

Oddly enough, this reasoning about the Olmec achievements was not questioned by some of us who were familiar with Peruvian archaeology. There the Peruvian Chavín style provided a perfect model for such apparent artistic and monumental "precocity" as that claimed for Olmec. The Chavín style horizon had been demonstrated as antecedent to the "Florescent," or "Classic," cultures in that area (Bennett 1943). But we did not draw the parallel of such a developmental possibility for Mesoamerica.

It was left for radiocarbon dates to resolve the matter. These showed, overwhelmingly, that the La Venta architecture and monuments dated back to as early as 800 B.C. (Drucker, Heizer, and Squier 1957, 1959), or to the Middle Preclassic Period. Subsequently, M. D. Coe's (1968) excavations at another major Olmec site, San Lorenzo, pushed dates for early Olmec monumental art back to 1200 B.C.

The effect of the Olmec dating on Mesoamerican archaeology was profound. Not only was there a Preclassic understructure to the Mesoamerican civilizations represented by ceramics and farming, but this understructure was now seen to contain many of the traits that had been reserved for those civilizations themselves. And this was not just a Late or Terminal Preclassic situation, but one which could be extended back into the past by several centuries, to the very beginnings of the Middle Preclassic Period. The effect was to turn archaeologists toward a closer consideration of the Preclassic, to look for Olmec connections or developmental parallels in other regions. What bearing did the Olmec discoveries and datings have on the Maya Lowland culture historical structure? To begin with, they posed questions about Maya origins, or at least about the origins of certain elements in Lowland Maya elite culture. Were the Olmec to be considered as ancestral to the Classic Maya? If so, where might the developmental linkages be traced? These questions were to lead archaeologists back to the general region of the Maya Highlands and, particularly, to their Pacific slopes.

Except for scattered finds of portable objects, such as carved jades, there were no indisputable Olmec-style remains in the Maya Lowlands at that juncture of research; and the same situation still obtains. Thus, if Olmec culture did have a part in the rise of Maya civilization, the transitional development, it was reasoned, must have taken place somewhere else than in the Maya Lowlands. Early on in Olmec research, it had become apparent that Olmec art, as seen in both monuments and smaller objects, described a widespread horizon style throughout much of south and central Mesoamerica (M. D. Coe 1962, 1965). There were, thus, several places where an Olmec-to-Maya transition could have taken place, but the most logical was in a region, or regions, somewhere close to the Olmec and Lowland Maya heartlands. M. D. Coe (1962, 1965, 1977) was the first to pursue the problem in detail. He began with a study of late or epi-Olmec remains in the Olmec country proper of the Gulf Coast. He drew parallels between this Late Preclassic (400–0 B.C.) Olmec, or Olmec-derived, art with the art and monuments of the Pacific Chiapas–Guatemalan Izapan culture, also of Late Preclassic age. This suggested a spread of Olmec, or Olmecoid, influences on a Late Preclassic time level across the Isthmus of Tehuantepec, from the Gulf Coast to the Pacific side. Subsequently, it has been shown that there were probably earlier passages of Olmec influence by this same route, but the data most germane to an Olmec-Maya transition, however indirect, involved the Late Preclassic time level and the sites and monuments subsumed under the label of the Izapan culture. It was Coe's thesis, neatly summed up by him in diagrammatic fashion (M. D. Coe 1965, fig. 57), that Middle Preclassic Olmec gave rise to the Late Preclassic Izapan style, with its two branches (or aspects), that of late Tres Zapotes, on the Gulf Coast, and of Izapa, in Pacific Chiapas. The Tres Zapotes branch led on into such styles as Cerro de las Mesas and Tajín, while the Izapan branch led into Classic Lowland Maya art. Not only art was involved in this Olmec-Izapa-Lowland Maya transfer, but also iconology and ideology, including bar-and-dot enumeration and Long Count calendrics. Linkages were traced from coastal Izapa and coastal plain sites in Guatemala to Kaminaljuyu, in the Guatemalan Highlands, where Late Preclassic stelae at the site (Miles 1965a; Parsons 1983) not only resemble those of the Classic Maya Lowlands in style and themes, but also incorporate hieroglyphics that are reasonably prototypical to those of the Lowlands.

Since Coe's interpretations of the 1960s, there have been other analyses that have questioned the simple linearity of the Olmec-Izapa-Lowland Maya model (Quirarte 1976, 1979; Graham 1977a,b, 1979). These would not dispute the chronological priority of Olmec art but would tend to see Izapan and Classic Lowland Maya styles as distinct growths from an Olmec base, each drawing upon a tradition of common elements and ideas that were differently arranged and emphasized. Graham, with his studies at Abaj Takalik, on the Guatemalan Pacific Piedmont, has argued this very definitely. He groups the monuments found at that site into Olmec, Izapan, and Early Mayan categories. He sees the latter stelae, some of which bear

Long Count dates, as the clear, obvious forerunners to the Maya Lowland Early Classic monuments. Following this interpretation, Izapan and Early Maya (of the Pacific Slopes) were contemporaneous developments for a time. Both then disappeared in the Pacific region, but the latter was responsible for the "seeding" of the Lowland Classic.

The problem of the Olmec-to-Maya transition is enormously complex. It is safe to say, however, that our conceptions of Lowland Maya culture history—especially insofar as these concern the origins of elite artistic and intellectual aspects of Maya civilization—have been significantly modified by the discoveries, analyses, and hypotheses just reviewed. One of the main ideas to emerge has been that the Lowland Maya area was a relatively "backward" one, in contrast to some of the neighboring regions of southern Mesoamerica. The Veracruz-Tabasco Coastal Lowlands, as early as the beginning of the Middle Preclassic Period (1200 B.C.), had sites which clearly reflect complex, nonegalitarian societies. At this same time, the Maya Lowlands are assumed to have been on a much simpler, village farming level. Later on, too, in the Late Preclassic, the cultures of Pacific and Highland Guatemala and Chiapas appear to be more complex and sophisticated than those of the Maya Lowlands, serving as their "donors" in matters of art, iconography, religious ideology, hieroglyphics, and calendrics.

This was the way things appeared by the end of the 1960s, and this still seems to be the conventional wisdom. But at least one caveat has been registered against it. L. R. V. Joesink-Mandeville and Sylvia Meluzin (1976) have suggested that some Olmec ideas, as expressed in art and iconography, may have been carried or diffused directly into northern Yucatan from Olmec sources in Veracruz and Tabasco, bypassing the round-about Pacific Highland route of the Izapan culture, as it were. This is a minority report, nagging at the more generally accepted conventional structure, but it is something to be kept in mind, for it will reemerge further along.

A Culture Historical Model ca. 1970

During the 1950s and 1960s, at the same time the Olmec question and related matters were being considered, Maya archaeologists were following a number of topical interests. These interests were new or enjoyed new emphases. They included settlement-pattern studies, inquiries into subsistence, a concern with the institution of trade, and significant new developments in hieroglyphic and iconographic research. Much of this research was done in connection with survey and excavation programs at Mayapan (Pollock et al. 1962), Barton Ramie (Willey et al. 1965), Tikal

(W. R. Coe 1965), Dzibilchaltun (Andrews 1965), Altar de Sacrificios (Willey and Smith 1969), and Seibal (Smith and Willey 1969).

Questions of Lowland Maya settlement densities and arrangements had worried some archaeologists earlier (Ricketson and Ricketson 1937), but the first full-scale attempt to attack the problem was at Barton Ramie, in the Belize Valley, where my colleagues and I were concerned with two aspects of settlement: (1) the nature and arrangements of residential households; and (2) the macrosettlement distributions of centers with reference to each other and to their supporting residential populations. A third aspect of settlement, the examination and analysis of centers, especially those large ones referred to as cities, was instigated by the Carnegie Institution, at Mayapan, and by the University of Pennsylvania, at Tikal (Haviland 1965, 1966a,b).

As a result of these and other settlement studies, we came to know that literally hundreds of thousands of small ruin mounds dot the Lowland landscape, demonstrating ancient Maya populations to have been much larger than we had formerly imagined. We found that many, or most, of the small mounds were houses and that they were often grouped into small patio units, suggesting extended family kin groupings, an interpretation that found support in modern Maya ethnography (Vogt 1964). While there are regional variations in house-type forms, as well as disagreements about kinship corollaries (Ashmore 1981; Kurjack and Garza 1981; Willey 1981b), house-mound studies have provided Maya archaeologists with a whole range of data pertinent to social behavior. On the macropattern, or regional, scale, we know that large centers and smaller centers were arranged into hierarchical networks (Marcus 1973, 1976; Adams and Smith 1981), implying graded hierarchies of social and political authority. Finally, we know now that some centers were indeed cities, with urban dimensions, rather than "empty" ceremonial centers.

Settlement quite obviously articulated with subsistence. That the Maya of the past had lived only by swidden maize farming was incompatible with house-mound numbers and densities. This led to the discoveries of remnants of other cultivation systems, such as artificial terraces (Turner 1979) and raised fields (Siemens and Puleston 1972; Turner 1978b); and it was also recognized that "garden-plot" farming and arboriculture were important parts of old Maya subsistence (Harris 1978).

As is the case in many other areas in the world, trade has been looked at anew by Maya archaeologists and analyzed in its systemic relationships with other institutions within the culture and as a dynamic factor in the rise of civilization (Rathje 1971, 1972, 1977; Tourtellot and Sabloff 1972; Sabloff and Rathje 1975 eds.; Ball 1977a, 1977b). While there is some disagreement on just how important trade may have been as such a factor in the Maya Lowlands, there is a considerable body of information about it, especially as regards the importation of obsidian from sources outside the Lowlands (Hammond 1972b; Rovner 1976; Sidrys 1977), as well as salt (A. Andrews 1980), marine shells (Moholy-Nagy 1963; Feldman 1974), and jade (Foshag 1954; Rands 1965). All such data have certainly given Maya archaeologists a new vision of the contacts of the Maya Lowlands with other regions, if nothing else.

As for hieroglyphics, calendrics, iconography, and major art, we have seen that Maya archaeology was concerned with these things from the very beginnings of the discipline; such studies have continued from that time forward (see, e.g., Proskouriakoff 1950; Thompson 1950). More recently, however, there have been what can justifiably be called breakthroughs in these fields, especially in that of hieroglyphic research. Heinrich Berlin's (1958) identification of "emblem glyphs," as the names or escutcheons of specific Maya cities, was one of these. It was followed by Proskouriakoff (1960, 1963, 1964) combining stelae dates, stelae portraits, and hieroglyphic texts to determine patterns of ruler succession and the glyphic clauses referring to these ceremonies. There could now be no doubt that the inscriptions referred to historical events, people, and places, enabling archaeologists to talk about rulers, dynasties, marriages, alliances, wars, and deaths; and to do this, in some instances, as far back as the Early Classic Period.

These new interpretations of Maya hieroglyphic texts were paralleled by linguistic and phonetic advances in their decipherment (Knorozov 1955, 1968; Lounsbury 1974a,b; Mathews and Schele 1974; Kelley 1976; Schele 1976), which greatly enriched their meaning and which hold the potential for a complete decipherment of Maya writing. Among the findings flowing from this research has been the revelation of interchanges among the great Lowland Classic city of Tikal, Kaminaljuyu in the Guatemalan Highlands, and distant Teotihuacan in Central Mexico. According to one interpretation of the art and glyphic texts of Tikal, a foreign lord, perhaps from Kaminaljuyu but also associated with symbols of Teotihuacan, allied himself with a ruling Lowland Maya dynasty in the Early Classic Period (Coggins 1979). In a word, by the 1970s the culture historical structure of Maya archaeology was beginning to become "humanized."

With the results of all of this research and new research directions of the 1950s and 1960s behind them, Maya archaeologists were ready, by about 1970, for some consolidation and synthesis of their findings; this was forthcoming in the results of two seminars, held under the auspices of the School for American Research, in Santa Fe, New Mexico, in 1970 and 1973, respectively. The seminar on *The Origins of Maya Civilization* (Adams, ed., 1977) summarized the earlier part of the culture historical structure. To begin with there was no information on an Early Preclassic Period occupation of the Maya Lowlands, a period which by 1970 had been identified elsewhere in southern Mesoamerica. The record began with the Middle Preclassic (1000–300 B.C.) Xe and Mamom ceramics, found in small farming villages; however, by the end of that period, small temple or special building platforms were known from a few sites. During the Late Preclassic-Protoclassic periods (300 B.C. to A.D. 250), there was both population growth and cultural and sociopolitical elaboration. That is, complex society came into being in the Maya Lowlands. This was the time of the Guatemalan Pacific-Highland region's contacts with the Lowlands, especially in the sphere of elite culture. In general the trends of these centuries were toward increasing elaboration and complexity; however, there were regional differences, with some parts of the Lowlands attaining complex sociopolitical status earlier than others and with some stabilizations and even setbacks in evolutionary trends. These variations in the Late Preclassic-Protoclassic story could not be satisfactorily explained in 1970, and they still cannot be.

The Early Classic Period (A.D. 250–500/600) was viewed in the 1970s model much as it had been before, as the period of the propagation of the stelae and Initial Series dating system, presumably from centers such as Uaxactun and Tikal, in the northeastern Peten. This was the time of the first florescence of corbeled-vault architecture and, in the south at least, of Tzakol-sphere polychrome pottery (Willey, Culbert, and Adams 1967). In retrospect it can be said that our views of a general uniformity of the Early Classic were much more confident than they are today. A phenomenon known as the "hiatus" had received some attention in the 1970s (Willey 1974). This referred to the period of 9.5.0.0.0 to 9.8.0.0.0 (A.D. 534–93), a time during which many major centers of the south ceased stelae dedication and major construction; I offered the speculation that this might have had something to do with the waning of Teotihuacan power and with the loss of these foreign contacts, which precipitated a crisis of some sort in Lowland Maya polities. But there was a vigorous recovery in the Late Classic Period, with the founding and rise to prominence of many new cities and a renaissance in many of the old ones. This occurred between A.D. 600 and 800, but after the latter date Classic Maya civilization, at least as seen in the elite spheres of activity, went into a rapid decline, from which there was no recovery.

This subject was explored in the second Santa Fe seminar, *The Classic Maya Collapse* (Culbert, ed., 1973). It was our opinion then that after the close of the ninth century A.D., only a few minor sites and reduced populations remained in the southern Lowland regions. Center or city construction was seen as continuing for a time in the northern Lowlands; however, even there Classic Maya civilization was seen as coming to a close, or at least experiencing a radical reorientation, with the advent of Toltec, or Toltec-influenced, peoples from the west, who invaded the area and established their power at Chichen Itza. From about A.D. 1000, the model of the 1970s remained essentially the same as that outlined by Thompson in 1945, continuing through two Postclassic Periods to the Spanish entry. There was, however, one strong dissenting voice to the way we dealt with the Classic-to Postclassic transition in the 1970 model—that of E. W. Andrews IV (1973), who saw things quite differently.

The Preclassic Again and Related Matters

We come down now to the last few years of research, to the late 1970s and the beginnings of the 1980s. Some of these results have been published; others have not and are known only through meetings, seminars, or even more informal, word-of-mouth communications among colleagues. Consequently, it is moot as to just what information precedes what and what should be the order of presentation. I will begin with the Preclassic part of the structure.

Our knowledge of the Preclassic has been substantially deepened chronologically. Hammond's discovery of the Swazey phase, at the Cuello site in northern Belize, has pushed back the Lowland Maya ceramic record to at least 2000 B.C., if not earlier (Hammond et al. 1979). If such a dating is accepted, it means that the Maya Lowlands had an Early Preclassic Period occupation as early as, or earlier than, other areas of southern Mesoamerica. Who were these Early Preclassic peoples of the Maya Lowlands? While ceramic comparisons between Swazey and other early complexes leave the matter in some doubt, one possibility is that the idea of pottery making was brought to the Maya Lowlands from the Guatemalan Highlands. If so, does this mark the first appearance of Maya speakers in the Lowlands? Historical linguistic findings offer some support for such a hypothesis. A proto-Mayan language, from which all later forms of Maya speech are believed to have been derived, is estimated to have been extant in the Guatemalan Highlands by 2200 B.C., and such proto-Mayans, or early Mayans, could have descended to the Lowlands at some time after that (Kaufman 1976). But some doubts must be raised about this reconstruction, in that very recent discoveries in the Lowlands indicate a long preceramic occupation there, antedating the Preclassic (MacNeish, Wilker-

son, and Nelken-Turner 1980). Were these preceramic Lowlanders of
Mayan linguistic affiliation or not? Could they have developed pottery
there prior to its appearance in the Highlands? At this point there are clearly
more questions than answers. What seems safest to say now is that Lowland Maya Early Preclassic archaeology looks about as old as that of any
other Mesoamerican preclassic culture and that, in Lowland territory, its
ceramics appear as reasonable prototypes for subsequent Middle Preclassic complexes (Willey 1982).

Our 1970 image of the Preclassic has also been changed, or at least
called into question, at the other end of its time scale. Are truly large constructions (temple and palace pyramids and platforms) to be confined solely
to the Late Preclassic or even to the Protoclassic? This has been the conventional wisdom, and David Freidel's (1981b) stimulating essay on the
rise of complex society in the Maya Lowlands would favor it. But very
recently there have been some disturbing discoveries at El Mirador, in the
northern Peten; the architectural mass at that site is so great that it actually dwarfs Tikal (Matheny, ed., 1980; Arthur Demarest 1983, personal
communication). El Mirador is supposed to be Late Preclassic in its mound
and platform constructions, and there seems little doubt that some of it
is; but is it all this late, or could there be Middle or even Early Preclassic
levels to this mammoth construction? This raises the point made by Joesink-
Mandeville, to which we have already referred: Could we have here linkages with or reflections of early Olmec construction to the west? Need
foreign elite inspiration have come to the Lowland Maya solely from the
Pacific-Highland Guatemalan region and only on a Late Preclassic time
level? The 1970 culture historical model has not yet been changed, but
there is a possible chink in the structure.

However this question of dating the beginnings of elite cultural activity in the Maya Lowlands is to be resolved, one strong fact has come out
of recent investigations—the impressiveness of Late Preclassic Lowland
ceremonial and politicoreligious activity. Some of this had been admitted
in the 1970 model, but I do not think we appreciated the full nature and
scale of the Late Preclassic activity, brought home to us since by Freidel's
writings (1978, 1979, 1981b,c). In fact, viewing the Maya developmental
continuum, a case could be made for two constructional crests, one in the
Late Preclassic and a second in the Late Classic, with the Early Classic
Period as something of a trough in between. Yet this generalization, too,
is an uncertain one, for there are regions, or individual sites, where Early
Classic developments are quite impressive (as at Tikal), even though there
are others where the process from Late Preclassic to Early Classic appears

to have been one of decentralization, a dissolution of large centers in favor of several smaller ones, as at Cerros (Freidel 1978, 1979; Potter 1985). Perhaps what we are viewing is a lack of chronological patterning in the rise and fall of Maya polities and, instead, a revelation of a peculiar instability in the evolution of state formations in the Maya Lowlands (Freidel 1983; Willey 1981c).

The Terminal Classic-Postclassic

Even more recent than the new findings and considerations concerning the Preclassic and the Preclassic-to-Classic transition, are questions and doubts, again, about the Lowland Maya Classic Collapse, its relationships with the Postclassic, and southern-northern Lowland relationships. This nexus of problems goes back a long way in Maya research. Were there "Old Empire" and "New Empire" separate climaxes in Lowland Maya civilization, as Morley, and later E. W. Andrews IV, have argued; or was Thompson correct in his belief that the southern Late Classic Tepeu phases were coeval with the Rio Bec–Chenes-Puuc developments of the north? When Andrews advanced this return to something close to the original Morley formulation, the majority of Mayanists were unconvinced and preferred to continue with the Thompson interpretation (Willey 1971). But in 1982 a seminar on the Lowland Maya Postclassic, held by the School of American Research, in Santa Fe, returned to the Morley-Andrews position in a consensus that well-known Puuc sites, such as Uxmal, Kabah, Labna, and Sayil, were to be dated after the southern Collapse. In addition, the seminar was largely in agreement that there was at least a partial and perhaps a complete chronological overlap between the Puuc sites and Chichen Itza.

These new revisionist interpretations raise numerous questions that I cannot go into here, but which will be presented in detail in the forthcoming seminar report (Sabloff and Andrews, eds., 1986). It is sufficient to add that one of the seminar leaders (Sabloff) concluded with the statement that Classic Maya civilization can be conceived of as having two developmental peaks: an earlier Late Classic (A.D. 600–800), southern one and a later Terminal Classic-Early Postclassic (A.D. 800/900–1100/1200), northern one. According to this view, the Terminal Classic-Early Postclassic period in the north is not seen as easily divisible but is, instead, a continuum (including both of Andrews's Florescent and Modified Florescent periods; the real break in the north came after the fall of Chichen Itza and immediately preceded the Late Postclassic Period.

Concluding Reflections

In this historical review I have attempted to recount what appear to me to have been the most significant conceptions about Lowland Maya culture history, together with changes in these conceptions. First was the idea that Lowland Maya civilization was an in situ evolutionary growth in the New World, an idea that has since been elaborated upon and essentially demonstrated.

Early on, Maya civilization was looked upon as something of a "mother culture," one giving rise to the other civilizations of Mesoamerica. This concept has since been rejected, for good reasons. The "Classic" civilizations have been demonstrated to be essentially contemporaneous, all resting upon an interrelated underbase of Preclassic cultures.

We have seen that the regularity and uniformity of a chronological-developmental scheme had its usefulness in helping to put the Mesoamerican archaeological house in order for a time—with Lowland Maya developments neatly placed within this framework. But the simplistic evolutionary aspects of the scheme proved misleading.

The problem of Olmec-Maya relationships gave rise to the Pacific-Guatemalan Highland (Izapan) transference model. While debated in its particulars, this model still seems serviceable, although recent Preclassic discoveries in the Lowlands keep open the possibility that Olmec-to-Lowland Maya communications might have taken place by routes other than the Pacific-Highland one.

The linked problems of the Classic Collapse and southern-northern relationships within the Lowlands have been reopened, with the balance of opinion now tilting toward a Terminal Classic-Early Postclassic climax in the north, following the Late Classic climax in the south.

In this brief presentation I have had to be selective. I have said nothing about the question of the Mayan-Christian calendrical correlation, except to mention Goodman's first work on it and his conclusions favoring the 11.16.0.0.0 interpretation, the one followed here. It is still generally favored by a majority of Maya archaeologists. The earlier 12.9.0.0.0 correlation has been largely dropped, but there has been recent interest in the possibility of a later correlation that would raise Initial Series dates by a little over two hundred years (Kelley 1983). If such a correlation should be proved, it would obviously have a significant effect on the Lowland Maya culture historical model we work with today. I have not dealt with historical linguistics, ethnohistory, or ethnography, except indirectly or fleetingly. All could have important bearing on the developments of, and changes in, our culture historical models, especially regarding Terminal Classic-Postclassic matters.

It is difficult to close a review of this kind without admitting that it has a cautionary quality. I suppose that in this respect there is nothing special or unusual about the Maya field. Any other healthily active branch of archaeology would probably show a similar pattern of development. New discoveries prompt new interpretations, new models. Somewhat more disturbing, perhaps, is the way certain problems seem to persist, to re-emerge a score of years after we thought they had been solved. A good example would be the matter of the relationships between the southern and northern Lowlands and the developments spanning Late Classic through Early Postclassic times. Neither our predecessors nor we ourselves have been able to satisfactorily, demonstrably settle it. How can we frame hypotheses about so obviously complex a phenomenon as the "Classic Collapse" if we cannot do better than we have done on this straight-forward archaeological question?

It shall be my qualified optimistic contention that our current, much-amended cultural historical structure for Lowland Maya archaeology is a pretty good one. As far as it goes, it has certainly been hard-won. Still, judging from the way the field has developed in the past, it is probably well to temper any optimism with caution and to be braced for surprises.

Bibliography

ADAMS, R. E. W.

1969 "Maya Archaeology 1958–1968, a Review," *Latin American Research Review,* 4:3–45.

1971 *The Ceramics of Altar de Sacrificios,* Guatemala, Papers of the Peabody Museum of Archaeology and Ethnology, Vol 63, no.1 (Cambridge, Mass.: Harvard University).

1973a "The Collapse of Maya Civilization: A Review of Previous Theories," in *The Classic Maya Collapse,* ed. T. Patrick Culbert, (Albuquerque: University of New Mexico Press, School of American Research Advanced Seminar Series).

1973b "Maya Collapse: Transformation and Termination in the Ceramic Sequence at Altar de Sacrificios," in *The Classic Maya Collapse,* ed. T. Patrick Culbert (Albuquerque: University of New Mexico Press, School of American Research Advanced Seminar Series).

1977 "Rio Bec Archaeology and the Rise of Maya Civilization," in *The Origins of Maya Civilization,* ed. R. E. W. Adams (Albuquerque: University of New Mexico Press, School of American Research Advanced Seminar Series).

1981 "Settlement Patterns of the Central Yucatan and Southern Campeche Regions," *Lowland Maya Settlement Patterns,* ed. Wendy Ashmore (Albuquerque: University of New Mexico Press, School of American Research Advanced Seminar Series).

ADAMS, R. E. W. (ed.)

1977 *The Origins of Maya Civilization* (Albuquerque: University of New Mexico Press, School of American Research Advanced Seminar Series).

ADAMS, R. E. W. and T. P. CULBERT

1977 "The Origins of Civilization in the Maya Lowlands," *The Origins of Maya Civilization,* ed. R. E. W. Adams, (Albuquerque: University of New Mexico Press, School of American Research Advanced Seminar Series).

ADAMS, R. E. W. and WOODRUFF D. SMITH

1981 "Feudal Models for Classic Maya Civilization," in *Lowland Maya Settlement Patterns,* ed. Wendy Ashmore (Albuquerque: The University of New Mexico Press, School of American Research Advanced Seminar Series).

ADAMS, R. E. W. and FRED VALDEZ, JR.

1980 "The Ceramics of Colha, 1979–80 Seasons," Mimeographed ms.

ANDREWS, ANTHONY P.

1980 "Salt and the Maya: Major Prehispanic Trading Spheres," *Atlatl* 1:1–17.

ANDREWS, E. WYLLYS, IV

1965 "Archaeology and Prehistory in the Northern Maya Lowlands: An Introduction," *Handbook of Middle American Indians,* Archaeology of Southern Mesoamerica, 2:(I) 288–331, ed. Robert Wauchope and G. R. Willey.

1973 "The Development of Maya Civilization after the Abandonment of The Southern Cities," in *The Classic Maya Collapse,* ed. T. P. Culbert (Albuquerque: University of New Mexico Press, The School of American Research Advanced Seminar Series).

ANDREWS, E. WYLLYS, IV and ANTHONY P. ANDREWS

1975 *A Preliminary Study of the Ruins of Xcaret, Quintana Roo, Mexico,* Pub. 40, (New Orleans: Middle American Research Institute, Tulane University).

ANDREWS, E. WYLLYS, IV, and E. WYLLYS ANDREWS, V

1980 *Excavations at Dzibilichaltun, Yucatan, Mexico,* Pub. 48, (New Orleans: Middle American Research Institute, Tulane University).

ARMILLAS, PEDRO

1948 *"A Sequence of Cultural Development in Mesoamerica,"* in *A Reappraisal of Peruvian Archaeology,* ed. W. C. Bennett, Memoir 4, Society for American Archaeology.

ASHMORE, WENDY

1981 "Some Issues of Method and Theory in Lowland Maya Settlement Archaeology," in *Lowland Maya Settlement Patterns,* ed. W. Ashmore (Albuquerque: University of New Mexico Press, School of American Research Advanced Seminar Series).

ASHMORE, WENDY, (ed.)

1981 *Lowland Maya Settlement Patterns* (Albuquerque: University of New Mexico Press, School of American Research Advanced Seminar Series).

BALL, JOSEPH W.

1974 "A Coordinate Approach to Northern Maya Prehistory: A.D. 700–1200," *American Antiquity,* 39:(1) 85–93 (Washington, D.C.)

1977a "The Rise of the Northern Maya Chiefdoms: A Socioprocessual Analysis," in *The Origins of Maya Civilization*, ed. R. E. W. Adams (Albuquerque: University of New Mexico Press, School of American Research Advanced Seminar Series).

1977b "A Hypothetical Outline of Coastal Maya Prehistory: 300 B.C.–A.D. 1200," in *Social Process in Maya Prehistory*, ed. N. Hammond, 167–96 (London: Academic Press).

1977c *The Archaeological Ceramics of Becan, Campeche, Mexico*, Middle American Research Institute, Pub. No. 43 (New Orleans: Tulane University).

1978 "Archaeological Pottery of the Yucatan-Campeche Coast," Middle American Research Institute, Publication 46, 71–146 (New Orleans: Tulane University).

1980 *The Archaeological Ceramics of Chinkultic, Chiapas, Mexico*, Papers of the New World Archaeological Foundation, No.43 (Provo, Utah).

BARROLL, M. A.

1980 "Toward a General Theory of Imperialism," *Journal of Anthropological Research*, 36:(2) 174–195 (Albuquerque: University of New Mexico).

BASCOM, W. R.

1969 *The Yoruba of Southwestern Nigeria* (New York: Holt, Rinehart and Winston).

BECKER, M. J.

1973 "Archaeological Evidence of Occupational Specialization Among the Classic Period Maya at Tikal, Guatemala," *American Antiquity* 38:396–406.

BECQUELIN, PIERRE

1979Ms. "Tonina, A City-State of the Western Maya Periphery," Paper presented at International Congress of Americanists, Vancouver, B.C.

BENNETT, W. C.

1943 "The Position of Chavín in Andean Sequences," *Proceedings of the American Philosophical Society* 86:323–27.

BERLIN, HEINRICH

1953 "Archaeological Reconnaissance in Tabasco," *Current Reports*, No. 7 (Washington: Carnegie Institution of Washington).

1956 *Late Pottery Horizons of Tabasco, Mexico*, Publication 606, Contribution No. 59 (Washington: Carnegie Institution of Washington).

1958 "El Glifo 'enblema' en las inscripciones mayas," *Journal de la Société des Américanistes* 47:111–19.

BERNAL, I.

1980 A History of Mexican Archaeology (London: Thames and Hudson).

BOSERUP, ESTER

1965 *The Conditions of Agricultural Growth: The Economics of Agrarian Change Under Population Pressure* (Chicago: Aldine Publishing Co.).

BRAINERD, GEORGE W.

1958 *The Archaeological Ceramics of Yucatan*, Anthropological Records, No. 19, University of Yucatan (Berkeley and Los Angeles: University of California Press).

BREWBAKER, J. L.

1979 "Diseases of Maize in the Wet Lowland Tropics and the Collapse of Classic Maya Civilization," *Economic Botany*, 33:101–118.

BRONSON, BENNET
  1966 "Roots and the Subsistence of the Ancient Maya," *Southwestern Journal of Anthropology* 22:251–79.
  1978 "Angkor, Anuradhapura, Prambanan, Tikal: Maya Subsistence in an Asian Perspective," in *Prehispanic Maya Agriculture*, ed. P. D. Harrison and B. L. Turner II (Albuquerque: University of New Mexico Press).
BROTHERSTON, GORDON
  1979 "Continuity in Maya Writing: New Readings of Two Passages in the Book of Chilam Balam of Chumayel," in *Maya Archaeology and Ethnohistory*, ed. N. Hammond and G. R. Willey (Austin: University of Texas Press).
BULLARD, WILLIAM R., JR.
  1960 "Maya Settlement Pattern in Northeastern Peten, Guatemala," *American Antiquity* 25:355–72.
  1970 "Topoxte: A Postclassic Maya Site in Peten, Guatemala," *Monographs and Papers in Maya Archaeology*, ed. W. R. Bullard, 61:245–309 (Cambridge, Mass: Peabody Museum Papers)
  1973 "Postclassic Culture in Central Peten and Adjacent British Honduras," in *The Classic Maya Collapse*, ed. T. P. Culbert (Albuquerque: University of New Mexico Press, School of American Research Advanced Seminar Series).
CASO, ALFONSO
  1938 "Exploraciones en Oaxaca, quinta y sexta temporadas," Publication 34, Institute of Geography and History (Tacubaya, Mexico)
CARR, R. F. and J. E. HAZARD
  1961 *Maps of the Ruins of Tikal, El Peten, Guatemala*, Tikal Rep. 11, (Philadelphia: University Museum).
CHANG, KWANG-CHIH
  1968 "Toward a Science of Prehistoric Society," in *Settlement Archaeology*, ed. K. C. Chang (Palo Alto: National Press).
CHARNAY, DESIRÉ
  1888 *The Ancient Cities of the New World* (New York: Harper and Brothers).
CHASE, ARLEN F.
  1976 "Topoxte and Tayasal: Ethnohistory in Archaeology," *American Antiquity*, 41:(2) 154–168.
  1979 "Regional Development in the Tayasal-Paxcaman Zone, El Peten Guatemala: A Preliminary Statement," *Ceramica de Cultura Maya et al.*, No. 11, 87–116.
CHASE, ARLEN F. and PRUDENCE M. RICE, eds.
  1985 *The Lowland Maya Postclassic* (Austin: University of Texas Press).
CHASE, DIANE Z.
  1981 "The Maya Postclassic at Santa Rita Corozal," *Archaeology*, 34:(1) 25–34.
COE, MICHAEL D.
  1962 *Mexico*, Ancient Peoples and Places Series, ed. G. Daniel (London and New York: Praeger).
  1964 "The Chinampas of Mexico, *Scientific American* 211: 90–98.
  1965 "The Olmec Style and its Distribution," *Handbook of Middle American Indians*, ed. R. Wauchope and G. R. Willey, 3:739–75 (Austin: University of Texas Press)
  1968 "San Lorenzo and the Olmec Civilization," in Dumbarton Oaks Confer-

ence on the Olmec, ed. E. Benson, 41–78 (Washington, D.C.: Dumbarton Oaks).

1977 "Olmec and Maya: A Study in Relationships," *The Origins of Maya Civilization*, ed. R. E. W. Adams (Albuquerque: The University of New Mexico Press, School of American Research Advanced Seminar Series).

COE, WILLIAM R.

1965 "Tikal: Ten Years of Study of a Maya Ruin in the Lowlands of Guatemala," *Expedition*, 8 (1) (Philadelphia: University Museum.)

1967 "Tikal: A Handbook of the Ancient Maya Ruins," (Philadelphia: University Museum).

COE, WILLIAM R. and MICHAEL D. COE

1956 "Excavations at Nohoch Ek, British Honduras," *American Antiquity* 21:370–82.

COGGINS, CLEMENCY

1979 "A New Order and the Role of the Calendar: Some Characteristics of the Middle Class Period at Tikal," *Maya Archaeology and Ethnohistory*, ed. Normand Hammond and G. R. Willey. (Austin: University of Texas Press.)

COLLEA, BETH

1981 "The Postclassic in Belize," Seminar in Middle American Archaeology (Cambridge, Mass: Tozzer Library, Peabody Museum, Harvard University) Manuscript.

COMAS, JAUN

1966 "Características físicas de la familia lingüística Maya," *Cuardernos: Serie Antropológia*, no. 20 (Mexico D.F.: Universidad Nacional Autónoma de México, Instituto de Investigaciones Históricas).

CONNOR, J. G.

1975 "Ceramics and Artifacts," *A Study of Changing Pre-Columbian Commercial Systems*, ed. J. A. Sabloff and W. L. Rathje, Monographs of the Peabody Museum, No. 3 (Cambridge, Mass. Harvard University).

COWGILL, GEORGE L.

1964 "The End of Classic Maya Culture: A Review of Recent Evidence," *Southwestern Journal of Anthropology*, 20 (2) 145–59.

1979 "Teotihuacan, Internal and Militaristic Competition, and the Fall of the Classic Maya," *Maya Archaeology and Ethnohistory*, ed. Norman Hammond and G. R. Willey (Austin: University of Texas Press).

COWGILL, URSULA M. and G. EVELYN HUTCHINSON

1963 "El Bajo de Santa Fe," *Transactions of the American Philosophical Society 53* (7):1–51.

CULBERT, T. PATRICK

1973a "Introduction: A Prologue to Classic Maya Culture and the Problem of Its Collapse," *The Classic Maya Collapse*, ed. T. P. Culbert, (Albuquerque: University of New Mexico Press, School of American Research Advanced Seminar Series).

1973b "The Maya Downfall at Tikal," *The Classic Maya Collapse*, ed. T. P. Culbert (Albuquerque: The University of New Mexico Press, School of American Research Advanced Seminar Series).

1977 "Early Maya Development at Tikal, Guatemala," *The Origins of Maya Civilization*, ed. R. E. W. Adams (Albuquerque: The University of New Mexico Press, School of American Research Advanced Seminar Series).

CULBERT, T.P. ed.

1973 *The Classic Maya Collapse*, (Albuquerque: The University of New Mexico Press, School of American Research Advanced Seminar Series).

CULBERT, T. PATRICK, P. C. MAGERS, and M. L. SPENCER

1978 "Regional Variability in Maya Lowland Agriculture," *Prehispanic Maya Agriculture*, ed P. D. Harrison and B. L. Turner II (Albuquerque; The Univesity of New Mexico Press).

DEMAREST, A. A.

1984 "Political Evolution in the Maya Borderlands: The Salvadoran Frontier," *The Southeastern Classic Maya Zone*, ed. E. H. Boone and G. R. Willey, (Washington D.C.: Ms. in press, Dumbarton Oaks).

1984 "The Harvard El Mirador Project, 1982–1983," *Mesoamerica*, No.7 (Antigua,Guatemala: Centro de Investigaciones Regionales de Mesoamerica).

1986 "The Olmec and the Rise of Civilization in Eastern Mesoamerica," *The Olmec and the Development of Formative Mesoamerican Civilization*, ed. R.J. Sharer and D. Grove (In press).

DEUTSCH, KARL

1969 *Nationalism and Its Alternatives,* (New York: Alfred A. Knopf).

DRUCKER, PHILIP

1952 "La Venta, Tabasco: A Study of Olmec Ceramics and Art," *Bureau of American Ethnology Bulletin 153* (Washington D.C.).

DRUCKER, PHILIP, R. F. HEIZER, and R. J. SQUIER

1957 "Radiocarbon Dates from La Venta, Tabasco," *Science* 126:72–73.

1959 "Excavations at La Venta, Tabasco, 1955," Bureau of American Ethnology Smithsonian Institution, Bulletin no. 170 (Washington D.C.: U.S. Government Printing Office).

EATON, JACK D.

1974 "Chicanna: An Elite Center in the Rio Bec Region," *Preliminary Reports on Archaeological Investigations in the Rio Bec Area, Campeche, Mexico*, Middle American Research Institute, Pub. No. 31 (New Orleans: Tulane University).

1978 "Archaeological Survey of the Yucatan-Campeche Coast," Middle American Research Institute Publication 46, (New Orleans: Tulane University).

EBRIGHT, R. H.

1981 "Mayapan, Yucatan, Mexico, The Archaeology and the Ethnohistory," Ms. Seminar in the Middle American Archaeology, Tozzer Library, Peabody Museum (Cambridge Mass: Harvard University).

ERASMUS, CHARLES J.

1968 "Thoughts on Upward Collapse: An Essay on Explanation in Archaeology," *Southwestern Journal of Anthropology,* 24:170–194, (Albuquerque: University of New Mexico).

FELDMAN, LAWRENCE H.

1974 "Shells from Afar: 'Panamic' Molluscs in Mayan Sites," *Mesoamerican Archaeology: New Approaches*, ed. N. Hammond (London: Duckworth).

FLANNERY, KENT V.

1972 "The Cultural Evolution of Civilizations," *Annual Review of Ecology and Systematics*, 3:399–426.

FOGEL, HEIDY

1981 "Cozumel," Ms. Seminar in Middle American Archaeology, Tozzer Library, Peabody Museum (Cambridge, Mass.: Harvard University).

FÖRSTEMANN, E. W.

1906 "Commentary on the Maya Manuscripts in the Royal Public Library of Dresden," Papers of the Peabody Museum 4(2) (Cambridge, Mass.: Harvard University).

FOSHAG, W. F.

1954 "Estudios minerologicos sobre el jade de Guatemala," IDAEH 6(1):3–48, (Guatemala City: Instituto de Antropología e Historia).

FREIDEL, DAVID A.

1976 *Late Postclassic Settlement Patterns on Cozumel Island, Quintana Roo, Mexico,* (Ph. D. Thesis, Department of Anthropology, Harvard University).

1978 "Maritime Adaptations and the Rise of Maya Civilization: The View from Cerros, Belize," in *Prehistoric Coastal Adaptations: The Economy and Ecology of Maritime Middle America*, ed. B. Stark, and B. Voorhies (New York: Academic Press).

1979 "Cultural Areas and Interaction Spheres: Contrasting Approaches on the emergence of Civilization in the Maya Lowlands," *American Antiquity*, 44: 36–55.

1981a "Continuity and Disjunction: Late Postclassic Settlement Patterns in Northern Yucatan," in *Lowland Maya Settlement Patterns*, ed. Wendy Ashmore (Albuquerque: University of New Mexico Press, School of American Research Advanced Seminar Series).

1981b "The Political Economics of Residential Dispersion Among the Lowland Maya," in *Lowland Maya Settlement Patterns*, ed. Wendy Ashmore (Albuquerque: University of New Mexico Press, School of American Research Advanced Seminar Series).

1981c "Civilization as a State of Mind: The Cultural Evolution of the Lowland Maya," in *The Transition to Statehood in the New World,* ed. G. D. Jones (Cambridge, England: Cambridge University Press).

1983 Political Systems in Lowland Yucatan: Dynamics and Structure in Maya Settlement," in *Prehistoric Settlement Patterns: Essays in Honor of Gordon R. Willey*, ed. E. Z. Vogt and R. M. Leventhal (Albuquerque: University of New Mexico Press and the Peabody Museum, Harvard University).

GAMIO, MANUEL

1913 "Arqueologia de Azcapotzalco, D.F., Mexico," Proceedings, 18th International Congress of Americanists (London: Harrison and Sons).

GANN, THOMAS

1900 "Mounds in Northern Honduras," *Bureau of American Ethnology, 19th Annual Report for 1897–98*, Part 2 (Washington, D.C. Smithsonian Institution).

GESELOWITZ, M. N.

1981 "Chichen Itza," Ms. Seminar in Middle American Archaeology, Tozzer Library, Peabody Museum (Cambridge, Mass.: Harvard University).

GIFFORD, JAMES C.

1976 *Prehistoric Pottery Analysis and the Ceramics of Barton Ramie in the*

Belize Valley, Memoirs, Peabody Museum Vol. 18 (Cambridge, Mass.: Harvard University).

GOODMAN, J. T.

1897 "The Archaic Maya Inscriptions," Appendix to Vol.I of *Biologia Centrali Americana,* Part 8, ed. A. P. Maudslay, (London: R. H. Porter and Dulau and Co.).

GRAHAM, J. A.

1972 *The Hieroglyphic Inscriptions and Monumental Art of Altar de Sacrificios,* Peabody Museum Papers, Vol. 64, No. 2, (Cambridge, Mass.: Harvard University).

1973 "Aspects of Non-Classic Presences in the Inscriptions and Sculptural Art of Seibal," in *The Classic Maya Collapse,* ed. T. P. Culbert (Albuquerque: University of New Mexico Press, School of American Research Advanced Seminar Series).

1977 "Discoveries at Abaj Takalik, Guatemala," *Archaeology,* 30(3):196–97.

1979 "Maya, Olmecs, and Izapans at Abaj Takalik," Proceedings, 42nd International Congress of Americanists, 8:179–1881. (Paris: Musée de l'Homme).

HAMMOND, N.

1972 "Locational Models and the Site of Lubaantun: a Classic Maya Centre." in *Models of Archaeology,* ed. David L. Clarke (London: Methuen).

1974 "The Distribution of Late Classic Maya Major Ceremonial Centres in the Central Area," *Mesoamerican Archaeology-New Approaches,* ed. Norman Hammond (London: Duckworth and Co., Ltd.).

1975a *Lubaantun, A Classic Maya Realm,* Peabody Museum Monographs, No. 2 (Cambridge, Mass.: Harvard University).

1975b "Maya Settlement Hierarchy in Northern Belize," *Contributions of the University of California Archaeological Research Facility,* no. 27:40–55.

1977a "The Earliest Maya," *Scientific American,* 236:116–33.

1977b "Ex Oriente Lux: A View from Belize," in *Origins of Maya Civilization* ed. R. E. W. Adams (Albuquerque: University of New Mexico Press, School of American Research Advanced Seminar Series).

1978 "The Myth of Milpas: Agricultural Expansion in the Maya Lowlands," in *Prehispanic Maya Agriculture,* ed. P. D. Harrison and B. L. Turner II (Albuquerque: University of New Mexico Press).

1981 "Settlement Patterns in Belize," in *Lowland Maya Settlement Patterns,* ed. Wendy Ashmore (Albuquerque: University of New Mexico Press, School of American Research Advanced Seminar Series).

1983 "Lords of the Jungle: A Prosography of Maya Archaeology," in *Civilization in the Ancient Americas: Essays in Honor of Gordon R. Willey,* ed. R. M. Leventhal and A. L. Kolata (Albuquerque: University of New Mexico Press and the Peabody Museum, Harvard University).

HAMMOND, NORMAN and WENDY ASHMORE

1981 "Lowland and Maya Settlement: Geographical and Chronological Frameworks," in *Lowland Maya Settlement Patterns,* ed. Wendy Ashmore, (Albuquerque: University of New Mexico Press, School of American Research Advanced Seminar Series).

HAMMOND, NORMAN, DUNCAN PRING, RICHARD WILK, SARA DON-

AGEY, F. P. SAUL, E. S. WING, A. V. MILLER, and L. H. FELDMAN
    1979 "The Earliest Lowland Maya: Definition of the Swasey Phase," *American Antiquity*, 44(1):92–110.
HARRIS, D. R.
    1973 "The Prehistory of Tropical Agriculture: An Ethno-Ecological Model," in *The Explanation of Culture Change: Models in Prehistory* ed. A. C. Renfrew (London: Duckworth).
    1978 "The Agricultural Foundations of Lowland Maya Civilization: A Critique," in *Prehispanic Maya Agriculture*, ed. P. D. Harrison and B. L. Turner II. (Albuquerque: University of New Mexico Press).
HARRISON, PETER D.
    1975 "Intensive Agriculture in southern Quintana Roo, Mexico: Some New Lines of Evidence and Implications for Maya Prehistory," paper presented at the Fortieth Annual Meeting, Society for American Archaeology, Dallas.
    1977 "The Rise of the *Bajos* and the Fall of the Maya," in *Social Process in Maya Prehistory: Studies in Memory of Sir Eric Thompson*, ed. N. Hammond (London: Academic Press).
    1978a "So the Seeds Shall Grow: Some Introductory Comments," in *Prehispanic Maya Agriculture*, ed. P. D. Harrison and B. L. Turner II, (Albuquerque: University of New Mexico Press).
    1978b *"Bajos* Revisited: Visual evidence for One System of Agriculture," in *Prehispanic Maya Agriculture*, ed. P. D. Harrison and B. L. Turner II, (Albuquerque: University of New Mexico Press).
    1979 "The Lobil Postclassic Phase in the Southern Interior of the Yucatan Peninsula," in *Maya Archaeology and Ethnohistory*, ed. Norman Hammond and G. R. Willey (Austin: University of Texas Press).
    1981 "Some Aspects of Preconquest Settlement in Southern Quintana Roo, Mexico," in *Lowland Maya Settlement Patterns*, ed. Wendy Ashmore, (Albuquerque: University of New Mexico Press, School of American Research Advanced Seminar Series).
HARRISON, PETER D. and B. L. TURNER II, ed.
    1978 *Prehispanic Maya Agriculture*, (Albuquerque: University of New Mexico Press).
HAVILAND, WILLIAM A.
    1965 "Prehistoric Settlement at Tikal, Guatemala," *Expedition* 7(3):7–14. (Philadelphia: University Museum).
    1966a "Maya Settlement Patterns: A Critical Review," Archaeological Studies in Middle America, Middle American Research Institute, Publication 26 (New Orleans: Tulane University).
    1966b "Social Integration and the Classic Maya," *American Antiquity*, 31(5): 625–31.
    1969 "A New Population Estimate for Tikal, Guatemala," *American Antiquity*, 34(4):429–33.
    1970 "Tikal, Guatemala, and Mesoamerican Urbanism," *World Archaeology*, 2(2):186–97.
    1972 "Estimates of Maya Population: Comments on Thompson's Comments," *American Antiquity*, 31:261–62.
    1981 "Dower Houses and Minor Centers at Tikal, Guatemala: An Investiga-

tion into the Identification of Valid units in Settlement Hierarchies," *Lowland Maya Settlement Patterns*, ed. Wendy Ashmore (Albuquerque: University of New Mexico Press, School of American Research Advanced Seminar Series).

HAY, C. L. et al., ed.
1940 *The Maya and Their Neighbors*, (New York: Appleton-Century).

HESTER, T. R., J. D. EATON, and H. J. SHAFER
1980 "The Colha Project, Second Season, 1980 Interim Report," Center for Archaeological Research, (San Antonio: The University of Texas).

JAECKEL, PAUL
1981 "The Western Maya Lowlands," Ms. Seminar in Middle American Archaeology, Tozzer Library Peabody Museum. (Cambridge, Mass.: Harvard University).

JOESINK-MANDEVILLE, L. R. V. and SYLVIA MELUZIN
1976 "Olmec-Maya Relationships: Olmec Influences in Yucatan," in *Origins of Religious Art and Iconography in Preclassic Mesoamerica*, ed. H. B. Nicholson. (Los Angeles: UCLA, Latin American Studies Series 31).

JONES, CHRISTOPHER
1977 "Innauguration Dates of Three Late Classic Rulers of Tikal, Guatemala," *American Antiquity*, 42:28–60.

JONES, CHRISTOPHER and ROBERT J. SHARER
1980 "Archaeological Investigations in the Site Core of Quiriqua," *Expedition* 23(1):11–20.

JONES, GRANT D., DON S. RICE and PRUDENCE RICE
1981 "The Location of Tayasal: A Reconsideration in the Light of Peten Maya Ethnohistory and Archaeology," *American Antiquity*, 46(3):530–547.

JOYCE, T. A.
1914 *Mexican Archaeology*, (London: Putman).

KAUFMAN, TERENCE
1976 "Archaeological and Linguistic Correlations in Mayaland and Associated Areas of Mesoamerica," *World Archaeology*, 8(1):101–18

KELLEY, D. H.
1962 "Glyphic evidence for a Dynastic Sequence at Quirigua, Guatemala," *American Antiquity*, 27:323–35.
1983 "The Maya Calendar Correlation Problem," in *Civilization in the Ancient Americas: Essays Honoring Gordon R. Willey*, ed. R. M. Leventhal and A. L. Kolata, (Albuquerque: University of New Mexico Press and the Peabody Museum, Harvard University).

KIDDER, A. V.
1940 "Archaeological Problems of the Highland Maya," in *The Maya and Their Neighbors*, ed. C. L. Hay and others (New York: Appleton-Century).

KIDDER, A. V. and J. D. JENNINGS
1937 "Guatemala Highlands," *Carnegie Institution of Washington Yearbook*, 36:9–10.

KNOROZOV, Y.
1955 "La escritura de los antiguos mayas," (Moscow: Ethnographic Institute).
1968 "Investigacion formal de los textos jeroglificos mayas," *Estudios Cultura Maya*, 7:59–65.

KUBLER, GEORGE

1974 "Climate and Iconography in Palenque Sculpture," *Art and Environment in Native America*, ed. Mary E. King and Idris R. Taylor Jr., Special Publication Museum University of Texas 7 (Austin: University of Texas).

KURJACK, EDWARD B.

1974 *Prehistoric Lowland Maya Community and Social Organization: A Case Study at Dzibilchaltun, Yucatan, Mexico*, Middle American Research Institute, Publication 38 (New Orleans: Tulane University Press).

KURJACK, EDWARD B. and T. SILVIA GARZA

1981 "Precolumbian Community Form and Distributions in the Northern Maya Region," in *Maya Lowland Settlement Patterns*, ed. Wendy Ashmore, (Albuquerque: University of New Mexico Press, School of American Research Advanced Seminar Series).

LANGE, FREDERICK W.

1971 "Marine Resources: A Viable Subsistence Alternative for the Prehistoric Lowland Maya," *American Anthropologist*, 73(3):619–39.

LEVENTHAL, RICHARD M.

1981 "Settlement Patterns in the Southeast Maya Area," in *Lowland Maya Settlement Patterns*, ed. Wendy Ashmore (Albuquerque: University of New Mexico Press, School of American Research Advanced Seminar Series).

LINCOLN, C. E.

1985 "Ceramics and Ceramic Chronology," in *A Consideration of the Early Classic Period in the Maya Lowlands*, ed. G. R. Willey and P. Mathews, Institute for Mesoamerican Studies, Publication No. 10, (Albany: State University of New York).

LONGYEAR, JOHN M., III

1952 "Copan Ceramics: A Study of Southeastern Maya Pottery," Carnegie Institution of Washington, Publication No. 597 (Washington, D.C.).

LOTHROP, SAMUEL K.

1924 "Tulum," Carnegie Institution of Washington, Publication No. 335 (Washington, D.C.).

1927 "Pottery Types and Their Sequence in El Salvador," *Indian Notes and Monographs* 1(4):165–220 (New York: Museum of American Indian, Heye Foundation).

LOUNSBURY, FLOYD G.

1974a "On the Derivation and Reading of the 'ben-ich' prefix," *Mesoamerican Writing Systems*, ed. E. P. Benson (Washington, D.C.).

1974b "The Inscription of the Sarcophagus Lid at Palenque," *Primera mesa redonde de Palenque*, 2 ed. Merle Greene Robertson (Pebble Beach, Ca. Robert Louis Stevenson School).

LOWE, GARETH W.

1977 "The Mixe-Zoque as Competing Neighbors of the Early Lowland Maya," in *The Origins of Maya Civilization*, ed. R. E. W. Adams (Albuquerque: University of New Mexico Press, School of American Research Advanced Seminar Series).

MACKIE, E. E.

1961 "New Light on the End of the Classic Maya Culture at Benque Viejo, British Honduras," *American Antiquity*, 27:216–224

MACNEISH, R. S., S. J. K. WILKERSON, AND ANTOINETTE NELKEN-TURNER
1980 *First Annual Report of the Belize Archaic Archaeological Reconnaisance,* (Andover, Mass.: R. S. Peabody Foundation for Archaeology).

MALER, TEOBERT
1901 "Researches in the Central Portion of the Usumatsintla Valley: Report of Explorations for the Museum 1891–1900," Memoirs of the Peabody Museum of Archaeology and Ethnology, vol. 4, no. 2 (Cambridge, Mass.: Harvard University).
1903 "Researches in the Central Portion of the Usumatsintla Valley: Report of Explorations for the Museum 1898–1900," Memoirs of the Peabody Museum of Archaeology and Ethnology, vol. 2, no. 2 (Cambridge, Mass.: Harvard University).
1908 "Explorations of the Upper Usumatsintla and Adjacent Regions: Altar de Sacrificios; Seibal: Itsimté-Sacluk; Cankuen," Memoirs of the Peabody Museum of Archaeology and Ethnology (Cambridge, Mass.: Harvard University).

MARCUS, JOYCE
1973 "Territorial Organization of the Lowland Classic Maya," *Science,* 180: 911–16.
1983 "Lowland Maya Archaeology at the Crossroads," *American Antiquity* 48:454–488.

MATHENY, RAY T.
1970 "The Ceramics of Aguacatal, Campche, Mexico," Papers of the New World Archaeological Foundation, 27 (Provo, Utah: Brigham Young University).
1978 "Northern Maya Lowland Water-Control Systems," in *Prehispanic Maya Agriculture,* ed. P. D. Harrison and B. L. Turner II (Albuquerque: University of New Mexico Press).

MATHENY, RAY T. ed.
1980 "El Mirador, Peten, Guatemala: An Interim Report," Papers of the New World Archaeological Foundation, 45 (Provo, Utah).

MATHEWS, PETER
1985 "Maya Early Classic Monuments and Inscriptions," in *A Consideration of the Early Classic Period of the Maya Lowlands,* ed. G. R. Willey and Peter Mathews, Institute for Mesoamerican Studies, Publication No. 10 (Albany, New York: State University of New York).

MATHEWS, PETER, and LINDA SCHELE
1974 "Lords of Palenque: The Glyphic Evidence," in *Primera mesa redonda de Palenque I,* ed. M. G. Robertson (Pebble Beach, Ca.: Robert Louis Stevenson School).

MAUDSLAY, ALFRED P.
1889–1902 Archaeology (Biologia Centrali Americana). 4 Volumes plates, 1 Volume text. (London: R. H. Porter and Dulua and Co.).
1892 "The Ancient Civilizations of Central America," *Nature,* 45(1174) 617–22.

MERWIN, R. E. and G. C. VAILLANT
1932 "The Ruins of Holmul, Guatemala," Memoirs of the Peabody Museum of Archaeology and Ethnology (Cambridge, Mass.: Harvard University).

MILES, S. W.
1965a "Sculptures of the Guatemala-Chiapas Highlands and Pacific Slopes, and

Associated Hieroglyphs," in *Handbook of Middle American Indians*, ed. R. Wauchope and G. R. Willey 2:237–75, (Austin: University of Texas Press).

1965b "Summary of Preconquest Ethnology of the Guatemala-Chiapas Highlands and Pacific Slopes," *Archaeology of Southern Mesoamerica, Handbook of Middle American Indians*, ed. G. R. Willey, 2:276–87 (Austin: University of Texas Press).

MILLER, ARTHUR G.

1977 "The Maya and the Sea: Trade and Cult at Tancah and Tulum, Quintana Roo, Mexico," *The Sea in Precolumbian World*, ed. E. Benson, (Washington, D.C.: Dumbarton Oaks).

MILLON, RENE

1973 *Urbanization at Teotihuacan, Mexico, Volume I: The Teotihuacan Map (Parts 1 and 2, Text and Maps)* (Austin: University of Texas Press).

MOHOLY-NAGY, HATTULA

1963 "Shells and Other Marine Material from Tikal," *Estudios Cultura Maya*, 3:65–83.

MORLEY, SYLVANUS G.

1946 *The Ancient Maya*, (Palo Alto: Stanford University Press).

MORRIS, E. H., JEAN CHARLOT, and A. A. MORRIS

1931 "The Temple of the Warriors at Chichen Itza, Yucatan," Carnegie Institution, Publication No. 406 (Washington, D.C).

NETTING, ROBERT McC.

1977 "Maya Subsistence: Mythologies, Analogies, Possibilities," in *The Origins of Maya Civilization*, ed. R. E. W. Adams (Albuquerque: University of New Mexico Press, School of American Research Advanced Seminar Series).

NIGH, R. B.

1981 "Review of *Prehispanic Maya Agriculture*," ed. P. D. Harrison and B. L. Turner II *American Antiquity*, 46(3) (Washington, D.C.).

PAHL, GARY W.

1976 "A Successor-relationship Complex and Associated Signs," *The Art, Iconography and Dynastic History of Palenque*, 3 ed. M. G. Robertson (Pebble Beach: Robert Louis Stevenson School).

PARRY, JAMES

1981 "Dawn Comes to Zama: The Postclassic in Quintana Roo, Mexico," Seminar in Middle American Archaeology, Tozzer Library, Peabody Museum, (Cambridge, Mass.: Harvard University).

PARSONS, J. J. and W. M. DENEVAN

1967 "Precolumbian Ridged Fields," *Scientific American*, 217:92–100

PARSONS, L. A.

1969 "The Pacific Coast Cotzumalhuapa Region and Middle American Culture History," *38th International Congress of Americanists*, 1:197–203 (Stuttgart-Munich).

1983 "Altars 9 and 10, Kaminaljuyu, and the Evolution of the Serpent-Winged Diety," in *Civilization in the Ancient Americas: Essays in Honor of Gordon R. Willey*, ed. R. M. Leventhal (Albuquerque, University of New Mexico Press and the Peabody Museum, Harvard University).

PENDERGAST, DAVID M.

1964 "Excavations en la Cueva Eduardo Quiroz, Distrito Cayo, Honduras

Britianica," *Estudios Cultura Maya*, 4:119–141 (Mexico, D.F.: Universidad Nacional Autonoma de Mexico).

1967 "Ocupacion post-classic en Altun Ha, Honduras Britanica," *Revista Mexicana Antropologicos*, 21:213–225. (Mexico, D.F.: Sociedad Mexicana de Antropologia).

1969 "The Prehistory of Actun Balam, British Honduras," Occasional Paper 16, (Toronto: Royal Ontario Museum).

1970 "A. H. Anderson's Excavations at Rio Frio Cave E, British Honduras (Belize)," Occasional Paper 20, (Toronto: Royal Ontario Museum).

1974 "Excavations at Actun Pobilche, Belize," *Archaeology*, Monograph 1.

1979 "Excavations at Altun Ha, Belize, 1964–1970," 1, Royal Ontario Museum.

1981 "Lamanai, Belize: Summary of Excavation Results, 1974–1980," *Journal of Field Archaeology*, 1(8):29–55.

POHL, MARY E.

1974 The Contribution of Hunting to Present-day Maya Nutrition. Paper presented at the 73rd meetings of the AAA, Mexico City.

POLLOCK, HARRY E. D.

1965 "Architecture of the Maya Lowlands," *Archaeology of Southern Mesoamerica, Handbook of Middle American Indians*, 2, ed. G. R. Willey (Austin: University of Texas Press).

POLLOCK, HARRY E. D., RALPH L. ROYS, TATIANA PROSKOURIAKOFF and A. LEDYARD SMITH

1962 *Mayapan, Yucatan, Mexico*. Carnegie Institution of Washington, Publication No. 619. (Washington, D.C.).

POTTER, DAVID F.

1977 *Maya Architecture of the Central Yucatan Peninsula, Mexico*, Middle American Research Institute, Publication 44, (New Orleans: Tulane University).

POTTER, DANIEL R.

1985 "Settlement," in *A Consideration of the Early Classic Period in the Maya Lowlands*, ed. G. R. Willey and Peter Mathews, Institute for Mesoamerican Studies, Publication No. 10 (Albany: State University of New York).

PROSKOURIAKOFF, TATIANA

1950 *A Study of Classic Maya Sculpture*. Carnegie Institution of Washington Publication 593 (Washington, D.C.).

1951 "Some Nonclassic Traits in the Sculpture of Yucatan," *Selected Papers of the Twenty-Ninth International Congress of Americanists*, 1 (Chicago: University of Chicago Press).

1960 "Historical Implications of a Pattern of Dates at Piedras Negras, Guatemala," *American Antiquity* 25:454–75.

1963 "Historical Data in the Inscriptions of Yaxchilan, Part I," *Estudios de Cultura Maya*, 3:149–66.

1964 "Historical Data in the Inscriptions of Yaxchilan, Part II," *Estudios de Cultura Maya*, 4:177–201.

PULESTON, DENNIS E.

1968 "New Data from Tikal on Classic Maya Subsistence," paper delivered at the Annual Meeting of the Society of American Archaeology, Santa Fe.

1971 "An Experimental Approach to the Function of Classic Maya Chultuns," *American Antiquity*, 36:322–35.

1973 "Ancient Maya Settlement and Environment at Tikal, Guatemala: Implications for Subsistence Models," (PhD. diss. University of Pennsylvania).

1974 "Intersite Areas in the vicinity of Tikal and Uaxactun," *Mesoamerican Archaeology: New Approaches*. ed. N. Hammond (Austin: University of Texas Press).

1977 "The Art and Archaeology of Hydraulic Agriculture in the Maya Lowlands," in *Social Process in Maya Prehistory: Studies in memory of Sir Eric Thompson*. ed. N. Hammond (London: Academic Press).

1978 "Terracing, Raised Fields, and Tree Cropping in the Maya Lowlands: A New Perspective on the Geography of Power," in *Prehispanic Maya Agriculture*, ed. P. D. Harrison and B. L. Turner II (Albuquerque: University of New Mexico Press).

PULESTON, DENNIS and OLGA S. PULESTON

1971 "An Ecological Approach to the Origins of Maya Civilization," *Archaeology*, 24(4):330–37.

QUIRARTE, JACINTO

1976 "The Relationship of Izapan-Style Art to Olmec and Maya Art: A Review," in *Origins of Religious Art and Iconography in Preclassic Mesoamerica*, ed. H. B. Nicoloson (Los Angeles: UCLA Latin American Studies Series, 31).

1977 "Early Art Styles of Mesoamerica and Early Classic Maya Art," *The Origins of Maya Civilization*, ed. R. E. W. Adams (Albuquerque: University of New Mexico Press, School of American Research Advanced Seminar Series).

1979 "Sculptural Documents in the Origins of Maya Civilization," 42nd International Congress of Americanists (Paris: Musee de l'Homme).

1983 "Outside Influence at Cacaxtla," in *Highland-Lowland Interaction in Mesoamerica: Interdisciplinary Approaches*, ed. A. G. Miller (Washington, D.C.: Dumbarton Oaks).

RANDS, ROBERT L.

1965 "Jades of the Maya Lowlands," in *Handbook of Middle American Indians*, 3, ed. R. Wauchope and G. R. Willey (Austin: University of Texas Press).

1967a "Ceramic Technology and Trade in the Palenque Region, Mexico," *American Historical Anthropology, Essays in Honor of Leslie Spier*, ed. C. L. Riley and W. W. Taylor (Carbondale and Edwardsville: Southern Illinois University Press).

1967b "Ceramica de la Palenque, Mexico," *Estudios de Cultura Maya*, 6:111–147, (Mexico, D.F.: Universidad Nacional Autonoma de Mexico).

1973a "The Classic Collapse in Southern Maya Lowlands: Chronology," in *The Classic Maya Collapse*, ed. T. P. Culbert, (Albuquerque: University of New Mexico Press, School of American Research Advanced Seminar Series).

1973b "The Classic Maya Collapse: Usumacinta Zone and the Northwestern Periphery," in *The Classic Maya Collapse*, ed. T. P. Culbert (Albuquerque: University of New Mexico Press, School of American Research Advanced Seminar Series).

1977 "The Rise of Classic Maya Civilization in the Northwestern Zone: Isolation and Integration," in *The Origins of Maya Civilization*, ed. R. E. W. Adams

(Albuquerque: University of New Mexico Press, School of American Research Advanced Seminar Series).

1979 "Comparative Data from the Palenque Zone on Maya Civilization," *Actes International Congress of Americanists*, 42(8) (Paris).

RATHJE, WILLIAM J.

1970 "Socio-political Implication of Lowland Maya Burials," *World Archaeology*, 1(3):359–74.

1971 "The Origins and Development of Lowland Classic Maya Civilization," *American Antiquity*, 36:275–85.

1972 "Praise the Gods and Pass the Metates: A Hypothesis of the Development of Lowland Rainforest Civilizations in Middle America," in *Contemporary Archaeology*, ed. M. P. Leone, (Carbondale: Southern Illinois University Press).

1973 "Classic Maya Development and Denouement: A Research Design," in *The Classic Maya Collapse*, ed. T. P. Culbert (Albuquerque: University of New Mexico Press, School of American Research Advanced Seminar Series).

1975 "The Last Tango in Mayapan: A Tenative Trajectory of Production-Distribution Systems," in *Ancient Civilization and Trade*, ed. J. A. Sabloff and C. C. Lamberg-Karlovsky (Albuquerque: University of New Mexico Press, School of American Research Advanced Seminar Series).

1977 "The Tikal Connection," *The Origins of Maya Civilization*, ed. R. E. W. Adams (Albuquerque: University of New Mexico Press, School of American Research Advanced Seminar Series).

REICHEL-DOLMATOFF, GERARDO

1976 "Cosmology as Ecological Analysis: A View from the Rain Forest," *Man* (N.S.) 11:307–18.

RICE, DON S.

1974 "The Archaeology of British Honduras: A Review and Synthesis," *Katunob*, No. 6, (Greely: University of Northern Colorado, Museum of Anthropology).

1978 "Population Growth and Subsistence Alternatives in a Tropical Lacustrine Environment," in *Prehispanic Agriculture*, ed. P. D. Harrison and B. L. Turner II (Albuquerque: University of New Mexico Press).

RICE, DON S. and PRUDENCE M. RICE

1979 "The Postclassic at Topoxte and Macanche," Manuscript.

1980 "The Northeast Peten Revisited," *American Antiquity*, 45(3):432–455.

RICE, PRUDENCE M.

1979 "Ceramic and Nonceramic Artifacts of Lakes Yaxha-Sacnab, El Peten, Guatemala. Part I The Ceramics, Section B, Postclassic Pottery from Topoxte," *Ceramica de Cultura Maya* 11:1–85.

RICE, DON S. and DENNIS E. PULESTON

1980 "Ancient Maya Settlement Patterns in the Peten Guatemala," in *Lowland Maya Settlement Patterns*, ed. W. Ashmore (Albuquerque: University of New Mexico Press, School of American Research Advanced Seminar Series).

RICKETSON, OLIVER G. and EDITH B. RICKETSON

1937 "Uaxactuan, Guatemala, Group E 1926–1937," Carnegie Institution of Washington Publication, no. 447 (Washington, D.C.).

ROBERSTSON, DONALD

1970 "The Tulum Murals: The International Style of the Late Post-Classic," *Pro-*

ceedings of the 38th International Congress of Americanists, 12 to 18 August, 1968, 77–89. (Stuttgart-Munchen).

ROVNER, IRWIN
1976 "A Method for Determining Obsidian Trade Patterns in the Maya Lowlands," *Katunob*, 9(1):43–51.

ROYS, RALPH L.
1933 "The Book of Chilam Balam of Chumayel," *Carnegie Institution Publication 438* (Washington, D.C.).

RUPPERT, KARL
1935 "The Caracol at Chichen Itza, Yucatan, Mexico," *Carnegie Institution Publication 454* (Washington, D.C.).

RUPPERT, KARL, J. E. S. THOMPSON and TATIANA PROSKOURIAKOFF
1955 "Bonampok," *Carnegie Institution of Washington Publication 602* (Washington).

RUZ, ALBERTO
1969 La Costa de Campeche en los Tiempos Preshipanicos," *Investigaciones 18*, Instituto Nacional de Antropologia e Historia (Mexico, D.F.)

SABLOFF, JEREMY A.
1973a "Major Themes in the Past Hypotheses of the Maya Collapse," in *The Classic Maya Collapse*, ed. T. P. Culbert (Albuquerque: University of New Mexico Press, School of American Research Advanced Seminar Series).
1973b "Continuity and Disruption during Terminal Late Classic Times at Seibal Ceramic and Other Evidence," in *The Classic Maya Collapse*, ed. T. P. Culbert (Albuquerque: University of New Mexico Press, School of American Research Advanced Seminar Series).
1975 "Excavations at Seibal Ceramics," *Memoirs of the Peabody Museum of Anthropology and Ethnology*, vol. 13, no. 2 (Cambridge, Mass.: Harvard University).
1977 "Old Myth, New Myths: The Role of Sea Traders in the Development of Ancient Maya Civilization," *The Sea in the Pre-Columbian World*, ed. E. P. Benson (Washington, D.C.: Dumbarton Oaks).
1983 "Classic Maya Settlement Pattern Studies: Past Problems, Future Prospects," in *Prehistoric Settlement Patterns, Essays in Honor of Gordon R. Willey*, ed. E. Z. Vogt and R. M. Leventhal (Albuquerque: University of New Mexico Press, and the Peabody Museum, Harvard University).

SABLOFF, JEREMY A. and E. W. ANDREWS V, (eds.)
1986 *Late Lowland Maya Civilization: Classic to Postclassic*, (Albuquerque: University of New Mexico Press, School of American Research Advanced Seminar Series).

SABLOFF, JEREMY A. and WILLIAM L. RATHJE
1975 "The Rise of the Maya Merchant Class," *Scientific American*, 233(4):72–82.

SABLOFF, JEREMY A. and WILLIAM L. RATHJE
1975 *Changing Pre-Columbian Commercial Systems*, Monographs of the Peabody Museum No. 3 (Cambridge, Mass.: Harvard University).

SABLOFF, JEREMY A. and GORDON R. WILLEY
1967 "The Collapse of Maya Civilization in the Southern Lowlands: A Consideration of History and Process, *Southwestern Journal of Anthropology* 23:311–36.

SANDERS, WILLIAM T.
1960 "Prehistoric Ceramics and Settlement Patterns in Quintana Roo, Mexico," *Publication 606*, Carnegie Institution of Washington (Washington, D.C.).
1973 "The Cultural Ecology of the Lowland Maya: A Reevaluation," in *The Classic Maya Collapse*, ed. T. P. Culbert (Albuquerque: University of New Mexico Press, School of American Research Advanced Seminar Series).
1977 "Environmental Heterogenity and the Evolution of Maya Civilization," in *The Origins of Maya Civilization*, ed. R. E. W. Adams (Albuquerque: University of New Mexico Press, School of American Research Advanced Seminar Series).
1981 "Classic Maya Settlement Patterns and Ethnographic Analogy," in *"Lowland Maya Settlement Patterns*, ed. Wendy Ashmore (Albuquerque: University of New Mexico Press, School of American Research Advanced Seminar Series).
SANDERS, WILLIAM T. and BARBARA J. PRICE
1968 *Mesoamerica: The Evolution of a Civilization* (New York: Random House).
SATTERTHWAITE, LINTON
1965 "Calendrics of the Maya Lowlands," *Archaeology of Southern Mesoamerica, Handbook of Middle American Indians* ed. G. R. Willey 3:603–31 (Austin: University of Texas Press).
SAUL, FRANK P.
1973 "Disease in the Maya Area: The Pre-Columbian Evidence," in *The Classic Maya Collapse*, ed. T. P. Culbert (Albuquerque: University of New Mexico Press, School of American Research Advanced Seminar Series).
SCHELE, LINDA
1976 "Accession Iconography of Chan-Bahlum in the Group of the Cross at Palenque," in *The Art, Iconongraphy, and Dynastic History of Palenque, Mesa Redonda de palenque*, pt. 3, ed. M. Greene Robertson (Pebble Beach: Robert Louis Stevenson School).
SCHELLHAS, PAUL
1904 "Representations of Deities of the Maya Manuscripts," Papers 4(1) Peabody Museum (Cambridge, Mass.: Harvard University).
SHARER, ROBERT J.
1978 "Archaeology and History at Quirigua, Guatemala," *Field Archaeology* 5:51–71.
SHARP, ROSEMARY
1981 "Chacs and Chiefs," *Studies in Pre-Columbian Art and Archaeology*, No. 24. (Washington D.C.: Dumbarton Oaks).
SHEETS, P. D.
1976 *Ilopango Volcano and the Maya Protoclassic*, University Museum Studies No. 9 (Carbondale: University of Illinois).
SHIMKIN, DEMITRI B.
1964 "National Forces and Ecological Adaptations in the Development of Russian Peasant Societies," in *Process and Pattern in Culture*, ed. R. A. Manners (Chicago: Aldine).
1973 "Models for the Downfall: Some Ecological and Culture-Historical Considerations," in *The Classic Maya Collapse*, ed. T. P. Culbert (Albuquerque:

University of New Mexico Press, School of American Research Advanced Seminar Series).

SIDRYS, RAYMOND

1977 "Mass-Distance Measures for the Maya Obsidian Trade," *Exchange Systems in Prehistory*, ed. T. Earle and J. Ericson, (New York: Academic Press).

SIEMENS, ALFRED H.

1978 "Karst and the Prehispanic Maya in the Southern Lowlands," in *Prehispanic Agriculture*, ed. P. D. Hammon and B. L. Turner II (Albuquerque: University of New Mexico Press).

SIEMENS, ALFRED H. and DENNIS E. PULESTON

1972 "Ridged Fields and Associated Features in Southern Campeche: New Perspectives on the Lowland Maya," *American Antiquity* 37:228–38.

SMITH, A. LEDYARD

1972 "Excavations at Altar de Sacrificios: Architecture Settlement, Burials, and Caches," papers of the Peabody Museum of Anthropology and Ethnology vol. 62, no. 2 (Cambridge, Mass.: Harvard University).

SMITH, A. LEDYARD and GORDON R. WILLEY

1969 "Seibal, Guatemala in 1968: A Brief Summary of Archaeological Results," 38th International Congress of Americanists 1:151–58 (Stuttgart-Munich: Klaus Renner Verlag).

SMITH, ROBERT E.

1936a "Preliminary Shape Analysis of the Uaxactun Pottery," Special Publication, Carnegie Institution of Washington (Washington, D.C.).

1936b "Ceramics of Uaxactun: A Preliminary Analysis of Decorative Technics and Design," Special Publication, Carnegie Institution of Washington (Washington, D.C.).

1940 "Ceramics of Peten," in *The Maya and Their Neighbors*, ed. C. L. Hay and others, (New York: Appleton-Century).

1971 "The Pottery of Mayapan, Vol. 1,2," Papers of the Peabody Museum of Archaeology and Ethnology, 66 (Cambridge, Mass.: Harvard University).

SPINDEN, H. J.

1915 "Notes on Archaeology of Salvador," *American Anthropologist*, 17: 446–87.

1917 "The Origin and Distribution of Agriculture in America," 19th International Congress of Americanists Smithsonian Institution (Washington, D.C.).

1928 *Ancient Civilizations of Mexico and Central America*, (New York: American Museum of Natural History, Handbook Series No. 3.).

STIRLING, M. W.

1940 "An Initial Series from Tres Zapotes, Veracruz, Mexico," Contributed Technical Papers, Mexican Archaeology Series, 1(1) National Geographic Society.

1968 "Early History of the Olmec Problem," *Dumbarton Oaks Conference on the Olmec*, ed. E. P. Benson (Washington, D.C.: Dumbarton Oaks).

SWANTON, JOHN R.

1946 *The Indians of the Southeastern United States, Bureau of American Ethnology Bulletin*, no. 137 (Washington, D.C.: U.S. Government Printing Office).

THOMAS, PRENTICE M., JR.

1974 "Prehistoric Settlement in Becan: A Preliminary Report," *Preliminary*

Reports on Archaeological Investigations in the Rio Bec Area, Campeche, Mexico, Middle American Research Institute, Publication 31 (New Orleans: Tulane University).

THOMPSON, J. ERIC S.

1939 *Excavations at San Jose, British Honduras,* Carnegie Institution of Washington, Publication no. 506 (Washington, D.C.)

1940a "Late Ceramic Horizons at Benque Viejo, British Honduras, Contributions to American Anthropology and History, Vol. 7, No. 35," Carnegie Institution of Washington, Publication no. 528 (Washington, D.C.).

1940b "Archaeological Problems of the Lowland Maya," in *The Maya and Their Neighbors,* ed. C. L. Hay and others (New York: Appleton-Century).

1941a "Dating of Certain Inscriptions of Non-Maya Origins," Theoretical Approaches to Problems, No. 1, Carnegie Institution of Washington (Washington, D.C.).

1941b "A Coordination of the History of Chichen Itza with Ceramic Sequences in Central Mexico," *Rev. Mexicana,* tomo 5:97–111.

1943 "A Trial Survey of the Southern Maya Area," *American Antiquity,* 9: 106–34.

1945 "A Survey of the Northern Maya Area," *American Antiquity,* 11:2–24.

1950 "Maya Hieroglyphic Writing," Carnegie Institution of Washington (Washington, D.C.).

1951 "The Itza of Tayasal, Peten," *Homenaje al Doctor Alfonso Caso,* (Mexico, D.F.).

1966 *The Rise and Fall of Maya Civilization, 2nd Edition,* (Norman: University of Oklahoma Press).

1967 "The Maya Central Area at the Spanish Conquest and Later: A Problem in Demography," *Proceedings of the Royal Anthropological Institute of Great Britain and Ireland for 1966,* 23–37.

1970 *Maya History and Religion* (Norman: University of Oklahoma Press).

1974 " 'Canals' of the Rio Candelaria Basin, Campeche, Mexico," *Mesoamerican Archaeology: New Approaches,* ed. N. Hammond (Austin: University of Texas Press).

TOURTELLOT, GAIR

1970 "The Peripheries of Seibal: An Interim Report," *Monographs and Papers in Maya Archaeology,* ed. W. R. Bullard, Papers of Peabody Museum of Anthropology and Ethnology, vol. 61 (Cambridge, Mass.: Harvard University).

TOURTELLOT, GAIR and JEREMY A. SABLOFF

1972 "Exchange Systems Among the Ancient Maya," *American Antiquity* 37:126–35.

TOZZER, ALFRED M.

1957 *Chichen Itza and Its Cenote of Sacrifice: A Comparative Study of Contemporaneous Maya and Toltec,* Memoirs of the Peqabody Museum of Anthropology and Ethnology Vols. 11 and 12 (Cambridge, Mass.: Harvard University).

TURNER, B. L. II

1974 "Prehistoric Intensive Agriculture in the Mayan Lowland," *Science* 185: 118–24.

1978a "The Development and Demise of the Swidden Thesis of Maya Agriculture," *Prehispanic Maya Agriculture*, ed. P. D. Harrison and B. L. Turner II (Albuquerque: University of New Mexico Press).

1978b "Ancient Agricultural Land Use in the Central Maya Lowlands," in *Prehistoric Maya Agriculture*, ed. P. D. Harrison and B. L. Turner II, 156–83 (Albuquerque: University of New Mexico Press).

1979 "Prehispanic Terracing in the Central Maya Lowlands: Problems of Agricultural Intensification," in *Maya Archaeology and Ethnohistory*, ed. Norman Hammond and G. R. Willey (Austin: University of Texas Press).

TURNER, ELLEN SUE, NORMAN I. TURNER and R. E. W. ADAMS

1981 "Volumetric Assessment, Rank Ordering, and Maya Civic Centers," in *Settlement Patterns of Maya Lowland*, ed. W. Ashmore (Albuquerque: University of New Mexico Press, School of American Research Advanced Seminar Series).

VAILLANT, G. C.

1927 "The Chronological Significance of Maya Ceramics," (Ph. D. diss. Harvard University).

1934 "The Archaeological Setting of the Playa de los Muertos Culture," *Maya Research* 1(2):87–100, Middle American Research Institute (New Orleans: Tulane University).

1938 "A Correlation of Archaeological and Historical Sequences in the Valley of Mexico," *American Anthropologist* 40:535–73.

1941 *Aztecs of Mexico* (Garden City, N.Y.: Garden City Press).

VOGT, EVON Z.

1964 "Some Implications of Zinacantan Social Structure for the Study of the Ancient Maya," 35th International Congress of Americanists 1:307–19, (Mexico: Instituto de Antropologia e Historia).

VOGT, EVON Z. and ALBERTO RUZ

1964 *Desarrollo Cultural de los Mayas*, (Mexico, D.F.: Universidad Autonoma de Mexico).

VLCEK, DAVID T., SYLVIA GARZA DE GONZALES, and EDWARD B. KURJACK

1978 "Contemporary Farming and Ancient Maya Settlements: Some Disconcerting Evidence," in *Prehispanic Maya Agriculture* ed. P. D. Harrison and B. L. Turner II (Albuquerque: University of New Mexico Press).

WAUCHOPE, ROBERT

1950 "A Tentative Sequence of Pre-Classic Ceramics in Middle America," Middle American Research Records 1(14) Middle American Research Institute (New Orleans: Tulane University).

WEBB, MALCOLM C.

1973 "The Peten Maya Decline Viewed in the Perspective of State Formation," in *The Classic Maya Collapse*, ed. T. P. Culbert (Albuquerque: University of New Mexico Press, School of American Research Advanced Seminar Series).

WEBSTER, DAVID L.

1974 "The Fortifications of Becan, Campeche, Mexico," Middle American Research Institute, Publication 31 (New Orleans: Tulane University).

1975 "Warfare and the Origin of the State: A Reconsideration," *American Antiquity*, 40:464–70.

1976 "Lowland Maya Fortifications," *Proceedings of the American Philosphical Society,* (Philadelphia).

1977 "Warfare and the Evolution of Maya Civilization," in *The Origins of Maya Civilization,* ed. R. E. W. Adams (Albuquerque: University of New Mexico Press, School of American Research Advanced Seminar Series).

1978 "Three Walled Sites of the Northern Maya Lowlands," *Journal of Field Archaeology,* 5(4):375–390.

1979 "Cuca, Chccchob, Dzonot Ake: Three Walled Northern Maya Centers," Occaision Paper Anthropology II (Philadelphia: Pennsylvania State University Press).

WILLEY, GORDON R.

1971 "A Commentary on: The Emergence of Civilization in the Maya Lowlands," Contributions of the University of California Archaeological Research Facility, No. 11.

1973a "The Altar de Sacrificios Excavations, General Summary and Conclusions," Papers of the Peabody Museum of Archaeology and Ethnology, Vol. 64, no. 1 (Cambridge, Mass.: Harvard University).

1973b "Certain Aspects of the Late Classic to Postclassic Period in the Belize Valley," in *The Classic Maya Collapse,* ed. T. P. Culbert (Albuquerque: University of New Mexico Press, School of American Research Advanced Seminar Series).

1974 "The Classic Maya Hiatus: 'A Rehearsal' for the Collapse," *Mesoamerican Archaeology: New Approaches,* ed. N. Hammond (London: Duckworth).

1977a "The Rise of Classic Maya Civilization: A Pasion Valley Perspective," in *The Origins of Maya Civilization,* ed. R. E. W. Adams (Albuquerque: University of New Mexico Press, School of American Research Advanced Seminar Series).

1977b "The Rise of Maya Civilization: A Summary View," in *The Origins of Maya Civilization,* ed. R. E. W. Adams (Albuquerque: University of New Mexico Press, School of American Research Advanced Seminar Series).

1977c "A Consideration of Archaeology," *Daedalus, Discoveries and Interpretations: Studies in Contemporary Scholaship* 1:81–95.

1978a "Prehispanic Maya Agriculture: A Contemporary Summation," in *Prehispanic Maya Agriculture,* ed. P. D. Harrison and B. L. Turner II (Albuquerque: University of New Mexico Press).

1978b *Excavations at Seibal: Artifacts,* Memoirs of the Peabody Museum of Anthropology and Ethnology Vol. 14, no. 1 (Cambridge, Mass.: Harvard University).

1980 "Towards an Holistic View of Ancient Maya Civilization," *Man* 15:249–266.

1981a "Spinden's Archaic Hypothesis," in *Antiquity and Man,* ed. J. D. Evans, B. Cunliffe, and C. Renfrew (London: Thames and Hudson).

1981b "Lowland Maya Settlement Patterns, A Summary Review," in *Lowland Maya Settlement Patterns,* ed. W. Ashomore (Albuquerque: University of New Mexico Press, School of American Research Advanced Seminar Series).

1981c "Coherence and Instability in Lowland Maya Socio-Political Organization," Paper presented at University of Texas at San Antonio.

WILLEY, GORDON R., WILLIAM R. BULLARD, JR., JOHN B. GLASS, and JAMES C. GIFFORD
1965 *Prehistoric Maya Settlements in the Belize Valley*, Peabody Museum Papers 54 (Cambridge, Mass.: Harvard University).

WILLEY, GORDON R., and RICHARD M. LEVENTHAL
1979 "Prehistoric Settlement at Copan, in *Maya Archaeology, and Ethnohistory*, ed. Norman Hammond and G. R. Willey (Austin: University of New Mexico Press*)*.

WILLEY, GORDON R., RICHARD M. LEVENTHAL, and WILLIAM L. FASH, JR.
1978 "Maya Settlement in the Copan Valley," *Archaeology*, 31:32–43.

WILLEY, GORDON R. and JEREMY A. SABLOFF
1980 *A History of American Archaeology, 2nd Ed.* (San Francisco: W. H. Freeman).

WILLEY, GORDON R. and DEMITRI B. SHIMKIN
1971a "The Collapse of Classic Maya Civilization in the Southern Lowlands: A Symposium Summary Statement," *Southwestern Journal of Anthropology*, 27(1):1–18.
1971b "Why Did The Pre-Columbian Maya Civilization Collapse?," *Science*, 173(3997):656–58.
1973 "The Maya Collapse: A Summary View," in *The Classic Maya Collapse*, ed. T. Patrick Culbert (Albuquerque: University of New Mexico Press, School of American Research Advanced Seminar Series).

WILLEY, GORDON R. and A. LEDYARD SMITH
1969 *The Ruins of Altar De Sacrificios, Department of Peten, Guatemala: An Introduction*, Papers of the Peabody Museum of Archaeology and Ethnology, Vol. 62, no. 1 (Cambridge, Mass.: Harvard University).

WILLEY, GORDON R., A LEDYARD SMITH, GAIR TOURTELLOT III, and IAN GRAHAM
1975 *Excavations at Seibal: Introduction: The Site and Its Settings*, Memoirs of the Peabody Museum of Archaeology and Ethnology, Vol. 13, no. 1 (Cambridge, Mass.: Harvard University).

WISEMAN, F. M.
1978 "Agricultural and Historical Ecology of the Maya Lowlands," in *Prehispanic Maya Agriculture*, ed. P. D. Harrison and B. L. Turner II (Albuquerque: University of New Mexico Press).

WRIGHT, A. C. S., D. H. ROMNEY, R. H. ARBUCKLE, and V. E. VIAL
1959 *Land Use in British Honduras: Report of the British Honduras Land Use Survey Team*, Colonial Research Publications, No. 24 (London: Colonial Office).

Index

Abaj Takalik, 7, 198
abandonment of settlements, 23–28,
    30–31, 73, 92, 121, 127, 138,
    160, 164, 169, 177, 181
Acanceh, 72
Adams, R. E. W., 5, 31, 34, 35, 43,
    60, 69, 84, 85, 86, 108, 109,
    117, 118, 124–25, 128, 129–30,
    134, 144, 151
agriculture: conventional model, 35,
    103; crop diversification, 36,
    84, 85, 93; development, 9,
    106; expansion, 45; and
    Lowland settlement patterns,
    109, 122, 133; and population
    growth, 8, 35, 110; problems,
    43, 45–46, 50; productivity,
    103; variability, 103–5. *See also*
    specific techniques
agriculture, intensive, 9–10, 35–36,
    58n5, 69, 84–85, 86–87, 93,
    95n6, 98, 103, 130, 140,
    141–43. *See also specific*
    techniques
Aguacatal, 178
Aguateca, 126
Ake, 127
alphabet, Landa, 148
Altamira, 125
Altar de Sacrificios: burial, 57n3;
    collapse data, 26–28, 163–64,
    182; Early Classic, 71;